15—

Planet Dora

PLANET DORA

A MEMOIR OF THE HOLOCAUST AND THE BIRTH OF THE SPACE AGE

YVES BÉON

EDITED WITH AN INTRODUCTION BY MICHAEL J. NEUFELD

TRANSLATED BY YVES BÉON AND RICHARD L. FAGUE

Westview Press

A Division of HarperCollins*Publishers*

Copyright © 1997 by Westview Press, A Division of HarperCollins Publishers, Inc. Introduction copyright © 1997 by the Smithsonian Institution.

Published in 1997 in the United States of America by Westview Press, 5500 Central Avenue, Boulder, Colorado 80301-2877, and in the United Kingdom by Westview Press, 12 Hid's Copse Road, Cumnor Hill, Oxford OX2 9JJ. French edition, *La planète Dora*, published in 1985 by Éditions du Seuil.

Library of Congress Cataloging-in-Publication Data
Béon, Yves
  [Planète Dora. English]
  Planet Dora : a memoir of the Holocaust and the birth of the
space age / Yves Béon ; edited with an introduction by Michael J.
Neufeld ; translated by Yves Béon and Richard L. Fague.
      p.   cm.
  Includes bibliographical references.
  ISBN 0-8133-3272-9 (hc)
  1. Dora (Germany : Concentration camp)   2. World War, 1939–1945—
Prisoners and prisons, German.   3. Rocketry—Germany—History.
4. V-1 bomb.   5. V-2 rocket.   I. Neufeld, Michael J., 1951–   .
II. Title.
D805.G3B45613   1997
940.53'18'0943224—dc21   96-29626
                                                              CIP

Text Design by Heather Hutchison

10   9   8   7   6   5   4   3   2   1

Contents

PREFACE TO THE AMERICAN EDITION

When the American army reached the city of Nordhausen, Thuringia, on April 11, 1945, the troops found hundreds of skinny corpses clad in striped uniforms. Prisoners. A few miles away, they learned, there was a concentration camp named Dora. There they discovered an empty camp with dead bodies scattered around and the most fantastic thing they ever saw: a gigantic tunnel that sheltered the factory where the V-1 and V-2 "vengeance weapons" had been made by prisoners. They had discovered one of the most horrific concentration camps that had ever existed.

At the end of the war, both the East and the West tracked down the German scientists, engineers, and technicians—the creators of the rockets—not to punish them but to use them. And Dora remained what it had been: secret, classified.

When I decided to write the story of Dora, I knew that it would not be easy—but I had to do it. Many people helped me—first of all, the inmates, my friends who suffered there. In order to include all of them, I did not mention any last names. Just first names. After all, what happened to one of them happened to all of them, including myself.

But I would also like to make a special mention of the 3rd U.S. Armored Division and the 104th Infantry Division that liberated Dora. John G. O'Brien and Glen E. Lytle are now the presidents of the respective veterans' associations.

I also wish to thank my good American friends who helped me and allowed my book to be published in the United States of America:

- Gretchen E. Schafft, the representative of our Mittelbau-Dora prisoners' association in the States, who does so much for us;
- Richard L. Fague, who helped me to translate my book into American English. He spent weeks, maybe months, doing that job;
- Linda Hunt, my good friend, who was among the first Americans who broke the silence about the German scientists brought to the United States after the war, many of them illegally;

- Eli M. Rosenbaum and Robert G. Seasonwein of the Office of Special Investigations of the U.S. Justice Department, which tracks Nazi war criminals in the States; and
- Michael J. Neufeld, curator at the National Air and Space Museum, Washington, D.C. Thanks to Michael and his friendship, this book is now published in America.

This book is just a book, about a pound of paper like so many other books. It can be read or ignored. What is the problem with that? Only, if we ignore such books, our civilization will disappear.

Yves Béon

Introduction: Mittelbau-Dora— Secret Weapons and Slave Labor

Michael J. Neufeld

"Twenty-five thousand in a year and a half," he said. He was seventeen years old, Polish. . . . "Twenty-five thousand in a year and half. And from each there is only so much." The boy cupped his hands together to show the measure. I followed his glance downward. We were standing at the edge of what had once been a large pit, about eight feet long, six feet wide, and I guessed at six feet deep. It was filled to the overflowing with ashes from the furnaces— small chips of human bone—nothing else. Apparently bucketsful had been thrown from a distance, as one might get rid of the ashes in a coal scuttle on a rainy day.

—**Charles A. Lindbergh,** Autobiography of Values[1]

The famous American aviator witnessed this scene at Dora's crematorium in May 1945. His interlocutor "was a hide-covered skeleton"— one of the few surviving prisoners who had not been forcibly evacuated before liberation. And the survivor's measure of the human cost of this concentration camp in central Germany was little exaggerated: By the best estimate, of the roughly sixty thousand prisoners who passed through the Mittelbau (Central Construction) camp system, at least one-third died. Dora was the center of that system.[2]

Yet, in the larger framework of Nazi crimes, those twenty thousand dead would scarcely be remarkable if they were not also linked to the production of the Third Reich's most advanced weapons: jet engines and aircraft, the V-1 "buzz bomb," and, above all, the V-2—the world's first ballistic missile. Mittelbau-Dora embodied one of the twentieth century's most horrifying lessons: that advanced industrial technology is perfectly compatible with barbarism, slavery, and mass murder. Out of the portals of the underground factory next to Dora came not only nearly six thousand V-2s in sixteen months but also dead bodies. Afterward, many of the leading German rocket engineers, headed by Wernher von Braun, were employed and even lionized by the United States, while the story of Dora was obscured, whitewashed, and at times suppressed altogether.[3]

Yves Béon's powerful collective memoir (he uses the memories of many of his friends but never appears as a character himself) captures what it was like to be an ordinary French prisoner in this hellish and amazing place. Born in Brittany in 1925, the teenaged Béon was arrested by the Gestapo in Le Mans on November 25, 1943, for resistance activities. Weakened by torture and malnutrition, he was shipped to the Buchenwald concentration camp near Weimar in central Germany in February 1944, where he was assigned number 43808 and forced to labor in the stone quarry. He was soon sent on to Dora—then a Buchenwald subcamp—and survived a year on the V-2 production line. At the beginning of April 1945, he was forcibly evacuated along with thousands of other prisoners before the American army could arrive. After a horrendous rail journey, he ended up in Bergen-Belsen, where he was liberated by British troops on April 15, 1945.

Origins

Before we examine how Yves Béon's memoir illuminates the everyday realities of Dora, however, we must turn to the origins of the German rocket program and its use of concentration camp labor. The program's roots go back to at least 1929, when Lt. Col. Karl Becker of German Army Ordnance became interested in reviving the rocket as a weapon. Through the use of higher-performance liquid fuels, rocketry might even make possible the ballistic missile, which he saw as a potentially devastating form of long-range artillery. In 1932, Becker lured Wernher von Braun, the most brilliant young member of the leading Berlin amateur rocket group, into starting an army liquid-fuel program. Soon thereafter, the Nazi seizure of power steadily increased army resources. By 1936, in collaboration with the Luftwaffe (German air force), Becker had received permission to build an ultrasecret rocket research facility at Peenemünde on the Baltic coast. Von Braun became the technical director of the army side; he reported to a new ordnance rocket section headed by Maj. (later Brig. Gen.) Walter Dornberger. Their primary objective was to develop a ballistic missile called the A-4, fueled by liquid oxygen and alcohol, that could carry a one-ton warhead about 270 kilometers (170 miles). Only in 1944 did it receive a second label from the Propaganda Ministry: "Vengeance Weapon (Vergeltungswaffe) 2," or V-2.

After Hitler provoked war in 1939, the army rocket program was greatly accelerated. Development of the A-4/V-2 became a priority, but production was hampered because the Führer only became more interested in the missile after mid-1941 and especially after November 1942, when the strategic situation of the Third Reich began to deteriorate. Hitler came to see the V-2—along with a competing cruise missile project started by the Luftwaffe and later dubbed the V-1—as a "wonder weapon" that could terrorize the war-weary British populace into quitting the conflict. At the turn of the year 1942–1943, Albert Speer's Armaments Ministry moved to take over and speed up V-2 production. In addition to the assembly plants at Peenemünde and the Zeppelin works on Lake Constance, a third plant was added at Wiener Neustadt in Austria.

The program needed a production labor force, but the relentless military demands of the Eastern Front had created a severe manpower crisis in Germany. Earlier plans to use mostly German skilled labor were tossed aside, and in spring 1943, key decisionmakers such as the chief engineer of the Peenemünde Production Plant, Arthur Rudolph, first decided to use Eastern European forced labor and Soviet prisoners of war for much of the work. However, they soon focused on SS concentration camp prisoners since this labor force appeared to be more readily available and offered a greater protection for the program's secrecy. After viewing the exploitation of SS prisoners (Häftlinge, literally "detainees") at the Heinkel aircraft works at Oranienburg, north of Berlin, on April 12, 1943, Rudolph recommended their use in the Peenemünde plant. Apparently, the Zeppelin works had already made a similar decision, and rocket program chief Dornberger and Speer ministry officials decided to use slave labor at the third plant in Austria as well. After the war, Dornberger, von Braun, and others implied or stated that the use of camp prisoners had been forced on them by Heinrich Himmler's SS months later, but it is now clear that they knew this was not the truth.[4]

Hundreds of prisoners had arrived in each location when Allied airpower intervened in the summer of 1943. Raids on neighboring plants that damaged the Zeppelin and Austrian factories were followed by the RAF Bomber Command's all-out assault on Peenemünde on the night of August 17–18, 1943. Although this attack did not destroy the army facility, as is often asserted, it did inflict enough damage to cause consternation in the Nazi leadership. Reichsführer-SS Himmler, who had been trying since the end of 1942 to gain influence over Peenemünde and the V-2 program, happened to be at Hitler's East Prussian headquarters at the time. He convinced the Führer that missile production should be done underground, using concentration camp prisoners almost exclusively. Armaments Minister Speer had to struggle to reassert his primacy in the program, but he agreed with the decision to go underground and had little choice but to accept the person Himmler named to carry it out: SS-Brigadeführer (Brig. Gen.) Hans Kammler, head of SS construction.

The location that Kammler, Speer, and Dornberger chose was a gigantic underground complex near Nordhausen in the central German state of Thuringia. Mining of anhydrite, which becomes gypsum when water is added, had begun there in 1917. In 1936, after the Nazi seizure of power, the innocuously named Economic Research Company, Ltd. (Wirtschaftliche Forschungsgesellschaft mbH, or "Wifo") took over the mines to create a highly secret central petroleum reserve for the Reich. Two main tunnels, A and B, each large enough to swallow two railroad trains, were begun. Connecting them at regular intervals were cross-tunnels 160 meters (500 feet) long holding two huge oil tanks. Wifo extended the ladderlike network before and during the war; some cross-tunnels were earmarked for poison gas storage but apparently were not used for that purpose. (See Map 1.)

In about July 1943, Paul Figge, an official of the A-4 Special Committee set up by Speer to push through the production program, first scouted the tunnels as an underground site in view of the danger of Allied air attacks. After the Peenemünde raid, there was a short-lived power struggle when Reichsmarschall Hermann Goering, who controlled Wifo, threatened Figge with dire consequences if the tunnels were seized. But Hitler overruled Goering. At the time of the seizure, main tunnel B had just been pushed through to the south side of the Kohnstein Mountain—a distance of 1.8 kilometers (over 1 mile). The total available volume underground was an astounding 1 million cubic meters (35 million cubic feet)![5]

The First Phase:
August 1943 to March 1944

On the very day that tunnel B was finished, August 28, the SS trucked the first 107 prisoners from Buchenwald concentration camp to begin refitting the tunnels. Thus began the first, catastrophic phase of "Work Camp Dora." In view of the perceived urgency of starting production of the V-2 "wonder weapon," SS-General Kammler, who had supervised construction of the Auschwitz gas chambers, took no interest in prisoner comfort or even survival. The barracks camp to be constructed on the south side of the mountain, near the entrance of main tunnel B, was the lowest priority. The unfortunates transferred by the thousand from Buchenwald, along with those sent from the dissolved Peenemünde camp in October, were given straw to sleep on in

Map 1   The Mittelwerk Tunnel System

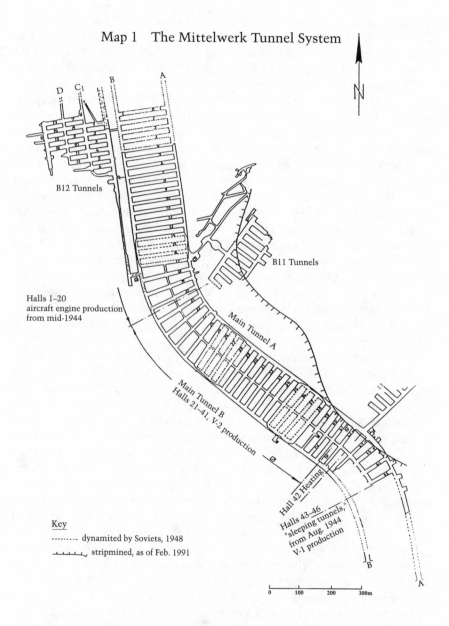

D C   B   A

N

B12 Tunnels

B11 Tunnels

Halls 1–20
aircraft engine production
from mid-1944

Main Tunnel A

Main Tunnel B
Halls 21–41, V-2 production

Hall 42 Heating

Halls 43–46
"sleeping tunnels,"
from Aug. 1944
V-1 production

B

A

Key
--------- dynamited by Soviets, 1948
᠆᠆᠆᠆᠆᠆ stripmined, as of Feb. 1991

0   100   200   300m

Map courtesy of the Kz-Gedankstätte Mittelbau-Dora.

the cold, damp tunnels. Using the forced labor of the prisoners themselves, Kammler's staff then created provisional underground barracks
by having bunks four levels high built into tunnels 43 to 46 at the far
southern end of main tunnel A, which had not yet been completed.[6]

What ensued was an almost unimaginable inferno—a hellish environment powerfully described by Yves Béon but only briefly experienced by him since he did not arrive until March 13, 1944. In addition
to the grueling work of moving heavy equipment in and out of the
tunnels at top speed, two circumstances led to especially horrible conditions. The first was the continuance of the mining of main tunnel A
through to the south side of the mountain. Construction and mining
work by SS camp prisoners most closely approximated the inhuman
Nazi concept of "annihilation through work" (Vernichtung durch Arbeit).[7] Strenuous physical labor for twelve or more hours a day, without adequate heavy equipment or concern for safety, was combined
with the usual starvation diet of the camps. Mining explosions were
carried out day and night adjacent to the "sleeping tunnels," robbing
the exhausted prisoners of what little sleep they could get. And dust
and poisonous gases from the explosions permeated the atmosphere of
the poorly ventilated tunnels, leading to many lung diseases among
the prisoners.

Catastrophic hygienic conditions rarely equaled even in the SS
camp system were Dora's second special circumstance. Since there
were no latrines available, oil drums were cut in half and topped with
boards. The stench was terrible, and the threat of cholera and other
diseases was so serious that the whole German civilian workforce had
to be immunized. There was no washwater at all, and the drinking
water supply for prisoners was extremely limited; they never bathed
and were constantly thirsty—some even resorted to washing themselves with their own urine. The straw mattresses in the bunks were
occupied in two shifts and often by more than one person simultane-
ously, since the "sleeping tunnels" became so crowded. By the end of
1943, there were ten thousand living underground. The mattresses became completely filthy and a haven for lice and fleas. The only time
most prisoners saw the outside world was during weekly roll calls,
when they often stood for hours in wind, rain, and snow while dressed
in thin uniforms that were little better than rags.

The inevitable result was a skyrocketing death rate—18 died in October, 172 in November, 670 in December. The typical causes of death
were pneumonia, tuberculosis, dysentery, or typhus, in combination
with malnutrition and physical exhaustion. The corpses had to be
trucked back to Buchenwald for cremation, giving Dora a fearsome
reputation there. A portable crematorium was brought to the camp in

January, and the permanent one was finished in the spring. The first three months of 1944 saw an escalating death toll—719 in January, 536 in February, and 767 in March—combined with three transports to Lublin-Majdanek or Bergen-Belsen, each composed of 1,000 seriously ill or exhausted prisoners. These transports were virtual death sentences for those "selected," with the result that Dora's death toll was effectively 6,000 in six months.[8]

The grueling pace of the work and the horrible conditions underground also exacerbated the more typical features of SS camps that Béon describes so well: rivalry among the nationalities verging on gang warfare, plus constant beatings and terror administered by the SS guards and their designated prisoner subordinates—the Blockältester (here translated as barracks chiefs), the Kapos (prisoners who served as team leaders, from the Italian word *capo*), and the Vorarbeiter (prisoners who acted as foremen). To save manpower, the SS had perfected a truly evil system of exploiting a few prisoners to control the rest. In addition, food, clothing, and other shortages, together with the brutality and the Nazi race hierarchy imposed on the prisoners ("Aryans" at the top, Slavs, Gypsies, and Jews at the bottom), created an enervating struggle of "all against all." During the first phase, Dora was a completely non-Jewish camp, with Soviets, Poles, French, and Germans forming the largest groups; the majority of these prisoners had been arrested for resistance or other "political" offenses. Béon reveals how language and cultural barriers, combined with the ruthless struggle for survival, divided the main nationalities into rival groups. His view is very much a French one; the "Russians" (many of whom were members of other Soviet nationalities, as he points out) were almost incomprehensible to the Western Europeans.

While some prisoners finished the mining, others removed the storage tanks and installed the V-2 assembly line equipment from Peenemünde, Zeppelin, and Wiener Neustadt. For missile production, the Speer ministry created a state-owned company, Mittelwerk GmbH (Central Works Ltd.), in September 1943. The name was a deliberately vague reference to the plant's geographic location. The ministry drafted managers from heavy industry to take over the company; the driving force in the tunnels was Albin Sawatzki, who had earlier been decorated for his work in Tiger tank production. Sawatzki was relentless with both the German civilian and prisoner labor forces and was known for sadistically beating camp inmates himself. It is no wonder Yves Béon symbolically gives his name (in corrupted form) to the company.

Under Sawatzki was Arthur Rudolph, who had been assigned from Peenemünde to be production manager of the Mittelwerk. Rudolph was a close friend of Wernher von Braun's and had worked under him as a rocket engineer since 1934. He had been a Nazi party member since mid-1931—two years before it became expedient to become one. Von Braun himself became a party member in 1937 and an SS officer in 1940 but was basically an apolitical opportunist. As the technical director of the army side of Peenemünde, he visited the Mittelwerk more than a dozen times during its short existence. Von Braun admitted in a TV interview not long before his death in 1977 that the "working conditions there were absolutely horrible" and that he had once seen the mining operations close up—it was "a pretty hellish environment," he said.[9]

By the end of 1943, assembly of the first Mittelwerk V-2s could begin. (Contra Béon, missile production did overlap with the sleeping tunnels period in the first months of 1944.) Fifty missiles were completed in January, but they were so flawed with bad welds, poor electrical and plumbing connections, and numerous other problems that they were virtually useless. The word *sabotage* first raised its ugly head at this time, as Mittelwerk managers and the SS camp administration, headed by commandant SS-Obersturmbannführer (Lt. Col.) Otto Förschner, sought scapegoats among the prisoners. No doubt sabotage did occur, in the form of both individual and organized acts of resistance, but the fundamental causes of poor missile quality were the underdeveloped state of the extremely complicated device, the numerous design changes coming from Peenemünde, general inexperience, and the terrible physical condition of the workforce in the horrific first phase of Dora.

The Second Phase:
April to October 1944

The middle period of the camp was marked by two main features: (1) a dramatic improvement in the death rate and (2) the creation of many new subcamps in the region to aid Kammler's construction of additional underground plants on the Mittelwerk model. Although the new camps—notably the two largest at Ellrich ("Erich") and Harzungen ("Hans")—nearly duplicated the murderous working conditions of Dora in the winter of 1943–1944, the end of mining and the gradual phaseout of the sleeping tunnels in the Mittelwerk removed the two most important causes of the catastrophic death toll there. Over the first five months of 1944, the prisoners were moved to the new barracks camp on the south side of the Kohnstein. (See Map 2.) The arrival of warmer weather and a slightly improved food supply helped, as did the shift of most workers to less strenuous, although still exhausting, production-line work. Dora recorded "only" 995 deaths in seven months in 1944, and the monthly total sank as low as 52 in August. (Total camp population hovered between twelve and fourteen thousand.) However, some weak prisoners were dumped on the other subcamps, artificially lowering the death rate.

After the war, Armaments Minister Albert Speer, among others, attempted to take credit for the improvement of health conditions and the creation of the aboveground camp. Speer's visit on December 10, 1943, may have led to slight improvements in the health care provided to the prisoners, but the barracks had been in the plans from the outset. Rather than taking energetic action to help the prisoners, Speer wrote to Kammler immediately after completing his trip to praise him for the astonishingly rapid transformation of the tunnels. It was, he said, an accomplishment "that far exceeds anything ever done in Europe and is unsurpassed even by American standards."[10]

As missile production came to the fore, the preservation of the prisoner workforce became a higher priority, especially as many now possessed semiskilled training in various assembly-line jobs. The Mittelwerk company made limited efforts to improve clothing and food rations, and Rudolph was involved in the creation of a premium-wage system that allowed some prisoners to earn prison scrip that could be used to buy a few extras at a canteen. Humanitarian concern had nothing to do with these measures, which were only aimed at getting better work out of the prisoners.

Such efforts did little to alter the fundamentally barbaric character of the Mittelwerk. On June 22, 1944, the company directors felt compelled to issue a secret decree to managers: "On the part of the camp doctor . . . it has been repeatedly determined that detainees who work in the offices or on the shop floor have been beaten by company employees because of this or that offense, or even have been stabbed with sharp instruments."[11] It reminded managers that the SS was there to do the beating. The five thousand or so prisoners laboring in two shifts in spring 1944 worked with about half that number of German civilians in the more skilled positions.[12] Many of the latter clearly had been corrupted by the vicious and racist atmosphere of the SS camp system, insofar as Nazi propaganda had not already laid the groundwork. A few civilians did surreptitiously pass prisoners food or do other small favors, but those who were inclined to be more humane were intimidated by the threat of denunciation by others and the possibility of sharing the prisoners' fate. Because of the highly secret character of the enterprise and the perceived life-or-death importance of the V-2 for the Reich, surveillance by the Gestapo/SD counterintelligence apparatus was all-pervasive and threatening.

XVIII

Map 2 Camp Dora

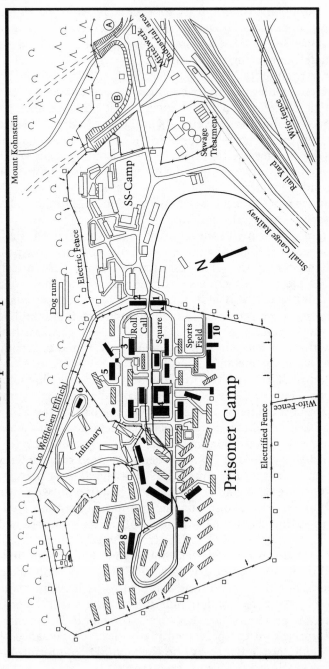

Key
Prisoner Barracks
Infirmary Barracks
Ⓐ Tunnel A (Mittelwerk)
Ⓑ Tunnel B (Mittelwerk)
Administrative Buildings
SS Buildings

1. Camp Administration
2. Political Section (Gestapo/SD)
3. Schreibstube (Administration)
4. Kitchen
5. Bordello
6. Crematorium
7. Showers
8. Movie Theater
9. Effektenkammer (Goods)
10. The Bunker

Derived from Wincenty Hein, 1945. Map courtesy of the Kz-Gedankstätte Mittelbau-Dora.

Sabotage naturally remained a central concern; the usual punishment was a gruesomely slow hanging on the roll call square, as Béon describes. In the 1947 Nordhausen war crimes trial, Sawatzki's secretary reported that Rudolph had passed along sabotage reports to the SS, although written evidence no longer exists to confirm this charge. Von Braun was less directly involved but was present with Rudolph and General Dornberger at a May 5, 1944, meeting in which Sawatzki discussed the necessity of enslaving 1,800 more skilled French workers to bolster the labor force. Von Braun was now in a difficult position because he had been arrested by the Gestapo in March and held for two weeks, presumably for refusing to go along with a Himmler plan to take over Peenemünde. (He was freed through the intervention of Speer and Dornberger.) Yet there is no doubt his involvement with concentration camp labor continued. In an August 15, 1944, letter to Sawatzki, he described how he had gone to Buchenwald and talked to the camp commandant as part of his effort to find skilled prisoners for a special workshop in the tunnels.[13]

In addition to sabotage, which had some indeterminate but significant effect on missile quality, the V-2's innumerable technical problems and political interference depressed the quality and quantity of production in spring and summer 1944. Production climbed to 437 missiles in May but then sank to as low as 86 in July. One reason was Kammler's new role in building underground plants for the aircraft industry, a response to the crisis provoked by Allied strategic bombing. The SS general ordered that the Mittelwerk cross-tunnels 1 through 20 be cleared so that the Junkers company could use them to produce jet and piston engines for fighters. The Junkers factory was called the Nordwerke (North Works); Mittelwerk had to squeeze its production into tunnels 21 through 46.

V-2 production also sank because Hitler ordered a shift in priority to the V-1 "buzz bomb," which the Luftwaffe began launching in large numbers against Britain a week after the June 6 Allied invasion of Normandy. The Mittelwerk had to take a subcontract to assemble the much smaller and simpler V-1s, which it did in the area of the old sleeping tunnels at the south end of main tunnel A, beginning in October and November. Toward the end of the summer, the Führer realized that the cruise missile would not produce the reversal in the course of the war he had hoped for, and he placed his hopes on the ballistic missile. After months of delay, the first V-2s were successfully launched against London and Paris on September 8. From September 1944 to February 1945, the Mittelwerk finally hit its stride, assembling six to seven hundred of them every month—more than twenty per day.

The Third Phase:
November 1944 to April 1945

At the end of September, the SS administration ordered that Dora be separated from Buchenwald and become the center of Concentration Camp Mittelbau—the last new SS main camp and the only one formed explicitly for weapons production. Under Mittelbau-Dora would be over two dozen subcamps and work commandos in the region. On November 1, 1944—the day on which the camp effectively came into operation—the total Mittelbau population was 32,471. Of these, 13,738 were in Dora, including 4,051 Soviets, 3,883 Poles, 2,373 French, 1,185 Germans, 557 Czechs, 472 Hungarian Jews, 377 Gypsies, 275 Italians, and 217 Belgians, plus a few hundred from a dozen other countries. The first Jews had come in May from the Nazis' mass deportation program in Hungary, which sent the majority straight to the gas chambers of Auschwitz. In typical SS fashion, most Jews in Mittelbau ended up with the absolute worst jobs, but some did labor in Mittelwerk production.[14]

As Béon describes, the failure of the Allies to liberate the camp in the summer and the arrival of cold and rainy weather in the fall were demoralizing for the prisoners. And these were harbingers of worse to come. The third phase of Dora would bring an epoch of suffering almost equaling that of the first winter, for three reasons: an increase in repression and executions after the Gestapo/SD counterintelligence office penetrated the camp resistance; massive overcrowding as a result of the arrival of many transports of camp inmates evacuated from the east; and a decline in food, clothing, and other rations caused by the final collapse of Nazi Germany.

Because of the fear of sabotage, the Gestapo/SD had recruited a network of informers, many of them from the ranks of the German criminal prisoners. At the beginning of November, many key leaders in the secret resistance groups of Soviet, French, Czech, and German political prisoners were seized and taken to the "bunker" (inmates' prison) in Dora or the Gestapo prison in Nordhausen. These loosely affiliated groups had organized some sabotage actions but mostly were only capable of using the prisoner-run parts of the camp administration to protect their own members. Most ordinary prisoners, like Yves Béon, were excluded from knowledge of these groups for security reasons; they regarded the more privileged inmates—and not without reason—with envy or mistrust. They could not envy the fate of those locked up, however; the resistance leaders were beaten, tortured, and jammed into incredibly overcrowded cells. From December on, hangings on the roll call square increased; other unfortunates were shot or tortured

to death. Criminal prisoners replaced German Communists and Socialists in the leading administrative positions, leading, in turn, to
even more brutality against ordinary prisoners.

In December 1944 and especially in January and February 1945, the
camp population began to swell with evacuated prisoners from
Auschwitz, Gross Rosen, Mauthausen, and other camps. A number of
the evacuees were Jewish, and virtually all were in horrible condition
as a result of forced marches and days spent in railroad cars without
food. Often, more dead bodies than live prisoners would be taken from
the trains. By March, Dora's population had risen to around 19,000
and the total Mittelbau population to over 40,000, even as the food
supply was getting ever more erratic.

The effects were predictable: over 5,000 recorded deaths from December 24 to March 23 alone (1,090 of them in Dora). By March, the
crematorium was overwhelmed, leading to the burning of bodies on
open pyres. The SS created a particularly horrific situation at the Boelcke Kaserne, a former barracks in the city of Nordhausen that was to
be a "recovery camp" for the sick. Instead, it became a dumping
ground for the hopeless cases from the transports and the camps—a
vast assemblage of the malnourished, diseased, and dying.

March 1945 also saw the horrifying apogee of the repression. In February, the last commandant of Auschwitz I, Richard Baer, replaced
Förschner as camp commandant and instituted an even more vicious
regime. Baer began a new round of executions. In desperation, a group
of 53 Soviet prisoners in the bunker broke out on the evening of
March 9. After killing a few SS guards, all were hunted down and brutally murdered. The SS then began to liquidate the other (mostly Russian and Polish) inhabitants of the bunker in gruesome mass executions: 57 on March 11 and 30 each on March 21 and 22, plus smaller
numbers on other days. At least once, the overhead crane that erected
the V-2s for vertical checkout in the tunnel 41 deep bay was used to
hang many prisoners at once. Béon did not witness this gruesome
show but encountered the horrifying aftermath when he came in with
the night shift. A few Peenemünde veterans who worked for the Mittelwerk, including Rudolph, did see it, however.

In the face of the horrific conditions for the prisoners and massive
disruptions in the war economy, it is astonishing that weapons production went on at full bore to the very last day of March. In February,
the Mittelwerk assembled 617 V-2s and 2,275 V-1s. Records are only
available for the V-2 up to March 18, by which time the facility had already shipped another 362. During the very last months, the company
also built a number of small, unguided Taifun (Typhoon) antiaircraft

rockets, assembled a couple of dozen Heinkel He 162 jet fighters, and put into operation an underground liquid-oxygen plant for the V-2 program. During February and March, on Kammler's orders, General Dornberger and Wernher von Braun also evacuated their staffs and much of Peenemünde's workforce to the SS-dominated region to avoid being overrun by the Red Army.

At the end of March, the Western Allies crossed the Rhine in large numbers. As the front collapsed, Kammler ordered the final evacuation of five hundred key personnel from the rocket program on Easter Sunday, April 1. They were to go to the Bavarian Alps, probably as a bargaining chip for Kammler's own survival. Meanwhile, the camp administration may have discussed annihilating the prisoners by blowing them up with the tunnels but instead ordered the evacuation that began on April 4. The preceding two nights, Royal Air Force Bomber Command burned down much of Nordhausen city in two fire raids that tragically killed about 1,500 sick prisoners at the Boelcke Kaserne as well.

The ensuing "death marches" and rail journeys had the same insane logic seen in other SS camp evacuations. Those who could not march were shot; many others spent days in railcars, often unprotected from the weather and without food, causing thousands more needless and wantonly cruel deaths; most prisoners ended up in other overcrowded, disease-ridden concentration camps, especially Bergen-Belsen, only to be liberated there. The worst crime of all took place at Gardelegen, where the SS and Luftwaffe guards locked over 1,000 marching prisoners from an outlying Mittelbau camp in a barn and set it afire. Those who tried to escape were gunned down. Only eight survived.

Elsewhere, liberation came for those in Bergen-Belsen on April 15, but some Mittelbau prisoners ended up as far away as Austria and were not freed until May.

Aftermath

On April 11, the first spearheads of the 3rd U.S. Armored Division reached Nordhausen and discovered the smoking ruins of the Boelcke Kaserne, at least 1,500 corpses, and 405 living skeletons. This shocking scene was duplicated in the late afternoon when other elements of the 3rd Armored and the 104th Infantry Division came into Dora, finding 600 sick prisoners and piles of corpses around the crematorium. The soldiers had already entered the vast underground V-weapons plant from the north, through the Junkers Nordwerke. The impression these plants left was stunning and haunting—in part because it looked as if the workers had just dropped their tools.[15]

Not everyone in the American army was as uninformed about the Mittelwerk as the troops at the front. U.S. Army Ordnance had formed a Special Mission V-2 to seize assets from the revolutionary German ballistic missile program. Although the V-2 proved to be a military failure that cost the Reich far more than it was worth, its rocket technology clearly heralded the coming of a new era in weapons. The ordnance team, headed by Maj. Robert Staver, arrived a few days later, armed with lists of people and empowered to seize one hundred complete V-2s for shipment back to the United States. Time was of the essence, as Mittelwerk stood in the future Soviet zone of occupation. Because few intact missiles could be found, troops threw a hundred each of as many parts as they could find into railcars, along with partially completed rockets. What Staver's team did not find were most of the key people. Wernher von Braun and Walter Dornberger finally made contact with American troops on May 2, while staying high in the Alps on the old Bavarian-Austrian border.

They, along with other key individuals from the program discovered in Bavaria and Thuringia, were gathered at the Alpine resort of Garmisch-Partenkirchen and were interrogated by many Allied intelligence teams. But U.S. Army Ordnance had the initiative; its interest in using the German rocketeers was instrumental in the Joint Chiefs of Staff's creation of Project Overcast in July. Overcast's aim was to temporarily exploit 350 German engineers and scientists to aid the war against Japan. The sudden end of that war in August made no difference, however, as the armed forces saw the technological riches of the German war machine to be too important—not least of all because of the perceived threat from America's erstwhile ally, the Soviet Union. In 1946, Overcast was expanded and renamed Project Paperclip. Wernher von Braun had already flown to the United States the preceding September. He and a handful of others were the advance men for about 120 Peenemünders to be reassembled at Fort Bliss, in El Paso, Texas, and White Sands Proving Ground, in New Mexico, to help the army launch its captured V-2s and gain insights into German technology.

Meanwhile, on May 5, 1945, Red Army units had fought their way into Peenemünde. They found the massive facility largely emptied of documents, people, and useful artifacts. It was not until, after some delay, the Soviet forces moved forward on July 5 that their intelligence teams could get access to the Mittelwerk and with it to the fruits of the German rocket effort. They brought their own lists of people, including Wernher von Braun, and were frustrated at the extent to which the United States had skimmed off the documents and top personnel. The Soviets did, however, capture a mass of material at Nordhausen. They began to assemble their own German rocket group nearby under the leadership of Helmut Gröttrup, a key member of the guidance group at Peenemünde.

To begin reconstructing and reassembling the V-2, the Soviets chose the former repair works at Kleinbodungen, where 500 prisoners had labored for the Mittelwerk company to refurbish and repair defective missiles. In spite of being hampered by a lack of documentation, the Gröttrup group created a large and successful operation, but on October 22, 1946, they were suddenly and forcibly deported to work in the Soviet Union. Over the next two years, the Soviets stripped the tunnels of much of their equipment before dynamiting them in the summer of 1948. As for the German rocket specialists, they were essentially prisoners and were only allowed to return to their homeland over the course of some years during the 1950s.

For the von Braun team in the American desert, their fate was a much happier one. There was some frustration in the late 1940s at the relatively low priority assigned to rocket research in the era of demobilization. But with the Cold War growing ever hotter, the army moved them to Huntsville, Alabama, in 1950 to form a new rocket center. The results of their wartime research were also influential on the new U.S. Air Force and any number of aerospace corporations. A decade later—in the wake of Sputnik and Huntsville's launch of the first U.S. satellite—the von Braun group was transferred to NASA, along with their big booster program, Saturn. The 1960s would be their second golden age. The Saturn V launch vehicle that put the first Americans on the moon was a Huntsville project—and its manager was Arthur Rudolph.

Disturbing questions about the Nazi records and Dora connections of Rudolph and his fellow engineers had been quickly and successfully suppressed. Pentagon authorities rewrote the security files of some, including von Braun and Rudolph, to permit their retention in spite of regulations designed to exclude ardent or active Nazis from Paperclip.[16] Ordnance also was not very cooperative with army war crimes investigators preparing for the Nordhausen trial at Dachau in mid-1947. Access to the Fort Bliss Germans was restricted to a few interviews and long-distance questionnaires, and a request that Wernher von Braun be sent to Dachau as a witness was rebuffed.

That trial ultimately convicted fifteen SS guards and Kapos; one was executed. But the former general director of Mittelwerk, Georg Rickhey, who had been installed in May 1944 to revamp the administration, was acquitted because of the narrow focus on individual crimes against inmates.[17] Embarrassingly for the U.S. Air Force, the war crimes investigators had found him at Wright Field in Dayton, Ohio, writing reports on underground factories. A few other leading perpetrators from Dora had earlier been killed or punished. Albin Sawatzki mysteriously died on May 1, 1945, in American captivity; SS-General Kammler was reportedly killed fighting Czech partisans a week later, although there is a chance he escaped; camp commandant Förschner was hanged by the United States in 1946 after a war crimes trial focusing on his period at Dachau in the last months of the war. Yet, as was true in regard to all the other Nazi camps, most of the perpetrators at Dora either were never tried or served only a few years in jail. Two decades later, the West German authorities tried two other infamous Dora guards; one—probably the man Béon calls "Ironface"—got a sentence of eight and a half years, the other seven and a half.

For the German rocket engineers in Huntsville and elsewhere, the issue essentially vanished after 1947. For obvious reasons, they spoke little about it, and there is not much evidence that it weighed on their consciences. For most but not all of them, events in Germany had indeed been beyond their control; in any case, the SS provided a convenient scapegoat for all the crimes committed in the V-2 program. Because of the Cold War and space race, the U.S. Army and other government bodies had a strong interest in whitewashing the Nazi issue, and the press was only too ready to cooperate. Wernher von Braun and his publicists did their part by creating an official history that stressed the spaceflight dreams of the German rocketeers and their alleged distance from Nazism. When a heavy-handed East German Communist exposé of von Braun's SS record and connections to Dora was published in the early sixties,[18] the American media ignored it. Only the efforts of French and Belgian Dora survivors in the late 1960s and 1970s really brought this suppressed history back to light in the West. Particularly noteworthy was the 1979 publication in English of *Dora*, a memoir by Resistance leader and survivor Jean Michel.[19]

A second watershed was 1984, when the U.S. Justice Department announced that Arthur Rudolph had left for Germany and renounced his U.S. citizenship rather than contest a denaturalization hearing over his role in the Mittelwerk. Congress had created the Office of Special Investigations (OSI) in 1979 with the specific task of pursuing Nazi war criminals still living in the United States. One of OSI's earliest investigations was of the German rocket engineers and Dora. (Von Braun had meanwhile died of stomach cancer in 1977.) Because of the scant surviving evidence, Rudolph's case was the only one that has been brought to a conclusion thus far. His responsibility as a top officer of the Mittelwerk was clear, and he chose to leave rather than fight. After his return to Germany, a prosecutor there investigated his case but found that under the narrow limits of the only German law for which the statute of limitations had not yet expired, "base motive murder," there was little chance of a conviction. Rudolph therefore was restored to German citizenship in 1987. His defenders tried to picture that as a vindication and attacked his voluntary agreement with OSI as coerced—but without success. On New Year's Day 1996, Rudolph died in Hamburg at the age of 89.[20]

Rudolph's case helped cement the links between the horrors of Dora and the technological triumphs of Peenemünde in popular memory—in large part because of the muckraking books and TV programs on Project Paperclip that followed. The complex questions of individual responsibility were certainly not solved by this sometimes sensationalistic journalism—but at least Mittelbau-Dora was no longer a historical footnote. Yet the voices of the actual survivors of this camp have scarcely been heard, especially in English—and there is no more poignant or powerful statement of the realities of life in Dora than the one you are about to read by Yves Béon. Moreover, it reminds us that the Nazi concentration camps engulfed gentile as well as Jewish prisoners, that America's hands were not entirely clean after the war, and that slavery and brutality were and are quite compatible with high technology. *Planet Dora* is thus more than a memoir of a past that must not be forgotten—it is a warning of a future that cannot be ignored.

Notes

1. Charles A. Lindbergh, *Autobiography of Values* (San Diego, New York, and London: Harcourt Brace Jovanovich, 1992), 348–349.

2. Manfred Bornemann and Martin Broszat, "Das KL Dora/Mittelbau," in *Studien zur Geschichte der Konzentrationslager* (Stuttgart: Deutsche Verlags-Anstalt, 1970), 154–198. This estimate includes the 1,500 killed by the British air raids on Nordhausen on April 3–4, 1945, and estimated deaths during the evacuations and the transports of the "selected."

3. This was certainly true of the standard works on the V-2 through the 1970s: Walter Dornberger, *V-2* (New York: Viking, 1954); James McGovern, *Crossbow and Overcast* (New York: William Morrow, 1964); David Irving, *The Mare's Nest* (Boston and Toronto: Little, Brown, 1965); and Frederick I. Ordway III and Mitchell R. Sharpe, *The Rocket Team* (New York: Thomas Y. Crowell, 1979). Thereafter, journalists altered the discussion drastically: Linda Hunt, "U.S. Coverup of Nazi Scientists," *Bulletin of the Atomic Scientists* (April 1985):16–24, and *Secret Agenda* (New York: St. Martin's, 1991); Tom Bower, *The Paperclip Conspiracy* (London: Michael Joseph, 1987); and Christopher Simpson, *Blowback* (New York: Weidenfeld & Nicolson, 1988). For my own attempt to integrate Dora into the history of the German army

rocket program, see *The Rocket and the Reich* (New York: Free Press, 1995; Cambridge, Mass.: Harvard University Press, 1996). See also Dennis Pisz-kiewicz, *The Nazi Rocketeers* (Westport, Conn.: Praeger, 1995), and most recently, Rainer Eisfeld, *Mondsüchtig: Wernher von Braun und die Geburt der Raumfahrt aus dem Geist der Barbarei* (Reinbek bei Hamburg: Rowohlt, 1996). For the last gasp of the old Huntsville history, see Ernst Stuhlinger and Frederick I. Ordway III, *Wernher von Braun: Crusader for Space*, 2 vols. (Malabar, Fla.: Krieger, 1994).

4. Neufeld, *The Rocket*, 184–189; Florian Freund und Bertrand Perz, *Das Kz in der Serbenhalle* (Vienna: Verlag für Gesellschaftskritik, 1987). The Rudolph documents are in the Bundesarchiv/Militärarchiv Freiburg, Germany, file RH8/v.1210.

5. For the history of the underground complex and camp, see: Manfred Bornemann, *Geheimprojekt Mittelbau*, 2nd rev. ed. (Bonn: Bernhard & Graefe, 1994), and *Aktiver und passiver Widerstand im KZ Dora und im Mittelwerk* (Berlin and Bonn: Westkreuz, 1994); Angela Fiedermann, Torsten Hess, and Markus Jaeger, *Das Konzentrationslager Mittelbau-Dora* (Berlin and Bonn: Westkreuz, 1993); and Bornemann and Broszat, "Das KL." Also useful but marred by an outdated East German Communist emphasis on the resistance is: Erhard Pachaly and Kurt Pelny, *Konzentrationslager Mittelbau-Dora* (Berlin: Dietz, 1990).

6. This "sleeping tunnels" area, which later became the V-1 production area, is now open for guided tours by the staff of the Mittelbau-Dora camp memorial. The crematorium and exhibits on the history of the camp and Mittelwerk can be seen at the former Dora site. The address is: Kz-Gedenkstätte Mittelbau-Dora, D-99734 Nordhausen-Krimderode, Germany.

7. Manfred Grieger, "'Vernichtung durch Arbeit' in der deutschen Rüstungsindustrie," in Torsten Hess and Thomas A. Seidel, eds., *Vernichtung durch Fortschritt* (Berlin and Bonn: Westkreuz, 1995).

8. For death statistics, see Bornemann and Broszat, "Das KL," 168.

9. Neufeld, *The Rocket*, 31, 178–180; 1976 TV excerpt presented in PBS *Frontline* special, "The Nazi Connection," broadcast February 24, 1987 (text from WGBH Transcripts). See also Eisfeld, *Mondsüchtig*.

10. Neufeld, *The Rocket*, 212.

11. The decree, which is included with a small collection of surviving Dora-Mittelwerk documents in the Bundesarchiv, record group NS 4/Anhang, is pictured in Bornemann, *Geheimprojekt Mittelbau*, 73.

12. Bornemann, *Geheimprojekt Mittelbau*, 68. In addition, another 6,000 to 7,000 prisoners worked for firms other than Mittelwerk GmbH at this time, supervised by only about 700 civilian workers. These firms must have included parts contractors working in the tunnels, as well as construction firms inside and outside the tunnel system. Over time, the number of German civilians in the tunnels tended to increase, while the number of prisoners working on production decreased, but there are no reliable numbers after May 1944.

13. Neufeld, *The Rocket*, 213–220, 227–228, and the sources cited therein. I discovered the von Braun letter on microfilm during the research for the book; the original has not been found.

14. On November 1, 1944, there were 1,170 Jews in all Mittelbau camps—the survivors of the group of 2,000 that had arrived in May and June. Bornemann and Broszat, "Das KL," 181–184. Most "nationalities" (as defined by the SS) split roughly according to the proportions of Dora versus the subcamps. But the Belgians were a peculiar case: 90 percent (1,800) of them were not in Dora. For a history of the Belgian prisoners, see Brigitte D'Hainaut and Christine Somerhausen, *Dora 1943–1945* (Brussels: Didier Hatier, 1991). Béon also mentions one black American, but he was apparently a Haitian.

15. Bornemann, *Geheimprojekt Mittelbau*, 149–150, and for American and Soviet intelligence teams, 150–164. For the U.S. side, see also the older account of McGovern, *Crossbow and Overcast*.

16. See the exposés of Hunt, Bower, and Simpson, cited in Note 3. However, there is reason to question their belief in a conspiracy in the Pentagon to violate the President's Paperclip order; the late John Gimbel argued that approval to fudge the rules came from the cabinet level at least. See his "German Scientists, United States Denazification Policy, and the '*Paperclip* Conspiracy,'" *International History Review* 12 (August 1990):441–485.

17. The trial records are on National Archives Microfilm Publication M-1079, available for purchase from the National Archives and Records Administration. On the trial, see Hunt, *Secret Agenda*, 57–77.

18. Julius Mader, *Das Geheimnis von Huntsville* (Berlin-East: Deutscher Militärverlag, 1963).

19. Jean Michel, with Louis Nucera, *Dora* (Paris: J.-C. Lattès, 1975; New York: Holt, Rinehart and Winston, 1979). It remains the only other major memoir about the camp published in English. Michel was a leading Resistance figure in France, and his connection to the camp underground allowed him to be quickly transferred to lighter duties in dentistry. His memoir is invaluable, but Béon's experience was much more typical of the ordinary prisoner. For an Italian prisoner memoir, see Carlo Slama, *Lacrime di Pietra* (Milan: Mursia, 1980).

20. On the case, see Hunt, *Secret Agenda*, and for a defense of Rudolph, see Thomas Franklin [Hugh McInnish], *An American in Exile* (Huntsville, Ala.: Christopher Kaylor, 1987).

An A-4 (V-2) test missile is launched from Peenemünde, 1943. (Photo courtesy of Deutsches Museum Munich)

Gen. Walter Dornberger and Dr. Wernher von Braun, the military and technical chiefs of V-2 development, read a telegram of congratulations, December 16, 1944. Hitler had awarded them the Knight's Cross of the War Service Cross, which they are wearing. (Photo courtesy of Smithsonian Institution, negative no. 85-17510)

Drawing (1945) by Italian Dora survivor Carlo Slama (prisoner no. 76374) of an entrance to the underground blocks, where thousands of prisoners lived and died under unimaginably horrible conditions in 1943–1944. (Drawing courtesy of Carlo Slama)

SS-General Hans Kammler, head of SS construction, was the brutal driving force behind the building of the underground plant and the Dora concentration camp. He later became operational commander of the V-weapons. (Photo courtesy of Archiv Jost W. Schneider)

Underground V-2 production in the Mittelwerk, a 1945 drawing by French Dora survivor Maurice de la Pintière (prisoner no. 31115). (Drawing courtesy of Maurice de la Pintière)

Even for the better-fed and better-dressed civilian workers in the Mittelwerk, conditions underground could be cold, damp, and unpleasant. (This photo may actually come from a postwar East German film, Frozen Lightning.*)(Photo courtesy of Deutsches Museum Munich)*

V-2 center-section assembly in main tunnel B, December 1944. For security reasons, entry was forbidden to all prisoners and workers not working in missile assembly, according to the sign at left. (Photo courtesy of Smithsonian Institution, negative no. 79-12324)

Hangings on Dora's roll call square were a frequent occurrence for offenses ranging from sabotage to resistance. In March 1945, prisoners were also hung en masse from the overhead crane in the Mittelwerk. Drawing (1945) by Maurice de la Pintière. (Drawing courtesy of Maurice de la Pintière)

Prisoners serving as Kapos were essential cogs in the SS machinery of intimidation and control in the concentration camps. Drawing (1945) by Dora survivor Maurice de la Pintière. (Drawing courtesy of Maurice de la Pintière)

The "death marches" and evacuations of April 1945 added thousands more dead to the horrifying toll of Mittelbau-Dora. Drawing (1945) by Maurice de la Pintière. (Drawing courtesy of Maurice de la Pintière)

Two sick prisoners abandoned by the SS and liberated by the U.S. Army in Nordhausen on April 11, 1945. (Photo courtesy of National Archives)

A V-2 is prepared for firing at the White Sands Proving Grounds in New Mexico, May 10, 1946. These launchings were crucial to the growth of missile development and space science in the United States. (Photo courtesy of National Air and Space Museum, Smithsonian Institution, USAF negative 32865AC)

An American GI inspects a nearly complete V-2 in the underground plant, spring 1945. The United States, the Soviet Union, Britain, and France quickly moved to seize German missile technology and personnel. (Photo courtesy of Smithsonian Institution, negative no. 75-15871)

Dr. Wernher von Braun with Col. Holger Toftoy, head of U.S. Army Ordnance rocket development, at Fort Bliss in El Paso, Texas, late 1940s. About 120 German engineers from Peenemünde and the Mittelwerk were brought to America, where they worked for the army and later NASA and various aerospace corporations. (Photo courtesy of Smithsonian Institution, negative no. A-14075A)

Planet Dora

The concentration camp known as Dora, near Buchenwald, opened its gates at the end of the summer of 1943. They were closed by Allied troops in April 1945. Between these dates, tens of thousands of prisoners from all over Europe and Soviet Asia passed through and perished in this accursed Nazi "model" camp. For most of them, Dora was the end of the road. The surface camp and the deadly tunnel they dug to house the underground factory where they constructed Hitler's V-2 rockets devoured the lives of whole shipments of prisoners—men who died by endless thousands under savage SS brutality. Their ashes fertilized the pleasant hills of the Harz Mountains in Thuringia.

Against all odds, some few managed to outwit the fate planned for them by their Nazi captors. Wasted by hunger and illness, numbing cold and continual beatings, they fought off the despair and destruction that would have made for an easier escape.

Each line in this account is written in homage to all those who, with unbelievable dignity, suffered and died in Dora.

—Y. B.

Author's Note: It should be pointed out that the foreign words and phrases occurring in this testimony are terms that were used and, all too often, deformed in the mixed slang of the camp. They do not necessarily indicate the normal form they might take in their original tongues.

THE SPIRIT OF DORA

My body doesn't look good and feels worse. On a scale, it would hardly weigh enough to move the dial. My skin is rotting away from the illnesses and misery of this unearthly place. I've become a tattered rag like all the other thousands here, and if my family had to look at me, they would be stricken with horror. This is what Dora, this Nazi "model" concentration camp, and its SS thugs, have made of us. We are the living dead—zombies who, with the slightest prod, can be sent tumbling into the yawning abyss beyond this "convict's paradise."

But don't be mistaken, you SS murderers, nor you, Dora, you accursed hole, the "glory" of Hitler's Third Reich. I know I won't get out of here alive; it's impossible. But you'll have to pay the price for my tattered body. Don't count on me to make the mistakes that will give you an easy "checkmate." I've been a prisoner here too long to fall into your traps. You'll have to earn my skin!

All of you around me, watching.

I swear: I will never give in.

NEVER!

THE UNDERGROUND CITY

March 13, 1944

Since morning, the train of twenty freight cars has made its way across the frozen German countryside. At 50 men per car, the total of 1,000 prisoners is just right for the SS.

Buchenwald has organized things well. For the prisoners in each freight car, it has been comparatively comfortable. They have been given new striped clothes. With heads, pubes, and asses freshly shaved, they have even been given some decent clogs for their feet. From the start, three groups have formed in each wagon: French, Russians, and Poles. The groups, united in hatred for each other, are shaken by quick jolts and restrained by rapid smashes from the rifle butts of the SS guards allotted to each wagon. One section per nationality is the norm.

Toward midday, the snow begins again, rushing in through the open wagon door. The men crowd together in silence against the bitter cold. In the afternoon, the train slows its pace. Michel, near the door, looks outside, protecting his eyes from the blowing snow. "Guys, I think we're arriving somewhere."

As the train jolts to a stop, he sees a prisoner in striped clothes outside, leaning on his shovel near the tracks. Bent in two, the man is fighting against the horizontally blowing snow.

"Hey, pal, what's the name of this camp?"

No answer comes back.

"Name Lager?" (What's the name of the camp?)

The prisoner turns his head toward Michel. "Dora."

Henri feels a lump from his throat to his stomach. "I'm finished," he thinks, "I'm done for." A sob comes from the corner where one of the Poles has wedged himself. From the Russians, the same sob, then a soft and progressively violent song from the steppes, a plaintive cry of deepest misery. It is the terminus, the end.

The first impression of Dora is terrifying. They discover a huge work-yard, the stores of a titanic metal dealer. There are masses of machines, railroad stocks, metal ducting, and other materials. They see massive piles of cement bags, rolls of electric cable, ominous stacks of reinforc-ing bars, and great stores of mining timber. Through and among these strange, formidable entities, the blizzard winds howl and echo.

At the end of the construction area, they see the entrance to a cave at the foot of the hill. It is covered by a camouflage net. From the opening, there comes a sort of panting—a mad amalgam of human cries, grinding metal, and explosions deep within the mountain. The impression is one of a beehive gone berserk.

Gray human forms enter and leave, some staggering under varied loads on shoulders and backs. Elsewhere, groups of ten struggle to carry lengths of railroad track at a run, some falling and all being mer-cilessly clubbed about heads, shoulders, and backs by Kapos (team leaders drawn from the prisoners) and Vorarbeiter (foremen, also pris-oners). The SS thugs strike relentlessly with their dreaded gummis (electric cables covered with rubber), bludgeoning every reachable body area. As if to escape the brutal attacks, the gray beings gallop with their cargo toward the cave entrance, even while wind-driven snow bites into their sides, ears, faces, and hands.

"*Los! Vorwärts!*" (Quick! Forward!) Adding to the hellishness, the "transfer" Kapos begin cursing and shouting to speed the new arrivals on their way. The terrified column rushes toward the cave, past a ma-chine gun, its magazine loaded, its gunner alert and ready. As an SS man counts them off, the prisoners, in rows of five, disappear into the mouth of the cave, methodically swallowed by Dora.

The air inside, oppressively thick with choking dust, fumes of burnt oil, and humidity, engulfs the newcomers. Here are hills of gravel, there valleys filled with water, and throughout the cave, pools of light alternate with suspicious areas of shadow. Gray beings shovel, hollow out, and tear away at the surfaces. Narrow hoppers loaded with stones and trash roll through a narrow passageway, pushed by men in filthy rags. In the unnatural light, lines of ghostly figures carry pieces of car-pentry on their shoulders. Others push, pull, and drag insane loads. Shouting and swearing, the SS, the Kapos, and the Vorarbeiter rush among them, whipping and clubbing the terrified prisoners. In the dis-tance, the sound of mine blasting adds to the chaos, and the air re-sounds with a thousand clamors.

Farther to the left, a transverse gallery lights up. It is a hundred and twenty yards long and twenty yards wide. The ground level there has been cemented, but overhead in the naked roof, the gleam of mica reflects light here and there.

In midgallery, several tables are lined up. Some clerical inmates record each arrival: last name, first name, nationality, prisoner ID number, age, profession. Neatly written index cards pile up, ready to go into the files.

At the far end of the gallery, a second hall, similar to the one through which they entered, is already finished. A railroad flatcar on standard-gauge track is moving forward. Its cargo is unfamiliar—enormous, green, and cigar-shaped. Voices exclaim, "It must be an aircraft fuselage." "No, it's a pocket submarine." "It looks like a rocket." "A rocket fifty feet long? What a crazy idea!" And as they wonder, the V-2 moves slowly forward.

The ID card business is completed, and the column regroups. The Kapos form the men in groups of fifty each, and it's "about turn!" and then "forward!" The newcomers now belong to a living furnace of endless abuse. Welcome to Dora!

★   ★   ★

"*Fertig! Abtreten!*" (Finished! Disperse!) Screams of joy greet the end of the roll call. Whole hordes rush toward the barracks, jostling each other, floundering in the melting snow. The square empties rapidly except for a few injured, poor specimens dragging along, some being helped by more able prisoners.

At the infirmary entrance, there is a considerable crowd. Those with diarrhea have a waxy tint to their skin and trousers soaking with yellow liquid; they smell foul. The TB victims and pleuritics shake with fever. There are men with frightening wounds on their necks and feet, wounds with putrefying smells. Some can't make it to the building and just languish nearby.

The infirmary corridor is overcrowded, but everyone wants to get in. A fight breaks out at the door, which closes with a bang. Two of the Polish Stubendienst (prisoners who served as orderlies), heavy and ruddy, rush forward, swearing and swinging their clubs. They strike at heads, backs, and arms, pushing the mass of prisoners back toward the outside. The weakest prisoners fall, their wounds oozing blood and pus. Others, their eyes bulging, rant and rave, unable to control themselves.

A shitter, dazed and miserable, stays alone in front of the door. "*Scheisserei, Kamerad, Scheisserei*" (I have the shits, comrade), he whines. His eyes are enlarged by illness, fixed and white. *"Kamerad, krank!"* (Comrade, I'm ill!)

One of the male nurses clubs him on the palm of his hand. "Fuck off, scum! You stink!" With a quick stroke, he smashes his club into the shitter's ear, and the man drops to the ground, howling in agony.

★   ★   ★

Charles is very pleased with himself. The open sore on his foot, acquired at Buchenwald, has taken on a horrible look. It is swollen with pus, and worrisome areolas have spread almost to his heel. To drain the pus, he has made two incisions in the wound and passed a bit of string through each incision. The pulling action is painful, but it brings him temporary relief.

He arrives at the infirmary where, curiously, the crowd is much thinner. As usual, the shitters are thrown out brutally because their smell upsets the orderlies.

"Franzous, komme!" The male nurse, a Russian youth, looks at Charles with a smile. With his white blouse and polished shoes, he is the picture of health. *"Franzous, lizopizdi 'pussy'?"* (Frenchman, you lick pussy?)

"Yes, you cunt. Stuff it." Charles returns his smile and takes off his canvas shoe and Russian sock (a sock made from a square piece of cotton fabric). His foot is visible, covered with white, green, and blue rings surrounded by an undefined redness. The middle swelling is crowned by the two bits of string. The Russian jokes and places Charles's foot in an enameled dish. "Pull the strings," he says.

Charles pulls. A jet of pus runs into the dish. The Russian takes scissors and, looking slyly at Charles, cuts in at one end of the swollen skin and continues quietly to the other. The pain is so excruciating that Charles thinks he will collapse or that his heart will stop. He feels a scream rise from deep inside, but the Russian works on, cutting out a circle of his flesh, keeping his smile. The scream doesn't emerge. *"Was ist Kunt? Kunt ist Kamerad Kommunist."*

While still laughing, the Russian takes a spatula, fills it with a sort of white cheesy paste, and spreads the mass over the huge sore area. Then he re-covers the mess with half a roll of toilet paper. He smiles at Charles. *"Zwei Tage Schonung!"* Two days off from work! Paradise!!

"Franzous, Transport!" The two Stubendienst look at Charles with sneering expressions. They're seated apart at a table, dipping their spoons into a bowl of thick, steaming soup out of which he sees them bring forth some potatoes and bits of meat. The barracks is otherwise empty.

Fascinated by the sight and smell of this soup, Charles forgets the shooting pains in his foot. His eyes widen with desperate hunger as they follow the spoons. Each one approaches the bowl, goes around the inside seeking a bit of meat or soft potato, and, with a full assortment, goes back to the already overfed mouths.

"Stinking swine," he thinks, "you gorge yourselves all day like the pigs that you are."

Since the night before, he has prowled the barracks, trying to get in, but each time, the Stubendienst have thrown him out. They spend their time eating soup and cooking potatoes on the stove. The day is only just starting; the kommandos (work teams) have left an hour before. Charles feels that his foot is soaking. The toilet-paper bandage is only a pulp.

"Was Transport?" (What transport?), he asks. One Pole looks up at him and mutters, *"Krankentransport."*

That's it, then. That's why there has been such a thin group at the infirmary. It has already been decided to "transfer" the ill, and the word has spread through the camp. Word has discreetly filtered from the Arbeitsstatistik (manpower records office), friends were alerted, and their friends in turn. It is imperative not to be in the infirmary or considered a "special treatment" case because the liquidation is imminent. *"Alle Schonung! . . . Antreten!"* (All those relieved from work! . . . Assembly!), comes the cry.

Led by the barracks chiefs, those relieved from work make their way across the roll call square, a muddy bog, and on upward to assemble a little higher, to the right of the camp. Even in their rows of five, they form a group of great length.

"I mustn't be taken!" Charles tries to overcome his anguish. He's badly placed in the first line, too visible. His shoe, only roughly laced, is slightly swollen by the dressing, his trousers hiding the rest. The pain is gone, or at least he no longer feels it.

Will the SS take everyone or only a selection? There's no way to know. Charles looks around. There are cripples with legs wrapped in rags and cement bags and men with gangrenous ears smashed in by Nazi clubs. Some have enormous swellings, and their trousers only exaggerate the evidence. They're done for, all of them. But then, he thinks, there are also the Lagerkommandos (camp maintenance teams), those who mend the shoes and do small chores. They're old and often unfit, but they have a restful air that gives them a look of good health. They won't be taken.

The man next to Charles speaks softly. "It seems they're sending us to a rest camp." Charles looks at him. The man isn't old, perhaps forty, but Charles senses that he has given up.

"Are you an idiot or what?" Charles sees the man's number, a 43,000 like his own. The man is pretty far gone.

"You know," he tells Charles, "they were going to send me back to my kommando, the diggers, but I haven't got the strength. I'd like to rest, and perhaps this talk about a rest camp is true."

The command comes: *"Stillgestanden!"* (Attention!)

A trooper arrives from the right, coming from the infirmary. Up there, it's finished. The SS doctor comes near the column, followed by the secretary, a prisoner who writes down the numbers. Charles feels the life running out of him; a lump sticks in his throat. Above all, he knows he must hold on. Eyes straight ahead, he can hear the group slowly approaching. There are stops and brief conversations, but he can see none of it.

Suddenly, a black silhouette is in front of him, the SS doctor. He looks at Charles, then puts a question to the secretary, who translates. "Frenchman, what's wrong with you?"

As if from afar, Charles hears his own voice. "A foot injury, but it's over with."

"Walk," orders the doctor. Charles takes three or four steps to one side, then returns. His walk is normal.

"Good. All right."

The troop moves on. Charles's eyes blur. He hears nothing, wishing only to stretch out and sleep.

★   ★   ★

The order is barked: *"Alle Schonung, Appelplatz!"* (All relieved from work, to roll call square!) An army of pitiful wreckage they are, rounded up from all the barracks, the ill and crippled temporarily excused from work. They look like a rabble of hoboes at the end of their run, leaning on makeshift crutches, spitting up the last of their lungs, or shitting out the remains of their guts. They find themselves lined up, worried looks on every face.

The Kapos, stiff within their double-thick jackets, seem less aggressive. They only strike with their clubs for good measure in this "Cours des Miracles" (the gathering place of the beggars in medieval Paris).

The pathetic group arrives at the Holzhof, a sort of work area where trees are cut up. In the middle of the clearing, there stands a gallows. The ropes are blowing this way and that in the biting wind, while snow drives into worn shoes and through every hole in the prisoners' ragged garments. A sudden disturbance at the entry to the camp enclosure attracts every eye. Accompanied by a group of dignitaries, the camp commandant and the Rapportführer, the SS officer who serves as a liaison between inmates and the camp administration, begin moving toward them. Their conversation is lively, even happy. Their boots are gleaming, uniforms fresh. They come to a stop a few yards from the gallows. Now the show can begin.

The actors appear, first the Lagerältester (camp chief, a prisoner), followed by two prisoners, their hands tied behind their backs. One is Russian, the other Polish. Both are ashen in appearance, and they trip over stones and roots hidden by the snow. Four SS guards surround them, bringing them to the foot of the gibbet.

The Rapportführer, accompanied by the Lagerdolmetscher (chief interpreter, a prisoner), advances to the front of the ranks. As the Rapportführer speaks, the Lagerdolmetscher translates into French, Polish, and Italian.

"These two prisoners," he says, "were surprised while sleeping in a barracks under construction, leaving their comrades to work in their place. This is a very serious form of sabotage. These are bad comrades. They are going to be hanged."

The Pole begins trembling all over. He falls on his knees, crying and crawling as he begs the Rapportführer for his life. The Lagerältester kicks him, swearing, beating him viciously. A kick of the gleaming boots caves in the man's ribs. Another kick smashes his face, and the Pole doubles up, howling in pain. Now the Kapos seize the condemned man and place him under the noose, quite straight, his feet on the stool.

The Lagerältester slips the noose around the Pole's neck, pulling carefully to make the show last longer. *"Prima!"* (First class!), he barks, and kicks the stool away.

The man drops, twisting in agony. His mouth is full of blood, and his eyes roll as he gasps in vain for air. He rears up, knees lifting to his chest, falling, then lifting again. The minutes pass as his strength ebbs. He moves only with a trembling that tightens the slipknot even more. His movements weaken and finally stop. It is over. The Kapos take the body down.

During the horror, the Russian has not moved. He looks at the executed prisoner and says, *"Pizdiak."* (Cunt.) Now it is the Russian's turn. He climbs onto the stool. The Lagerältester comes up, speaks to him with a smile, adjusts the noose, and kicks the stool away. The agony is long.

★   ★   ★

"Look at that, Sonny! It's pyramids of shit! Better than in Egypt. It's unbelievable; it's a once-in-a-lifetime thing. You have to see it. There's at least a ton. I don't mind coming to Dora; otherwise, I'd have missed this. Oh, there are artists here!"

In fact, there is roughly a ton of shit per pyramid. Fifty-gallon barrels have been cut in two, then placed one atop another: four on the bottom, then three, two, and one. Full to the top, that makes a good ton. Roland, toolbox in hand, looks at the strange scaffolding from a technician's point of view. "You see that, Sonny? The guys who stacked these up had a good eye. Just imagine a banana peel over there. What a mess that would be!"

Roland and Georges have worked together for a few weeks as electricians, while insane chaos rules in the tunnel. They work amid the roar of dynamiting, breathing choking air thick with dust. Close by, kommandos panic-stricken by endless beatings climb mountains of gravel or carry enormous, strange things on their backs, making their way around great piles of mining timber. Fights erupt between Russians, Poles, and Frenchmen even while the Kapos swing their gummis at backs, arms, hands, and heads. Many a man's feet are crushed by falling loads. Others, straining to hold heavy air-ducting in place, have their shoulders dislocated and flesh torn as protruding irons dig into their bodies. In areas not lighted by the dim, yellowed bulbs, prisoners stumble against rocks or discarded shards of planking, endless traps waiting to shred a man's feet or tear into his flesh.

Georges has complete confidence in Roland. Having a working companion makes him feel protected. At the same time, he finds it difficult to admit that he, a professional electrician and much older than Roland, has no authority. At least he knows his job; Roland had never seen an electric wire. On one bad morning, he takes the bit in his teeth. "Listen, Roland, you're pissing me off, always calling me 'Sonny.' I'm forty, and you must be barely twenty."

"Well, what's wrong with that, Sonny? You see, kids bore me, but if I had a son like you, in his forties, and with skill like yours, I'd be proud of that."

A blast roars from farther back in the cave, throwing a hurricane of thick dust toward them. The light in the dirtied bulbs above blinks off and on. "Let's get the hell out of here," says Georges, "before some Kapo jumps us."

"Sonny," continues Roland, "you haven't understood a thing. Look around. You see all these guys? What do they have in their hands? Nothing. So they have to break their backs with loads they can't carry. Then they fall, and the Kapos beat them to death. But we're different. We're electricians, see? We have our toolbox. When a mine blast tears out an electric cable, all the drills stop and everything goes black. Then what do we hear, Sonny? 'ELEKTRIKER!' The SS holler like hell, and the Kapos start beating up your kommando. But do they beat you? Never! You see, you're more important than the kommando. You're even more important than those trashy SS bastards. They can kill anyone; in fact, it can earn them promotions, but they don't know anything about electricity, those dumb cunts. So when the line is torn down, everything stops . . . and they're responsible for keeping the work moving! So they come looking for you without any fuss; they only stop short of kissing your hand. So you, with your toolbox, you go, calm and collected, and get them more electricity. That toolbox is the thing; it keeps trouble away!"

"But, Roland, you don't know anything about electricity."

"Sonny, there are days when I ask myself if it isn't me who's the best engineer in the team."

★   ★   ★

Swinging and jolting, the cart rolls along sloping rails into the tunnel. With its long shaft and small wheels, it is a small version of railcarts you can see from Germany to Russia.

Jacky puts his cap back on his head. It's a Russian chapka, a fur hat with its ears turned up into the top, giving him the look of a caricature of a president of the Court of Justice. Grinning and running up and down the tunnel, he is the "Vorarbeiter der Todträger" (chief of the undertaker's gang), finding and collecting bodies, then moving his cartful to the morgue.

Like a skilled sea captain who knows the rocks and shoals like the back of his hand, Jacky avoids the dead ends, bogs, and potholes. With two aides pulling, the cart arrives at Block 4. He pulls back the canvas door and goes inside. What a spectacle!

Block 4 is 130 yards long and 20 yards wide. Like the other three, it holds 3,000 men, split into 2 teams. Large rows of trilevel bunks are used nonstop by the teams. A constant rainfall comes from both infiltrating water and the condensation of human breath. The lights, always on, are veiled in clouds of swirling dust. Among the back alleys and "flea markets," thieves are sheltered, as are saints, the dying, and the dead. Cries break out in one corner, frantic galloping in another. Shoes, bread, and bowls have disappeared; even bunks are collapsing in the ensuing din. Every racial and ethnic group from the Atlantic to the depths of Siberia finds itself pulled into this nightmarish Babel.

Finding all the bodies for removal requires a flair for perception as well as talent, and Jacky has both. First, he visits the barracks chief, who has done most of the easiest work. A dozen bodies lie near the door; they were found where they had been thrown at the foot of the bunks. Jacky begins his rounds. First, the basics. At the ends of the alleys, he picks out the denuded silhouettes. These aren't "sleepers" seeking the warmth but already stripped corpses. Then he checks under the bunks, finding another dozen "clients."

Now comes the specialized part of his work. He moves slowly along the corridors, climbing bunk levels until he sees what he's looking for. The Russian is sleeping with clenched fists on a straw pallet, but his position is unstable. The pretense of deep sleep doesn't fool Jacky, who lifts a corner of the straw and sees the mummified body next to the Russian. He calls for his helpers, who pick up the body while the Russian hurries away out of their sight.

Jacky knows what hunger is. He even accepts the extremes to which prisoners can be driven by its ever-present torture. But when it comes to a prisoner hiding a dead body so as to have his rations as long as possible, Jacky cannot agree with that.

*   *   *

In this month of March 1944, Dora cannot be said to have a proud look. Of course, the tunnel, that witches' cauldron, seems complete. All during construction, in its chaotic madness, it filled the role of an insatiable man-eater. No one could imagine that one day, it would become a factory producing finished articles.

The surface camp is only a rough outline. Beyond the tunnel is a modest-sized valley, closed in at the far end to the right of the hill that houses the future underground rocket factory. To the left, an empty plain without houses stretches as far as the neighboring town of Nordhausen, a few miles distant. An electrified perimeter fence, with guard towers at its beginning, bars the entrance to the small valley. The fence climbs the hill and comes down again, thus marking the limits of the prison quadrilateral within which men from all across the continent are dying by the thousands, only to be replaced by new slave laborers. The entry, a simple wood barrier covered with barbed wire, recalls nothing of the "glorious" entrance to Buchenwald, the "Capital City of Death." The two adjoining buildings house the SS guard post, the Schreibstube (secretarial office), the Arbeitsstatistik, and the Politische Abteilung (political section). The roll call square in the center of the quadrilateral is still only a rough field where the snow hasn't yet covered the holes and bumps. Directly to its left is the bunker, the camp prison that holds those who have managed to be further imprisoned, even within a concentration camp. Farther on are the cobblers' and joiners' shops. To the right are the decontamination building and the Effektenkammer, the striped-clothes store filled mainly with ragged remnants of prison garb, which the cripples employed there mend with care. For Dora hasn't seen any of the fabulous riches like those at Buchenwald—where frightened prisoners from all over Europe arrived with full luggage and where successive layers of goods were quickly amassed. Here at Dora, newcomers arrive already stripped of everything they once possessed. Here they will now live, and die, entirely at the expense of the camp administration.

After the Effektenkammer, there is the kitchen with its row of shining chrome autoclaves. For the prisoners, though, the heavily guarded kitchen is a very dangerous place to approach. Halfway up the hill are construction sites for the crematorium and the infirmary. Only a few barracks destined as prisoners' quarters are scattered around the limits of the camp. Just as a small community doesn't become a real village until it has a church, a concentration camp doesn't become a real camp without a crematorium. Since Dora still suffers from this deplorable inconvenience, it is necessary to send truckloads of each day's dead bodies to Buchenwald. The tunnel produces an endless, growing number of corpses, and the infirmary, with its own unbelievable death rate, no longer knows what to do with its bodies.

However, several days ago, a furnace arrived and has been roughly placed on the left side of the roll call square. Uncovered as it is, with its oil tank on one side and an accompanying hold for corpses, it resembles something between a large liquor still and a small engine tender. It has been put into service without waiting for the crematorium that will house it with several others. This is a slight relief to the overworked SS truck drivers.

A warmly clothed prisoner in charge of the oven chooses a body from time to time. After carefully noting the number on the corpse's stomach, he takes up a sort of shovel to propel the body into the oven. With each new load, a puff of smoke and soot rises into the cold sky. Around the unit, the heat has melted the nearby snow.

Somehow we feel that in this month of March 1944, things are beginning to move. Certain signs show that Dora is about to give birth to a new entity. Now the majority of prisoners sleep in the tunnel, emerging only once a week for roll call. Only a few kommandos and some administrative services remain on the surface.

The Barakenbau-Kommando (barracks construction team), sappers, carpenters, and electricians have made up a good part of the last transfer. The roll call square, until recently deserted during the day, now holds several busy groups. SS and German civilians explain things with much gesturing: Cut down timber, clear the land, level the soil, then lay the concrete—and quickly! Always quickly! *Schnell!*

They send the kommandos to work. Land surveyors in tattered rags take their readings. Cement, metal, and mixers arrive with wheelbarrows, shovels, and pickaxes. Dora is stirring on the surface; a second hell is taking shape.

★   ★   ★

The Barakenbau-Kommando is a hell of a unit, all of them joiners and carpenters, promised, sworn. Michel looks at them worriedly. He wonders if these are the builders of cathedrals. Oh, God, we're in for it. If they're going to build the city of the future, we're not at the end of our troubles.

Their average age is perhaps about twenty-five, especially the newcomers from transports 40,000 to 45,000. There are a few old ones, such as Michel, from transport 30,000. Some already know each other and regroup in families according to the prison from which they came: Fort du Hâ, Le Pré-Pigeon, Montluc, and others. They know survival in this warped place depends upon possession of a manual skill. François the journalist from Bordeaux, Marcel the hatter from St. Malô, Guy the student, and Louis the professional soldier have signed on as carpenters. But only Michel has a bit of genuine experience in building.

The French form about half the kommando. The rest is made up of Russians, Poles, and those of uncertain nationalities. Their numbers alone favor the French, but their lack of concentration camp maturity and philosophical attitude, plus their bad temper and lack of discipline, threaten to cause problems for them.

The Russians, fewer in number, are a formidable group, ever complaining and quick to act. Their wild reactions are a constant threat. The Poles are united by a hatred for all other nationalities, so they are avoided like the plague. Cooperation between these groups is difficult, to say the least.

Rudi the Kapo looks at the miserable team with disgust. They are hulks, primitives, middle class, and intellectuals, all the scum of Europe. Tapping his club against his left palm, he asks if there is a Frenchman, Russian, or Pole who can speak German. Three men step from the ranks and stand before him. Snow has begun to fall.

"I've been in the camps eight years, and I'm your Kapo. Whoever doesn't toe the line will regret having been born. We're going to build blocks (barracks). There will be a lot, at least a hundred. You're the 'specialists,' but don't bullshit me, you don't know anything. You've signed on as carpenters. Well, you'll get those blocks up or I'll beat you to death, understood? OK, to work."

The kommando leaves the camp perimeter and heads toward the huge building site. There are mountains of planks, stacks of doors, windows, panels, and partitions all covered with snow. It isn't possible; we aren't meant to carry all that! "Los! Zu vier!" (Quick! By fours!)

In the confusion, Michel finds himself with two Frenchmen plus a Russian smaller than any of the three others.

"My God, this Russian is so small he won't carry a thing. Fuck off, Jackal! Raus! Weg! (Get out! Scram!), or I'll kick your ass!"

"Ebany, Franzous" (Fuck you, Frenchman), sneers the Russian. He is fine.

Michel is about to blow everything when he is suddenly staggered by a burning shock on his ears. The Vorarbeiter is already behind him, his club poised as he barks, "Schnauze, Franzous!" (Shut up, Frenchman!)

There is nothing left but to carry out his orders. In one great throng, amid shouts and curses echoing every corner of Europe, men climb the snowy stockpiles, knocking them down and causing panels to slip from hands too weak to hold them, falling clumsily to the ground. The clubs strike out in all directions.

Michel has his shoulder supporting a panel that cuts into his flesh. "This fucking thing weighs a ton, and this Russian isn't carrying a thing. We'll have to get rid of him. Fast."

The work teams are improvised without anything like good sense. We see teams made up of three big men and one small one who carries nothing or three small ones with one big man who carries everything. As the latter bends his legs or back to be at the same level as the others, it looks as if he is cheating, so he is beaten and clubbed. The very height of German efficiency!

"Get going!"

The column moves off at a steady pace, but the loads are awkwardly balanced. The four-hundred-pound panels shift their mass erratically on the uneven shoulders, accentuated by the irregular military-type march. Some men fall, setting off an explosion of shouting and beatings.

How many blocks did the Kapo say we'll build? More than a hundred? How many trips will it take to build just one? Michel regrets signing on as a plasterer and carpenter. He has seen no plaster in Dora; it doesn't seem to be used here. He could have signed up as an electrician. There would be nothing heavy to carry, and that wouldn't be bad. He's seen hundreds of splices and junction boxes. He'll have to look into that possibility later. Michel lifts up his head. It is March 15th, and it is snowing.

★   ★   ★

Inside the tunnel, the miners have driven into a side gallery. The transport kommando, those who will clear the rock, are there as well. The pneumatic drills, compressed-air lines, lamps with their electric lines, and scaffolding planks and tubes are massed in the middle. The gallery is completely without light. The men wait. A rumbling is heard from far off, but here there is no noise. The men are pressed against each other, stuck to the wall. The Germans are going to blow the mines. Will the roof hold? Or will slabs of rock and tons of stone fall upon them?

Suddenly, there is an enormous explosion, and a hurricane blast of stones and flying rocks, a whirlwind of dust and sheets of debris from the main gallery strikes the men, cutting into their flesh. The whole mountain shakes. "God, have mercy on us!"

The rumbles echo a hundred times, soften, and die. It's over, thank God! *Los! Arbeiten!* (Quick! To work!)

The Kapos, hidden in fear, reassert their authority. Electric lines are reconnected. The group leaves its shelter under renewed beatings. The main gallery air is thick and yellow, almost solid, irritating eyes, nostrils, and lungs, burning the mucous linings. The explosion has blasted a sort of funnel that will have to be leveled with heavy drills. Huge rocks are piled in a heap in front of the opening. Smaller stones from the blast cover the ground and create confusion under the strange lighting.

Amid the clubbings, a Vorarbeiter groups prisoners together. They are detailed to get the sections of narrow-gauge railroad and small wagons to carry off the stone. The others will clear the floor and break up rocks too big for loading into the trucks. The choice of tools becomes important. Shovels are popular, for they allow the amounts picked up to be lighter, if no one is spying. By going to the area farthest from the explosion, one can shovel reasonable amounts, being careful that the load is well distributed. There is also less risk of the roof caving in, and the SS, knowing the dangers of the drilling area, go about their brutal business more readily among the shovelers and sweepers. Prisoners scramble atop the mountain of rocks, some of which weigh several tons and have to be broken up. Men heave on the mining rods, break the largest boulders clear, and roll them away, thus spreading the pile, while others wield sledgehammers and picks. Men pant from their efforts, lungs gasping for air but instead filling with silica. They are handicapped by poor lighting, and their feet slip and stones fall, cutting into flesh unable to heal.

Distant outcries come closer. The railroad gang is returning, hemmed in by SS on one side and Vorarbeiter on the other, the Germans shouting hellishly, clubs striking at everyone they can reach. The men run, eyes bulging with fear, trying to hide behind the rails they struggle to carry. Still, their feet slip clumsily, and their hands and shoulders are unprotected from the rain of crushing blows.

The arrival of the SS spreads new terror, intensifying the frantic pace of work. Prisoners swing their sledgehammers, picks, and mining rods in a mad rhythm, lifting, placing, and smashing rocks that shatter in murderous bursts. In mass panic, they lay, wedge, and bolt the railroad track upon which carts soon begin to arrive. It's no longer a question of lifting small shovel loads or of carrying modest-sized stones. Now it's load the shovels to the limit, take the biggest stones, and throw everything into the hoppers, filling them with maniacal speed.

Catastrophe! In the mad rush, the front hoppers have been loaded. On the single track, they can't move out with empty cars behind them. Cursing with rage, the SS, Kapos, and Vorarbeiter drive the terrified prisoners to lift the empty hoppers and carry them to the opposite end of the track.

In the rush, the track has not been fully secured in place but in spots simply laid out along the ground, sections joined together as well as possible. It stretches along the rough, gravel-covered floor, which is riddled with holes, dangerous slopes, and sharp bends. While prisoners push the small trucks, they meet other teams carrying materials, laying drains, or drilling the walls. As a truck travels over a hole, the track lifts up at its opposite end and the truck sinks, then slams back to the surface with a heavy bang as the living scarecrows push it forward again.

Suddenly, a rail gives way and a hopper car derails, dumping its tons of stone on a prisoner. His scream, followed by groans, can be heard from under the pile. The Vorarbeiter bellows orders, and the men straighten the small truck. They load it again and put the victim on top. The man is in great agony.

"Forward!" The truck moves. They'll get rid of the poor wretch at the entrance. It isn't important; he'll be dead.

★   ★   ★

Dora is part of the last generation of Konzentrationslager (concentration camps). Due to circumstances beyond the control of its designers, the "thousand year Third Reich"—which is only to last for twelve—cannot be carried further. From a purely intellectual standpoint, this might seem regrettable if one were interested in exploring two aspects of the human condition: sadism exercised without constraint and the level of resistance that might be reached by a group of men subjected to extremes of suffering, constant physical misery, and sickness, aggravated by a starvation diet. Naturally, it is understood that the victims of such generously administered brutality will have a quite different point of view.

The first concentration camps were established soon after Hitler's rise to power. At first, the Nazis convicted and confined active and known opponents of the National Socialist regime, then those who simply might become obstacles to the setting up of the system. Once these people were imprisoned behind barbed wire, other groups were added, classified as "antisocial" or as "parasites," all of whom were described as a useless burden and a "bad omen" for the country. Then the gates opened still further to swallow up criminal prisoners, conscientious objectors, homosexuals, Gypsies, and members of other groups.

The goal of the first generation of camps was the repression of freedoms considered dangerous by the Nazi leaders. A site would be chosen, generally near a stone quarry. Prisoners would begin arriving, surrounded by perimeter fencing of electrified barbed wire and guard towers equipped with machine guns. The prisoners would be driven and terrorized unceasingly as they constructed the camp with whatever building materials the SS supplied. They took part in no useful activity for the country, industrial or otherwise; they were simply in the camp to disappear, and this they did. There were also a few originals who, *nolens volens*, became perverted, serving as SS auxiliaries and making up the prisoner hierarchy of the camps.

The birth of the second generation began around 1942, coming to fruition with the construction of Auschwitz. The idea was simple, logical, and efficient. The Nazi rulers took the position that millions of parasitic human beings existed throughout occupied Europe. In conformance with National Socialist doctrine, it was thus necessary to liquidate them. The Jews would be the first to be erased, then ethnic minorities, and then social groups that the Führer considered "disturbing elements."

Business was done briskly. The Jews of Europe were seized and shipped by trainloads from their homes to Auschwitz—men, women, children, old people, and babies. After sorting out the solid types who would be useful as laborers, the SS led the rest to their deaths in the gas chambers—no lost time, no paperwork. Prisoners moved the bodies to the crematoria, where they were burned. Often, one group would be leaving the chimneys as puffs of smoke while another arrived. The stationmaster at Auschwitz must have been a very busy man since more than a million "travelers" entered his establishment in some two years.

The third generation of camps opened with the outbreak of war. From 1939 onward, as all Germany was mobilized, factories found themselves short of manpower. Nazi planners decided prisoners could fill that need. They would die, in any case, but the Reich would profit from their labor until then. German industrialists, hardly worried about ethics, found the idea ingenious, and armaments factories opened in most of the camps.

Thus, Dora was created to construct the secret weapons, the V-1s and V-2s Hitler hoped would devastate England. The secret would be well guarded; no prisoner would survive. Between the arrival of prisoners in September 1943 and the arrival of the American army in April 1945, the slave-labor workforce of about 12,000–15,000 men at Dora was replenished at least three or four times due to the horrific death rate among the prisoners. From the standpoint of "SS efficiency," this result was good! Under the Nazi system, prisoners had but one common destiny—death, however and whenever it occurred.

It has been said that when there isn't enough to eat, rats will kill one another. This wasn't the case among the slaves of Dora, but it could be said that cooperation between nationalities was difficult. The conditions within a concentration camp—the compression of humans who would normally live far apart, from the Atlantic to the Pacific, the daily deaths from beatings, accidents, sickness, or starvation, and the endless suffering and terror—made a very explosive mixture.

The Czechs, for example, the first foreigners in the camps, had distrusted the French since the Munich Agreement that put their land into the hands of the Nazis. They had equal distrust for the Russians, whom they considered descendants of Attila. While few in number, they made up an elite that maintained a disdainful distance from the rest wherever possible.

The Russians arrived in huge, blustering lots, brutal and supreme, an indigestible proletarian mass within the prison population.

The Poles, who were also very numerous, simply hated everyone.

The French, along with a few Belgians, made up a good third of the prisoners. Their numbers helped them resist the hate, envy, and misunderstandings of the Slavs. Aside from the Poles, no one seemed to hold it against the Russians for having been allied with Hitler. But France's abandonment of its friends, the Czechs, its loss of the war, and its request for an armistice were beyond accepting.

The French image was also tarnished by a sexual fantasy that, in any other time or place, would have been of no consequence. In the mad cauldron of Dora, however, it took on enormous proportions. It seems that somewhere in Naziland, a Frenchman had confided to a Slav that he enjoyed *la minette* (pussy-licking) very much. Well, the "secret" crossed Europe like a shot, supposedly shocking camp inmates who were quick to add this "serious" propensity to their usual list of grievances. They concluded that Frenchmen—who came from a nation that forsook its allies and lost a war in six weeks and who themselves played *la minette* with their wives—could not really be trusted.

Relationships among Western Europeans were no problem. Belgians and French lived together with an understanding made easier by sharing the same language. The Dutch, with a few from Luxembourg—even though more reticent—knew their camp. The Spanish were few in number, for the Republicans arrested in France usually found themselves in Mauthausen. As for Anglo-Saxons, they were represented, as a reminder, by an Englishman who lived in Germany before the war. And there was one black American, who apparently was living in Europe at just the wrong time.

We should mention the Italians. After General Badoglio's seizure of power, many Italian units were taken prisoner by the German army and sent to work in Germany. One of these units arrived at Dora after having made many stops. They had an enormous death rate, but the survivors looked to the Western Europeans for support. This wasn't only necessitated by the huge Slav bloc; it was survival. What was normal in societies outside the wire would not be valid, wouldn't even exist in Dora. It was a world apart from normal humanity, run by murderous rules, dominated by the SS, the Kapos, and the Vorarbeiter. For prisoners, each day's survival required a mixture of size, skill, friendship, and cunning. When you are due to die together, then you must manage, like it or not, to live together.

Under the SS, principal authority was in the hands of Germans, whether political or criminal prisoners. They had the jobs of Lagerältester, Kapo, Blockältester, and so on. The Poles were predominant in lower duties, which were good jobs because they offered huge advantages without inconvenience. They were Stubendienst and messengers. They worked in the kitchens, in the Effektenkammer, and in the shoe-mending shops. These were key jobs that gave them enormous power without the weight that would usually accompany such jobs. The French, due to the presence of men of high value among them and because of their early arrival, managed to get jobs in the infirmary and in the administrative services. These advantages weren't always felt by the average prisoner, but at least he wasn't completely downtrodden. As a rule, someone would be able to help him in some way. As for the Russians, they represented the lowest level and, apart from holding a few minor posts, carried no weight. Their only force was in their numbers, in their inertial power, and in their "I couldn't care less" attitude.

The great majority of prisoners thus had no way of reaching the top of the camp hierarchy. It was too far above, too far away, too abstract.

When you reek with the stink of shit and death, you don't try to approach an administrator. No. You stay in your corner and try to be forgotten.

★   ★   ★

Stachek was looking out of the window. He felt well. The Tischlerei (joinery) where he stood overlooked the roll call square, where he saw a digging kommando hurrying about with their wheelbarrows. The prisoners were shoveling frantically both to avoid the vicious clubbing of a cursing Vorarbeiter and to fight against the cold, which had not yet relented, even in this month of April.

"It's high time," he thinks, "for this fucking roll call to be finished. There's been enough mucking about night and day in this dirty hole." Stachek feels the gentle heat in the hut as it radiates from the little stove that has been carefully filled with wood cuttings. He looks around at the other prisoners with satisfaction. Nearly all are Czechs; it is almost a reserved area. He realizes that there are also a few Poles, who hold their heads up and speak with affectation in an effort to fit in with the Czechs. Even so, he thinks, they're just lousy oriental primitives, brought up on potatoes and onions. The Vorarbeiter is a German criminal prisoner in his thirties. He is homosexual, has a mocking look, and has never lifted a hand against anyone. Often he is absent, having a beer with his colleagues in nearby areas.

Stachek admires his scaled plan. He will do a good job, even though it isn't the cabinetry he prefers. He doesn't mind doing carpentry from time to time; it is like a return to basics and reminds him of his beginnings in the profession. The SS will come this afternoon, so he has just enough time.

He planes the uprights with a sure touch, then carefully cuts them to size. For this job, he has been able to obtain fine straight-grained timber from the heart of beech, stout enough to resist splitting even under extreme stresses. Wisely, he measures several times at each step. In good joinery, Stachek knows, if an error shows up after the wood is cut, it's too late. With pencil and marker, he outlines the mortises, which he cuts with a mallet and chisel. The chips come away, giving off a fine aroma. Then he cuts the tenons with a handsaw. The hours pass to the sound of band saw, turning lathe, and tappings of the mallet.

By late afternoon, the job is finished, apart from the final assembly, which he carries out. To his great satisfaction, everything goes perfectly. He drills out the last holes with a brace and bit, then puts in the pins, the transversal and the joints, and finally the six rope hooks. It is done. He straightens out the assembly, remembering the framework that stood in the schoolyard of his youth. There he had loved the trapeze, the ring work, and climbing the rope. It hasn't really been so long ago, but it was all in another world.

The SS arrives with the Lagerführer. "Attention!"

Every activity in the joinery workshop stops at once. The Germans' flat cigarettes give off an oriental odor. The SS men look contentedly at Stachek's work, obviously well pleased. "Prima! A first-class job!" With the Kapo at their heels, they leave the shop. The Vorarbeiter comes to Stachek, an amused look on his face. "You've had the compliments of the top people, all overwhelmed. You've made life easier for them."

Stachek enjoys the compliment. "Well, with this framework they'll be able to get good exercise, ropework and climbing."

"But you haven't understood a thing!" hisses the Vorarbeiter. "Do you know what you've built? You fucking idiot, it's a gallows for six. Thanks to you, Dora can now move into the industrial age!"

Suddenly, Stachek feels numb all over.

★   ★   ★

The infirmary has been practically emptied as one "transfer" of patients departs. Their time has run out. But the hospital is filled again the very next day. Considering the frequency of the life-or-death selections, those who are admitted have about a month in which to be cured or die, and the second is more likely than the first.

It is on the side of the hill, close to the crematorium under construction. With German efficiency, the proximity of the two buildings will shorten future journeys. The infirmary building is large and besieged with men at the breaking point every evening. The infirmary is divided into two sections. One holds the tuberculosis patients, and the other houses medical and surgical cases. Both sections have three-tiered bunks, so that some gymnastics are required by doctors when they look at patients in the top bunks.

The tuberculosis section is, in fact, mostly a death room for those already at the end. Within a few days, it's over for most of them, but in that time, they have had to endure the brutal sadism of the male nurses. Food rations rarely even reach them.

On the other side is the "Cours des Miracles," a frightening mixture of faces badly swollen by erysipelas (skin infections), of swellings that horribly deform limbs and necks, of shocking wounds both suppurating and necrotic in nature, broken arms and legs, crushed ribs, hands, and feet. The rank smell of rotting bodies drifts throughout the room, and always there are the continuous groans of the helpless. There is no medicine, and there are no analgesics. The chosen few might hope for a dose of aspirin, but even this pitiful dosage creates great envy from one bed to the next.

Aside from the nurses—brutish thugs with little humanity and less decency—the hospital staff consists of two doctors, two real ones, a Dutchman and a Czech. With humanity, they try to do their best, which is to say virtually nothing at all. When they pass, the inflamed eyes of their suffering patients momentarily lose their look of haggard desperation and for a moment appear more human, as if to say, "So long as you're here, doctor, nothing will happen to me."

The "surgical" staff, however, is completely different. In compliance with SS doctrine concerning the use of qualified personnel in concentration camps in this month of April 1944, our surgeons are—if the grapevine is correct—a mason and a baker or the like. After months of practice, they have evolved a jolly technique that is astonishing to see.

With a pleuritic within their reach, no problem. The huge needle is thrust merrily between the ribs. If it is well directed, a jet of liquid spurts onto the floor, bringing a chorus of praise. If not, the hapless patient will die quickly from an internal hemorrhage mixed with pleurisy fluid.

The most serious operations, such as amputations, are done with the same serenity. Anesthetics are nonexistent, so they are replaced by a solid blow to the head, repeated whenever necessary, which certainly costs much less than drugs.

Dressings, though, have reached a higher level of evolution. Once wounds have been opened widely with scissors (lancets haven't arrived here at our model Nazi camp), creams and mysterious ointments are applied copiously, and the wound area is covered with toilet paper.

So the infirmary of April 1944 is a tragic illusion of infernal quality. Saints, martyrs, and bastards meet and cross each other's paths in the few days left to them—saints tortured with desperation because they can do so little, martyrs with the eyes of injured beasts looking for a den in which to die quietly, and bastards perfectly integrated within the system—necrophagous, living off the decomposing and unstringing flesh, off the mouths of those crying and begging, and off the rotting meat about to lose its soul, for trading, for getting a bit of fat.

Dora is studded everywhere with moments of truth, but without a doubt, the infirmary is the most hideous of all its areas.

*   *   *

"My God, what's that cunt doing? He'll get us in for it again! Forward, asshole!"

The men of a kommando carrying half-fuselages for a V-2 are being pushed along by a menacing Vorarbeiter. But men in the front section of their unit are blocked by still another team that, while sliding a machine across their path, has blocked it and created chaos. At once, the Vorarbeiter and Kapos storm into the prisoners, raining curses and blows in all directions. Good manners and self-control among the prisoners vanish quickly, and even the elite use pithier expressions than they had ever needed in their former social circles.

The worksite swarms with Dora's slaves, lit by searchlights. It is three o'clock in the morning. The kommandos have been at work since nine the evening before, so six hours remain before they are relieved by the day shift. The weather has turned mild, and a cutting rain gradually replaces the snow. It soaks into the prisoners' garments and turns the ground into a freezing slush.

The tunnel driving has advanced, and handling kommandos begin storing materials that arrive night and day. Commandeered from the four corners of Europe, lathes, drills, soldering gear, large jigs packed in crates, and loads of technical gear pour into Dora. So many delicate instruments can be damaged by the weather that they have to be sheltered. A standard-gauge railroad is being built into the tunnel but has not yet penetrated very deeply. So the heaviest, most awkward machines are either carried on prisoners' backs or pulled over wooden rollers.

Work is behind schedule, so the pace is accelerated. At the innermost end of the tunnel, miners are digging madly, dynamiting is done at an ever-faster pace, and stones are being cleared away even as they fall from the rock face. Clearing kommandos constantly pass other groups bringing materials into the mountain. From a distance, they resemble two lines of ants, one going up, the other coming down, as if working a layer of food.

Civil engineers, indifferent to the pitiful condition of the prisoners near them, are continually measuring the galleries according to the plans they carry. They move about, climbing the piles of rubble, going around machines and reels of cable, past turning concrete mixers, but never looking at the tattered men around them, nor even hearing the shouts, the vicious clubbings, or screams of pain. Quietly, they indicate location points desired for machines, for junctions, for joints and fixing points for the electric and pneumatic air ducts.

The future outline of the tunnel begins taking shape. Two parallel galleries are cut into the mountain for about two thousand yards. These will be interconnected with forty-six transverse galleries that will serve as workshops and storage areas. The right-hand tunnel will be used for receiving materials and spare parts, the left for the assembly and exit of V-2 missiles, Hitler's "vengeance" weapons against the British. Each rocket will be forty-five feet long and weigh thirteen tons.

The perpendicular galleries will be set aside for the machining and assembly of the different parts. The last hall is far deeper than the others. Here, the rocket can be placed in an upright position. This unique factory, sheltered deep beneath its covering mountain, will be immune to all attacks from the air, unlike the installation that the RAF so effectively ravaged at Peenemünde.

There is much yet to be accomplished. While the drilling nears its end, the tunnel installations are traced out to completion. Innumerable technical problems become apparent, and these have to be resolved in the least time possible. Although the overhead of the tunnel has been profiled, the rock is fragile in some spots under concentrated heat and moisture. Several times, whole sheets of rock break loose above the welding teams, crushing men to paper-thinness. This doesn't, of course, disturb the Germans. After all, prisoners are cheaper than decent cigarettes; but if a costly machine were destroyed, that would be serious!

It is also necessary to hermetically seal electric installations and junction boxes. All must be absolutely watertight to resist leakage that concentrates in the channels after having soaked the walls. All in all, the tunnel has to stand up to conditions similar to a deeply submerged submarine, resisting the outer pressure of a hostile environment waiting for a chance to crush everything within.

Berlin, we know, has great hopes for these secret weapons as well as the productive capacity of Dora. Upper Nazi circles think the rockets can and should lead to a redressing of the military situation. In a sense, then, the slaves of Dora have become the potential saviors of Hitler's Third Reich!

To save time, a simulation of V-2 production has been undertaken. Parts of a rocket (known as the "Torpedo") saved from destruction at Peenemünde have been brought in. These consist of fuselages still bearing their original stenciled markings. There are fins shaped like those of sharks, tanks for oxygen and alcohol—special aluminum containers that are difficult to handle—and instrument sections with removable doors that contain the electronic elements for command and guidance in flight. Only the explosive warhead is missing. This will come from another factory for installation prior to launching.

Certain assembly halls have been completed under high priority. Each unit has received a finished model, wherein the placement of machinery and electronic and pneumatic components are fixed. A twin of the model, built in almost a homemade manner, has been placed on the assembly line along the length of the second tunnel. As it emerges from the depths, the Torpedo resembles a gigantic metal fish that, as it passes through various workshop areas, will receive its bones, tail, fins, air bladder, and head. Production has yet to begin, but the machinery is coming together. Soon, each hour will see the exit of a new V-2. If all meet Hitler's plan, these rockets against which there is no defense will spread death and terror throughout England.

★   ★   ★

The roll call square fills with prisoners. Barracks by barracks, the prisoners group in the glare of searchlights. It is raining, and a glacial wind heightens the chilling effect.

The ground underfoot is a quagmire where a few beet roots stick out, glazed by the frost. Some prisoners have brought stones to put under their feet, to keep the freezing mud from penetrating their shoes. Their coats and jackets, soaked through twelve hours of rain, have formed ice copings on their shoulders and stuck to calves and thighs. It is roll call, the day's last formality before returning to the barracks, sleep, and oblivion. In five-man-deep formations, the groups stretch out parallel to the camp gate. There are six thousand prisoners at the moment, at two hundred per barracks, which means only thirty small calculations. After that, back to the dry barracks until the next day. Sleep first, and forget everything else!

"*Achtung!*"

Everyone comes to attention, heads bared. The SS officer approaches the Blockältester, whose head is also bared as he presents his register. The SS looks at the figure, then starts from the left. Tapping his truncheon on the shoulders of those in the first rank, he begins counting, "*Zehn, zwanzig, dreissig, vierzig* . . ." (Ten, twenty, thirty, forty . . .) Arriving at the end of the column, he checks the number of the day's dead, dying, and sick who are laid out on the ground, all neatly aligned, of course.

"*Stimmt!*" The count is correct. For once, it shouldn't drag out, perhaps an hour. The SS will take the numbers to the tower. Added to the others, a total will be reached, and everything will be finished for the day.

Instead, the waiting drags on. The cold intensifies as the wind strengthens. Flakes of snow engulf Les Misérables de Dora. "It can't be! That fucking snow can't be starting again!"

The rain has given way to snow falling from one side, blown on an icy wind. It bites into their eyes and tears at their ears. The winter they thought past has returned, bringing lumps to thousands of throats. A powerful blizzard takes Dora in its grip as soaked clothing hardens. Cloth shoes and Russian socks, already soaked with mud, bring piercing cold to the men's extremities, the pain of which quickly becomes unbearable.

A voice nearby speaks up. "When we're back in France, the first time some guy starts to tell me about wonderful winter sports, he's gonna get his ass stripped in the snow, and then I'm gonna beat the bastard to death! These guys are bastards!"

No one was impressed. "We'll all die if this doesn't end soon." The ranks begin to move about. The Blockältester scowls and raps a few heads. The lines reform fairly well again. At the gate, there is no activity, but under the searchlights, whole ranks are slowly breaking up. At the end of the columns, the dead and dying prisoners are swiftly being covered by snow. "The Rapportführer to the gate!"

"Oh, God, what now?" is the question in every mind. "Is the count wrong? Has there been an escape?" If there has, that man will bear the hatred of all the thousands suffering in this freezing snow. Even one escapee or one prisoner missing for whatever reason means hours of counting, then recounting the prisoners, and then doing it again. Men unable to go on cease fighting to stay alive, which is fine with the SS. There are always more slave laborers available.

Many prisoners on the brink of existence cling to life, barely knowing how or why. Perhaps they dimly sense that everything human and inhuman must be endured before admitting, one by one, "I've had it; there's nothing more I can do."

For two hours, they have waited, swept by the blizzard, agonized by icy gusts cutting into bodies already weakened by hunger and brutality. Involuntary sobs from tortured lungs are drowned in the winds, and one man's prayer might be that of thousands. "Oh, Lord, do something for us. It can't be that you've invented these things. You can see quite well that we're going to die. But why pick on us? What have we done to You?"

In the third hour, a brisk movement stirs the barracks chiefs, who reestablish the lines of men. Can it be over soon? Some prisoners have fallen, dying, to the ground. They are put with the bodies already laid out, which form a heap in the snow. The Blockführer (SS man in charge of barracks) returns, rechecks his register, and counts again. There have been changes, of course. Now there are fewer men standing, and more are stretched out in the snow. The count is the same. "*Stimmt!*"

The waiting begins again, but the Blockältester can no longer control the situation. Like swarms of migrating bees, balls of clustering humanity begin to form—moving, living things into which those outside try to enter, seeking the warm center, where life can flow and be preserved a while.

During the fourth hour, bodies are thrown from the swarms, lifeless things that have to be eliminated. The dead are walked upon and pushed away. Life and safety are here inside the ball, where wind and snow cannot penetrate. Those outside try to force their way inward to escape the cold as well as they can.

In the fifth hour, there is a brisk call: "Assembly! Close the ranks!" The shouts from the barracks chiefs are slightly different, almost human. During the past hours, they were not, but the chiefs must have relived some of the agonies of their own first years here. The ranks re-form, and the results are horrifying. The numbers of dead have doubled and tripled. The bodies are taken from the snowy mound, while those fit enough stand upright in straight ranks.

There is a crackling sound in the loudspeaker: *"Fertig!"* The roll call is finished.

★   ★   ★

Using the tunnel darkness as camouflage, the SS man searches for his prey. Tall and thin, he has a horse-shaped head that instills terror among the prisoners. His boots have been shined until they gleam whenever light crosses their surface. Some prisoners secretly call him "Horse head," others know him as "Ironface." He is an absolute terror—the worst, most experienced killer in Dora. He has arrived at this level of existence because he is unable to control himself; the rage within him can only momentarily be calmed with the death of some hapless prisoner.

In the usual tunnel chaos, two prisoner columns going in opposite directions somehow cross into one another. In the mix-up, they slow into utter confusion amid clamoring and shouted insults.

On the narrow-gauge rails, the hoppers run nonstop, loaded with stones, gravel, and waste. The route is winding and repeatedly deformed as the small wagons cause the rails to shift. The prisoners push, arching their backs each time the track hits a pile of rubbish, and then hold back lest the hoppers run loose on the downslope. At the hastily laid track joints, the hoppers bump and derail. Then swearing erupts anew, and blows fall wildly as the desperate men lift, pull, and push to set each hopper back on the rails and get it moving again.

From opposite directions, men in columns hunch along carrying units on their backs for the Torpedo. These will be stockpiled in warehouses at the far end, near the point where digging is still in progress. Members of one kommando stagger under grotesque, horrible burdens. These are the tanks for liquid oxygen and alcohol, enormous containers. Each is carried by four men, two ahead and two behind. Back to back, the prisoners have to join hands, whereupon the tank is placed in the resulting cradle.

Within seconds, their shoulders have become dislocated as hideous pains shoot through backs and necks. Hands begin to slip, but, above all, they must not let go. They move ahead blindly, feeling the way with their feet, avoiding deadly potholes. Their hands are numb, and sharp pains knife downward along their sides, but they must press on.

Hidden in darkness, Ironface watches. It's all too easy. He could act quickly, but then the tank-carriers wouldn't see him, bent in two as they are. He waits.

Soon two Russians arrive carrying a plank on their shoulders. They seem busy but are walking slowly and laughing. They come near, look to both sides, then move back into the dark. They put down the plank, and one produces a Makhorkov cigarette and a lighter. The man looks up to see Ironface just in front of him. He freezes, as if paralyzed, then begins to move from side to side like a sniffing rabbit.

The SS killer senses that his day is made; the unholy fury fills his being completely. Now to act! Insults on his tongue, his hand moves toward his gun. This startles the Russians, and they bolt, running madly, shoving through the columns, jumping over the gravel, racing frantically for the far end of the tunnel. Ironface, surprised for a moment, tears after them, firing his Luger wildly. Panic strikes everywhere as kommandos break up in fright, men running this way and that, and the furious Kapos strike out at everyone.

In the confusion, Ironface realizes he has lost his prey; they have disappeared. So. Others will pay. He picks up a piece of reinforcing steel and begins striking out right and left. A prisoner in his way falls, rolls up, and cries for mercy, but Ironface in his madness strikes the victim again and again, panting with the fury of his effort. The prisoner screams in his agony, again and again with each new blow. Then he stops moving.

2

THE INITIATION

Hunger is the one continuing, haunting reality. The average inmate, if he has followed classic prison-camp routine, is confronted with it daily. It affects everyone, especially those who have already spent weeks or months imprisoned in their own countries. There, in Gestapo and other German cells, they have been ill treated at best and sometimes tortured to an irremediable degree. Their food rations have been below survival limits, and conditions of detention have made them physical wrecks. On leaving the cells, one might face the execution squad with head held high, shouting whatever he would, yet be unable to run a hundred yards.

Thrown upon the evil Planet Dora, the Häftlinge (prisoners) arrive having already exhausted their means of physical defense. Of course, one could be hanged, clubbed to death, or crushed by a deadly overload. Many have been victims of national rivalries or have succumbed to various illnesses, but between all these German devilries, one has to manage to live and survive. To do that, one has to eat.

Dora is filled with physically devastated men. Those who, in civilian life, had a comfortable layer of fat, soon notice an apron of skin across their stomachs. The fat has melted, but the skin has not been reabsorbed. Others with flat stomachs and nothing to lose become skeletons within weeks. Yet all these have one point in common: hunger! It torments each one every second, minute, and hour. Its persistence reminds us that hunger is well entrenched. Its very triumph is ostentatious. It is never at rest, even in dreams. During the day, it pervades the bowels, legs, and arms. It breaks down men's morals, empties their heads, and shortens their breathing. Even the toughest men with balanced brains swing back and forth in pitiful phantasms.

Dora holds men once used to foods ranging from rustic meals to refined cuisine. Yet to a man, all of the thousands share the same compulsive desire for fat, for enormous cooked meals, for luscious stews swimming in thick sauces. The dreams of food are endless. Impossible recipes are passed back and forth, so beautiful that we believe them, dreaming of the day when we will be back home again and have our fill of them all.

In starvation fantasies, intellectuals and professional types decide to take up animal husbandry. They'll raise pigs, chickens, and cattle. Property from legal and insurance offices and consulting rooms will be sold in order to buy everything that can be used for making meat, which they plan to eat up every two hours. As the mad dreams expand, the shattered spirits feel warmer. The men envision acres of rich earth from which tantalizing pies are growing, great stews of irresistibly delicious aroma, legs of veal sprouting up like mushrooms after a shower, and more. "We'll invite each other," they promise and swear, "and we'll have the Feast to end all Feasts!"

As soup-time nears and visions fade, thoughts return to the present. Will there be any potatoes? How many men will share a lump of bread? Three? Four? Those who can calculate, using sane mathematical functions in a totally irrational world. Differing schools of thought conflict, until the madhouse becomes completely paranoid.

Once the rations are shared, the soup (with or without potatoes) and the bread split between three or four people, everything is gulped down hungrily. Each man keeps his eye on his neighbor's bowl, thinking, "That bastard, he has some potato in his soup, but I have a bit of meat in mine. It must make him shit; I can see him brooding over it. Anyhow, this soup is only dishwater, nothing but the slops. For Christ's sake, how will we hold out until tomorrow? Think of the soup in the kitchens, with all the meat and potatoes still in it. Yet it's these filthy Stubendienst who'll eat it all. God, let me live to the end of the war, and I'll smash all their faces in!"

The bowls are emptied. The bread, margarine, and slice of sausage have been swallowed. Each man feels as if his stomach has leaped upon the bits of food, weighed them and noted that they are all but worthless, put the trash aside, and found that there is little left. Hunger quickly returns, having never left. Even the mad dreams of food that haunted them an hour earlier have fled. Tears from within shake their bodies. Looking at each other, past the scrawny beards, men notice that their buddies have rotting flesh. With graying skin, they look to be old men, yet few are past thirty. And what of me? Yesterday, I noticed that the skin on my buttocks flops when I walk. Luckily, it happens where I can't see it.

After the war, I'll find an apartment above a restaurant and eat there every day. It will be one where they make up delicious stews, succulent veal, and the like. And I'll get a good stock of food at the market because, you never know, between midnight and one A.M., sometimes you want something to eat. And if my buddies show up, I'll make them a feast, and fuck the hour. They can even stay to sleep if they want. In the morning, we'll have fried eggs with bacon, honey, butter, and jam. What a dream!

One's thinking processes deteriorate. After the miserable so-called rations, reality reappears. You'll starve to death in Dora.

Meantime, roll call is next. There will be damage, as usual. Worse yet, there will be no rations before roll call or in the next twenty-four hours, nothing to sustain you while your body screams for food, any food at all. How I'd like to find some peelings, I don't care what. I want to eat. If I don't eat, I'll starve. Help me, God, they want to kill me!

★   ★   ★

A voice rasps, "Watch out! The Romanian!" as the SS man emerges from the gusting snow. Standing before the kommando, the Romanian is like the fox in the hen coop, except that this fox has come not to feed but to massacre. He likes that, plus the fact that no one can escape. A small, ferret-eyed, dark-complected man, he searches for prey. His peaked cap and grin are all too familiar. He looks, knowing a victim will offer himself. It's easy; he only has to look at one of these ragged wraiths and the man will become distracted, slip, and make a mistake to set off the Romanian's fury.

He watches the diggers making the barracks base. They have to pull roots, break up rocks, and level the ground. The picks strike sharply on the stones; some of the ancient shovels break against the roots and come up empty. The prisoners become agitated, and the Vorarbeiter swings his club left and right.

Paul isn't far from the Romanian. This is bad because he is picked out at once. He pushes the wheelbarrow with all his strength, trying desperately to reach a group where he can melt from view. Paul's forty-five years, crooked glasses, and intellectual air combine to make him look like a ridiculous puppet, almost a caricature of a rake returning from a strange costume party. His hands, which once held a pen and corrected notes, are now bitten away and deformed by cuts and the cold. His foot catches on a root, he trips and falls, the wheelbarrow, too. The Romanian lunges at him, striking with the truncheon and cursing. He clubs Paul on his back, his sides, and his head. Paul is in agony; he knows he's done for.

But a distraction occurs—shouts and outcries just beyond the curtain of falling snow. The Romanian straightens up, panting. He leaves his prey and hurries through the snow toward the noises. Paul slowly manages to get to his feet. He can feel his flesh swelling, his fingers are crushed and bleeding, one eye is swollen and closing. His glasses are twisted, one leg can no longer take his weight, but above all, he must not stop because the Romanian, intoxicated by the start of the killing, is more than ready to finish it. Hobbling, Paul takes up the wheelbarrow, but nobody speaks to him. He is as one under a curse.

★   ★   ★

Heinz the barracks chief is glad to encounter Philippe. "Ach, French-man, little cunt, you are still alive! *Arschloch* (Asshole), you always astonish me." He taps Philippe lightly on the back with his truncheon. He likes Philippe a lot because the Frenchman was born in Cayenne. And for Heinz, Cayenne is the mecca for criminals, the ultimate symbol. Of course, Philippe isn't a criminal, being much too young. He just happened to be born of a father stationed there on military duty.

This mad Heinz, however, is impressed by the romanticism of the place. The inimitable Cayenne: *wunderschön* (lovely, exquisite), the great French bandits! Yet Heinz wasn't a criminal, he was a soldier. He'd seen the Foreign Legion and Spanish Civil War, always a good soldier; there was nothing to be reproached in him. Then chance led him to Buchenwald and Dora, and he began turning rotten. He swayed between a pitiless savagery and a severe, strict nature. So when they met, Philippe would rummage among youthful memories of Cayenne, give a few details to the chief, and add some more, and this earned him a degree of relative peace. Philippe was almost the youngest in the camp, at least among those from Resistance groups. There were younger prisoners, Gypsies of twelve and thirteen, somehow spared from the gas chambers in the East, and some Russians not much older. Philippe became concerned only with his own survival when he saw those who might have defended him march off to the Stalags (POW camps) in columns of five.

At one point, certainly not for humane reasons but more for those of organization and statistics, the SS regrouped prisoners under eighteen in a barracks on the perimeter of the surface camp. All the kommandos sought youths who worked like their elders, fighting and dying like grown-ups. They weren't exempted from SS rules, so they worked as before but had a barracks to themselves.

Every night or morning, according to the shift he worked, Philippe went back to the youth barracks. In other barracks, no matter what their ethnic or sociological makeup, the sharing of the same hope for survival generated at least a minimal cohesion of spirit. But prisoners here couldn't care less. The law of the jungle reigned—and worse. These children, torn from families lost in the gas chambers and crematoria, behaved like wild creatures. They didn't give a shit about anything and had little or no social or moral sense. For weeks and months, their education had been beaten and terrorized into them—that of Dora. For them, survival wasn't won through solidarity but at knifepoint. Heated arguments or open attacks exploded into bloody confrontations. They became expert thieves, and woe betide anyone asleep who hadn't stowed his gear securely; he'd soon find himself stripped of shoes, bowl, and spoon, which would be sold at the flea market near the kitchens.

The young Gypsies and Russians, with their little angel faces and long eyelashes, were very sought after by the Kapos and barracks chiefs, who were almost all homosexuals. They would give the young men potatoes and soup for their services. It didn't seem to upset the youngsters, who would go and drool around their potential clients. The young had unbelievable vitality and adapted to the camp with remarkable ease, unable to worry about what would become of them. It was as if these boys had no souls, their thoughts never reached as far as the next day; they were fixed in the present moment only.

Ration issues would start fights, and the Stubendienst would halt them with strong blows to the head, using the heavy soup ladle as a club. Bread or sausage imprudently placed on the table would disappear instantly, passing from hand to hand to find itself welcomed into a far-off pocket, generating new battles and loud shouts. Heinz would erupt and strike savagely at these horrible monkeys, who would run and disappear.

Heinz cursed the day he was made chief of the youth barracks. It was easy to control adults. At the slightest argument, he'd appear with his club, and everything would snap back into place. He didn't even need to hit them unless he did it for pleasure.

However, he felt helpless with these kids who cared for nothing. As soon as he caught one to deliver a beating, the kid would let out deafening screams, twist loose, and hide under a table. The others, drawn by the noise, would shout for joy in a bullring atmosphere, hoping for a kill. Without pity or morals, they were extremely dangerous, ready for anything.

Amid this violence, Philippe was almost a father figure, an ancestor. After twelve hours of brute labor in the tunnel and a roll call that left him weak, he would find himself among savages ready, at the least chance, to strip him blind. Holding his bowl in one hand, he would slip the bread and sausage inside his shirt while keeping an eye on his margarine, also in danger of disappearing. In the dormitory, he would wrap his shoes and bowl in his jacket by tying the sleeves together, then put the lot under his straw pallet after checking to be sure the planks of his bunk were securely in place.

Happily, there were a few other French youths, captured Resistance people like himself, who formed a team. One other member was a Gypsy who fit into the group. To survive, the group adopted a united front, similar to settlers in Westerns who would circle the wagons against attack by the Sioux.

This continual frenzy covered an unpleasant reality. The death rate among the young savages was high, though offset by new arrivals. As a result, the block was always full, with the average age of its inhabitants nearer twelve or thirteen than eighteen. The Buchenwald Arbeitsstatistik, knowing Dora's reputation, could well have kept such children at the larger camp, where conditions were better, but that office didn't hesitate to be responsible for their liquidation.

★   ★   ★

The kommandos are assembled on the square, awaiting the end of roll call to leave for the tunnel. As he does each day, Claude, the small Lyonnais, carries the kommando banner like a standard-bearer. He, Luc, and Michel are always in front because there the marching pace is clean and unbroken. From rank to rank, the cadence falls apart, and the clubs fall painfully back there. Underfoot, frozen spittle forms small bumps on the walkway.

"Did you see that shitty soup?" asks Michel, from Brittany. "Dishwater, nothing but slops! Not even a bit of potato. Wait till I catch one of these filthy cooks; you'll see what I'll do to him." A professional plasterer, Michel is a nice guy. He really likes everyone, but once you hear his modest grievances, you have to admit that a lot of lowlifes are taking advantage of every prisoner here. But the fateful word *soup* starts a chain reaction. The starvation rations have created a burst of interest in cooking—or at least in dreaming about it. The most flabbergasting recipes get by with no argument.

A voice from the third rank is heard. "You're right. Those miserable cooks know nothing. I'm a cook by profession. With anything, I'll make up a feast. Say, for example, with turnips. Take just one, not too big. Of course, you have fresh cream and some thin slices of bacon."

Silence descends. Each one feels like crying, "Stop it, you bastard. No, don't stop. This abominable torture is too good. Make us ill, make us dream . . . "

A voice complains, "Yes, but your slops, your fresh cream, and your bacon aren't enough."

"Well, just wait," continues the cook. "You have a lovely Bresse duck, fifteen or sixteen pounds. First of all, you prepare it with some onions; not too many, just three or four. You add a large glass of brandy to melt the sauce and then a small glass of Kirsch, for the flavor."

Another voice adds, "And you need some vegetables."

"Wait, I haven't finished. You slice the bacon and let it simmer. Now, you put a good two pounds of potatoes and the same amount of macaroni in a casserole dish, and you add three or four spoonfuls of cream. Then, while that's cooking, you take some Gruyère cheese, about two pounds; grate it and put it over the duck."

Sobs break out in the columns. Russians, Poles, and Czechs, none of these savages exist anymore. One can't see them, doesn't want to see them. France is there, united around one man. Everyone listens to the culinary messiah as he speaks of the Promised Land.

A slightly timid voice asks, "And the chocolate? Don't you put in a little chocolate?"

There. You feel that something is wrong; it smacks of high treason. The head cook stops. Cursed be the imbecile who dared interrupt Scheherazade! You wait. Happily, the cook continues.

"All right, Toto, if you want to be funny, I'll let you have the place. Me, I've looked after ministers, famous actresses, and people of whom you have no idea. My God, chocolate in a duck! If one day you come to my restaurant—and that would astonish me—you'd have your chocolate. I'd throw a bucketful in your face!"

So. After a moment, our man takes up his exciting dream again. Like an actor in his theater, he senses that his audience is with him.

"Another thing I'll add, for finishing touches and connoisseurs, and that's truffles. They add to the flavor of a dish, and they prepare the palate for the next course."

The next course! My God, he'll tell us more fabulous things! The poor devils turn toward him, their legs giving away.

"Fertig!"

Shit, roll call is over. The kommandos will leave for the tunnel. It's cold. Nobody even asked what wine there would be. Nobody gives a shit about the wine.

★   ★   ★

The male nurses have come up with a new game. It's fun, and at the same time, it keeps their muscles in trim. All they need is a corpse that has just given up its soul, and there's nothing easier to find. They make the rounds of the beds in the infirmary, and there are always some.

They write the dead man's number on his stomach, following administrative regulations, then take the body by arms and legs and drag it off to the showers. They put a stretcher at the opposite end of the room, and one man takes the corpse by the arms, the other by the legs. The game consists of carefully balancing the body and trying to throw it onto the stretcher. A stiff weighs on average about seventy-five to eighty-five pounds, just the right weight for amusement without making the nurses too tired.

Obviously, they don't get it right every time. Either the body falls to one side, a miss, or lands on the stretcher sideways, not really a hit. After each turn, they call out the quality of the throw, give themselves points, and start again. Of course, the improvised "ball" suffers in the game. First, its nose breaks, quite normal, but then the arms become dislocated, which makes the next throw a bit awkward. The corpse doesn't bleed, though, just a little oozing but not enough to force the sportsmen to scrub down the room.

This is a bit worrisome to the bedridden. Who'll be next? If you die, it isn't really important since, a few hours later, your body will have been transformed into heat, light, and smoke in the crematorial furnace. Still, you have the impression that, though dead, you may still feel pain. The lifeless bodies that you see have twisted faces, seeming to cry out in suffering that hasn't stopped. The guy next to you, the one who has just gone to the next world, doesn't look saved. On the contrary, his open face and staring eyes appear more anguished than before.

Paul made up part of the group of onlookers in the infirmary, and his spirit had taken a hard knock. He had told himself he would never go to the infirmary; it was too dangerous. However, after the brutal beating by the Romanian, the Vorarbeiter, Kapos, Russians, and Poles used him as their scapegoat. He would be downed like an animal with a well-aimed blow from a stick. In a matter of days, he had become a punching bag, on the receiving end of all the killing madness. He was doomed. So one night in desperation, he went to the surgery after roll call.

He was examined by a doctor who didn't care about bruises but who looked at him, touched all the scars, then admitted him as a nephritis case. It was a catastrophe. He was put on a diet. There would be no bread, no starchy food such as the marvelous potatoes sometimes found at the bottom of the soup can. There was no hope of getting the "diet," which was the dream of the whole camp—a sort of sweetened soup thickened with powdered milk. Instead, he would get nothing better than a clear broth.

His trampy look and prominent jawbone covered by his beard drew sarcasm from the male nurses and Stubendienst. They dubbed him *"Scheisse Professor"* (Shit Professor) and served his watery rations with grins as they told him repeatedly that the crematorium was getting impatient for him.

Yet despite his physical state, Paul has a card up his sleeve; he is serious. It is the dedication of Social-Radicals, a left-liberal political philosophy that had taken the French, Czechs, and Poles to new heights.

Paul is a Social-Radical, has finished high school, and knows how to speak to people. He is listened to and sometimes even called "sir." It is a tribute here, where no titles exist. There are a few Frenchmen around him who, to forget hell, listen to his thoughts. The conversation turns to the Resistance—a rare commodity. It's quite simple. The French Resistance consists of Radicals, most of the Socialists, and all of the Communists. Finished. Around him, high school students, collegians, bosses, and directors ask themselves what the hell they're doing in Dora. It must be a mistake. Finding himself again, Paul adds a European dimension to his master's lesson. With a combination of Germanic, Russian, and Polish dialects, he translates for the Eastern groups, frequently punctuating his words with *"Ponimaich?"* (Understand?) to be certain that his meanings are clear. The Slavs double up with laughter. *"Scheisse Professor, k'ebionoi materi, yopa!"* (Shit Professor, go and see your mother fucked, you ass!) And *"Du bist ein gross Partisan!"* (You're a great partisan!)

Just imagining the Scheisse Professor spreading terror in the German army is enough to trigger fits of glee. *"Professor, wo ist dein Maschine Pistol? Ein Partisan hat ein Maschine Pistol! Du, Professor, du bist ein pussy Partisan!"*

Fits of laughter break out. Even the dying Russians begin chuckling. It worsens their chances to stay alive, but at least they're getting a good laugh. The Polish male nurses, drawn by the unusual atmosphere in the ward, abandon their games and come to this new one. Their pals put them in the picture; then bursts of laughter fill the room.

As for the Scheisse Professor, he suddenly finds an inspiring rise in popularity. The ways of the Lord are strange. Yesterday he was the victim being pushed toward death while being used as a laughingstock and scapegoat. Now he's the hero of the day. But for the nurses, the fun has just begun. One finds a broom. *"Los, Hurensohn"* (Quick, son of a bitch), he says, giving the broom to Paul. "Stand straight. Show us how you attack a Panzer division."

Paul, his prick tossing about under his too-short shirt, gets up. His leg hurts, but he must play his part. With hair and beard half an inch long, with toilet paper on his wounds and spectacles askew, he doesn't look like a fighter. He takes the broom, recalls some training memories, and gives a demonstration of presenting arms. The result is pitiful, but the ward, heated by the atmosphere, makes it a triumph for him. Here's the great strategist that Stalin, the *skourvisyn* (son of a bitch), should have had as an adviser. The great Russian army would be in Berlin. Everyone would be in Berlin, and all the Germans would be in Dora! *Bliadj!* (Whore!) "Why didn't you go and see the great leaders? *Potchemou?"* (Why?)

The mood in the infirmary is extraordinary, never seen before. Here and there, the dying pop off laughing. It's the first time. Carried away by enthusiasm, a male nurse brings Paul a bowl of soup! Paul doesn't care whether it suits his condition; it is thick enough so that the spoon sticks up, so he swallows the lot, it is so good. He has heard of such soup but has never seen it. He had rather thought—he the Cartesian, the intellectual—that it was one of the phantasms of a humanity not too concerned about the present in forgetting about the tomorrows that are calling. He devours the potatoes and soup with hungry lickings and inexpressible pleasure. Tomorrow or the next day, who knows—depending on the whims of so many—he'll be the helpless victim of more cruelties, but here and now, he has two pints of soup such as you don't get anymore. It's like grandmother's; nothing else counts. The left-wing parties and Popular Front are forgotten. Exhausting tomorrows are far away, and he devours every bit without thinking of offering a piece of potato to anyone.

★   ★   ★

In the barracks refectory, the soup is quickly swallowed and rations handed out. On this day, they consist of a quarter of a small, round bread loaf, an ounce of margarine, and a helping of cumin-flavored white cheese. Claude, Luc, and Michel use the handles of their spoons to spread it on the lot and wolf it down. They'll have nothing else till the next evening, but it's better to eat it all at once than to have it stolen.

Suddenly, there are loud voices in a corner. It seems that a fragment of cheese has broken off a ration and fallen on a neighbor. Since the loser is French and the gainer Russian, it becomes a casus belli, and the tones of voices rise in anger. "Let's get the hell out of here. There'll be a brawl!"

The three quickly reach the exit. They pass Helmut, the barracks chief, who tears in, club in hand. Cursing, he attacks the pack of prisoners. Margarine and cheese are squashed, bowls fly about, throwing splashes in all directions. Panic spreads, and the refectory empties in chaos. Outside, grumbling begins over the lost rations.

"There are some types who never really know where they are."

Luc sums it up. "Look at all these guys saying 'it's not right.' They talk. There are doctors who want to get into the infirmary, engineers who want to make plans, workers looking for a site—and they don't understand that everyone is in this shit. They all want it their way!"

"You wouldn't like to open a high school here?" asked Michel. Luc frowned. "Don't shit me. What I said is true. When I got to Buchenwald, I was in Barracks 61, the worst hole of all. You couldn't even begin to count the fleas per square inch; there were millions. Beside me, there was a bishop. He didn't say a thing, a likable guy. One day, he was taken to the tower, and we never saw him again. There was also another bishop, a vicar-general."

"You had some nice people with you." Michel is in a good mood, having eaten all his ration, which is more than many can say.

"Me, I like fine people," retorts Luc. "So this second bishop had an idea for a public prayer meeting. You should have seen the barracks chief's face. It didn't last long. He and his Stubendienst clubbed everybody and reestablished order. Imagine it, celebrating Easter at Buchenwald! There was also a team of Vichy military officers who'd been rounded up—no idea why—and they swore that Marshal Pétain himself was going to tell off the Krauts and get them back to their offices, where their pencils and erasers were getting bored."

"That's a good one, Luc. In fact, some guys daydream . . ."

"Wait, I haven't finished. The best bit was an air force colonel, an ace from the last war, and he'd shot down many German planes. He was skinny but must have been fat before he was arrested because the skin on his belly was like an apron. He was looking for an orderly, an orderly in Buchenwald! Unfortunately, I said someday I'd like to be a pilot, so he told me that with his connections, it was a sure thing! He just asked me to toast his bread and reheat his bowl on the stove near the barracks chief's bedroom. Well, when I got fed up with taking the blame in his place, I let it drop, and he soon found another sucker." Luc's memories were clear. "Well, I felt bad seeing all these guys going to the dogs so quickly without even knowing what was happening. When I saw the bishop and the colonel get up on the table to show us their prick and ass to look for fleas, I was shocked, not because of their social position in France but because they thought they could keep it in Buchenwald. And the day when, into the bargain, the colonel had a straw in his ass from out of his mattress, I understood where I was, but not them."

"Luc, the guys you're talking about, they were already fucked; they couldn't adapt. With their ages and past, they were only ready for a quick trip to the crematorium."

"They weren't the only ones. They only lasted a couple of weeks and went straight up the chimney. I also saw bigheaded plebeians who didn't last much longer. The unions and civil organizations—nothing prepared them for all this."

The camp whistles sound. All the Zawatsky kommandos assemble on the roll call square. So much for the philosophical discussions. The tunnel is there, awaiting its people.

⋆　　⋆　　⋆

Flavio is in bad shape. He is in a handling kommando, and every day, he carts material from the main site to the tunnel. He is not choosy, but if he has any preferences, he has never been asked. One day, he totes rolls of fiberglass; though they're very light, they turn you into a bleeding teddy bear. Another time, he'll carry liquid-oxygen tanks or sheet iron or metalwork. He carries everything and asks no questions.

Filthy life, *mondo cane!* Unfortunately, he works with some Russians who are far from being choirboys, and Flavio is Italian, *povero di lui* (poor guy). He's one of the last survivors of the Italian unit that arrived earlier. His khaki uniform and feathered cap make him the target of the Russians who want to make him pay for the Italian divisions on the Russian front. As if by chance, blunt, sharp, or pointed steel objects happen to fall right where he stands, and until now, only his suspicion and agility have enabled him to sidestep the deadly traps. He's courageous, but having seen all his buddies disappear quickly, he knows his turn isn't far off, especially with teammates like these. Now that he's practically the last to represent his country, he'll face the mass of Slavs who surround him. His insults will spring from the foulest lingo of the ports of Naples and Genoa.

Yesterday, however, he relaxed for one fatal moment. An iron sheet broke loose and tore his uniform open. At first, he felt nothing, then wondered why he was pissing in his trousers. But he wasn't pissing; he was bleeding, for his body was carved from the abdomen to his knee. The wound was deep, and blood was escaping as if a razor had done the job.

When he was taken to the infirmary, the operating theater was filled with ill men waiting their turns for lumbar puncture or to have boils drained. The air reeked of decomposition.

Our two supersurgeons, the jolly mason and his troll, saw Flavio arrive and rubbed their hands. An interesting case! The host of boils and other trifles were forgotten. Here, at least, they could further their knowledge. That magnificent wound, that superb tear, would let them glance inside to see how a man is made. No problem—they felt capable, these rare sadists incarnate, since their twisted minds found satisfaction in the shadow of Mercury's rod. For a little while, they would have, with a tear in one eye, recited the Hippocratic oath.

After washing the wound, they lifted the skin with a pin, and there, where the belly was open, they looked inside. There was a lot of blood; they soaked it up with a compress but saw nothing inside to attract their attention.

Flavio was still lucid. He wanted to hold on. He wanted to show these scum that Italians weren't just mandolin players, practical jokers, or running champions when they wore a uniform. It wouldn't be easy, he knew. He saw other patients who appeared both worried and interested. They were witnesses who could later confirm that he wasn't afraid and was just as good as the others!

The mason-surgeon threaded catgut on a curved needle and, after putting in a drain, started sticking it into the fleshy parts while his troll pulled the edges of the wound together, all without anesthetic. The pain was unbearable. Flavio felt the sweat flowing from all his pores. He knew he'd scream or faint. No. Not that! He was being watched. So he started singing! It was a broken song, the pain blocked his lungs, and his heart stopped, but he restarted the song again and again till the end. The surgeons laughed. Holy Italian, he was completely mad, but he was good for a laugh!

Flavio has now been in the infirmary two days. Things aren't going right. His toilet-paper dressing has nasty yellow stains and smells rotten. He has shooting pains in his lower stomach, and his ganglia are enormous. Yesterday, the surgeons came and undid the dressing. The wound has a strange look with blotches and bad colors all along. They powder it with sulfamide and, with their usual happy air, tell him to eat up. *"Immer fressen, mein lieber Mann!"* (Always eat up, my dear man!) In a nearby bed, a Czech repeats nonstop, "Italiano, spaghetti, spaghetti!" but he isn't really bad and helps Flavio to turn over. Flavio doesn't even think about the spaghetti remarks. His fever is too high and wears him away.

The room holds many nationalities but none that Flavio can contact. Among your own countrymen, you can speak, exchange thoughts, support one another. But Flavio is alone. He can't count on anyone. His vocal efforts during the operation had earned him an amused sympathy, however brief. So he will die all alone, but now he no longer gives a shit. Adieu, Naples, and adieu, Dora, you filthy shithole! The gangrene has now set in. It progresses rapidly, and Flavio drifts into his last delirium.

★   ★   ★

In the night, the dogs howl in their hillside kennel. They are excited by the cold and by the odors of the human prey they smell nearby. These dogs are a source of obsessive dread for the prisoners. They have nothing to do with the tame animals one sees in every town, whose main function seems to be to shit on as many areas as possible. Here, the dogs are vicious killers, trained by even more vicious men. They revive within each prisoner the same ancient dread that wolves have inspired since the dawn of time.

Their howling reminds prisoners of their midnight arrival at Buchenwald. The "welcoming committee" waited on the railway platforms to greet them, with their clubs and killer dogs. Upon opening the railcars, the prisoners were flung to the ground before the hunters and dogs. But could these half-demented beings covered with excrement, piled atop one another by the hundred the past three days— could they still be men?

No. They were the spoils. In the hunting sense of the term, it was the Big Moment. The prisoners were the quarry, already worn out after days of hellish "tracking" aboard the train. As they fell, haggard, starved, and dazed, the hunters and dogs attacked. The SS swore, swinging their clubs everywhere to the sounds of breaking bones and tearing flesh, driving the terrified prisoners to their feet. The dogs leaped at their human prey, sinking their tearing fangs into flesh as their victims screamed in agony. From the station to Buchenwald, it had been no less than a race bathed in blood.

The dogs are also here at Dora, as in all the camps. Held on leashes by their masters, they growl ferociously whenever a prisoner is near. One word or gesture from the SS and the dog will tear the prisoner apart. They are really more efficient than their masters; a prisoner seeking death could cross the line without worrying too much about a bullet in the back or head, but the dogs are a terrifying, visceral fear.

They are everywhere, all around sites outside the electrified wire. The Posten (SS guards) have the dogs at their feet. The beasts growl, their ears pricked, watching the comings and goings of their prey.

The Posten hold them back firmly, for a dog attacking a kommando would create an enormous panic. Prisoners maddened by fear would run off in all directions. It would be a wild flight and an insane massacre. In the extremely rare cases of evasion or even attempted avoidance, the very thought of an escapee being chased by killer dogs generates uncontrollable fears in the prisoners' minds, of fangs ripping into their own flesh!

One gets used to seeing an SS man coming into a worksite. Sure, they bring anguish, that is one thing; but the mere idea of a dog is intolerable. Men who were to be hanged would climb onto the stool on their own, silently. Most of those who were bludgeoned felt their bones snapping, their skin breaking off as life ebbed away. But no prisoner being attacked by the dogs could keep from screaming, so terrifying was the very sight of the growling, slavering beasts.

The SS often make their rounds beyond the wire with man's best friend. Their understanding and friendship are obvious; they know one another well. An SS man will caress, excite, or worry the dog, which will nip him affectionately in return. The man throws a stone or twig, and the beast rushes forward, brakes to a stop, picks up the object, and returns it to the master, who strokes its side. The beasts are well trained, knowing they mustn't go near the fatal barbed wire. The killer dogs seem to know all about Dora and the terror that must be sustained. They are cogs in the New Order that grips Europe implacably. They are confident in it; it will never fail them.

★   ★   ★

"Eh, Franzous, chto ta koi?" (Hey, Frenchy, what is it?), queries the Russian.

Gilbert looks at the straw pallet ruffling curiously. Something moved, but there's nothing on top or underneath. He opens the side of it and comes nose to nose with a surprised rat, which scurries off and escapes.

Gilbert replies, "That, Serghei, my little Russian cunt, is a rat. *Ponimaich? Er hat viel Russki gefressen, Capito? Mnoho kouchat Russki."* (He has eaten many Russians. Got it?)

Looking on, Pierre laughs. Gilbert comes up with strange explanations, and they're usually amusing. Here's a guy who doesn't give in and sees the brighter side of things when he can.

Apparently, the Crusaders brought rats back from the East. Pierre wants to show his knowledge of history. "Yes, my little buddy, they brought the rats back at the same time as the pox. You can say that now, thanks to them, we're all tooled up. There's even a chance that he might be somewhere there, our crusader. If Jacky hasn't been doing his job, there shouldn't be a shortage of dried-up crusader in there."

Pierre and Gilbert are on the night shift of a handling kommando, far from ideal work. For a long time, they've been trying to get into something less dangerous. Handling means working in rain, snow, and foul weather and struggling with insane loads while being beaten and clubbed from all directions.

As production began in some of the galleries, the two asked for assignment as engineers, fitters, electricians, or painters but without success. They got an abusive going-over from the Kapo when they told him they were specialists in these areas and would be more useful as production-team members.

Tonight, carpenter volunteers are asked for. Pierre, Gilbert, and others raise their hands but are held back with two Russians, Sergei and Yuri. The Kapo laughs as he points them out, for, as an old inmate, he knows what these "declarations of profession" are worth. Carpentry can also be dangerous where drilling and blasting are under way, but the Kapo holds them because they are four reliable workers, no more, no less. At least, the Frenchmen made the effort. If they didn't keep trying, they'd be on the kommando until the end of time.

A Vorarbeiter takes them to Barracks 4, one of the four galleries that has been transformed into dormitories. It is big and now devoid of people. The job involves lifting the straw pallets, dismantling the empty bunks, and clearing the entire gallery. It's silent now, this place that echoed like a drunken ship with cries and brutal beatings day and night, with its incredible mix of races and types, its demented promiscuity, and inhabitants who never undressed so as to avoid being robbed.

To the left of the entrance is the barracks chief's office. Once it seemed luxurious with its stained door, square bed, and engravings stuck to the wall. Now it looks more like the abandoned den of some tramp. The empty bays—never seen in that state—now show their true aspect, the face of tragedy.

Above them, the tunnel roof is now dry. The continual rain generated by the condensation of breath upon cold stone has finally stopped.

One fact strikes the small team again and again. Wherever people on the Planet Earth had stayed, from the poorest Gypsy camp to the miserable shacks of Calcutta, they had left traces of their stay. They had abandoned a certain number of things, such as bottles, empty tin cans, old boxes, bits of wood, rags, papers, and any number of odds and ends.

But here, in the depths of the Planet Dora, there is nothing. Absolutely nothing. Here the prisoners are so deprived that a bit of string, a paper bag, or even a scrap of rag is a treasure no one possesses. Thus, such things are fiercely coveted and protected. In departing, they have left nothing behind. But, ah, yes, they have left something: fleas!

Millions of fleas are jumping about like mad on the abandoned straw pallets. They miss the prisoners, for they had a good life and an abundance of food twenty-four hours a day. From habit, they learned the changing shifts at Dora. At wake-up time, they leave their human prey to dive back into the warm nest of straw. When the substitute arrives, they swarm onto his body, racing along trouser legs and the wrists and neck of his shirt, and it's a new feast for the ravenous insects. Many less happy creatures enter a prisoner's ears, become caught within earwax, and struggle for hours. Prisoners awaken covered with bloody lumps likely to become infected.

The Barracks 4 Vorarbeiter isn't very zealous. He's had a bellyful of handling kommandos, of going out into that filthy rain, and even of the shouting and clubbing he's done, twelve hours a day for years. He'd like a little rest.

He gives instructions. First, pick up the straw pallets and load them on the trolleys. They must be loaded to the maximum—that is, at least twenty-five per trolley—to cut the number of trips. That's still a lot of trips. There will be no shouting and no cries. All will be done as ordered and in good spirit. If the SS man or Kapo arrives, the Vorarbeiter is to be alerted at once! "Otherwise, you bunch of bastards, I'll make you regret having been born! *Verstanden?*" (Understand?) At the unanimous reply, "*Jawohl!*" (Yes sir!), the Vorarbeiter disappears into a corner.

To throw these straw pallets over your shoulder and back, then carry them to the trolleys, is very light work. It might be a cushy job but for these damnable fleas! Already worried by the sudden lack of food, then being moved, the insects become aggressive. Hordes of them jump upon each prisoner. They attach themselves to men's eyebrows and eyelashes, get inside their shirts, and bite them everywhere. Within a few minutes, the men are covered in blood from both directions to the waist.

"Good God, we're going to be eaten alive!" Gilbert rages. The "cushy" job is a nightmare! He'd imagined himself as self-employed, a craftsman quietly loading his trolley and taking it out of the tunnel in zigzags to avoid truncheons, gummis, and clubs. "Sure, it's quiet here," he thinks, "and the Vorarbeiter doesn't look troublesome, at least for a while. But don't work too fast, either, or he'll have to be awakened, and then he'll make a scene because he hasn't enjoyed his share of sleep."

The fleas, however, couldn't care less about the feelings of Gilbert and the others. They are voraciously hungry and not concerned about anything else. Everyone has his own problems.

Scratching himself furiously, Gilbert guesses the number of pallets at a glance. It's not possible, he muses; there must be at least a thousand. At this rate, by the time we finish work, we'll be bone-cleaned, good subjects for an anatomy class!

★   ★   ★

Since the March 13, 1944, arrival, which increased the size of the surface squad, the death rate has been high, with no real incoming transfers to offset the losses. The population is dropping, yet the construction work must advance, no matter what the cost.

The SS believe the perfect cure for the drop in prisoner numbers is—more beatings! With a good truncheon, miracles can be achieved, provided it is wielded by an expert.

If one looks from the viewpoint of a prisoner or kommando, it might seem that the clubbings, hunger, and deaths disorganize the worksite and only slow the progress of the work.

But in the SS mind, if you put aside any sensitivity, which has no place in a concentration camp, and look at things from a higher level, you notice the enormous changes that have taken place in only two months.

Dora, which was a sort of country stopover in March, is now beginning to look like a town. It isn't like Buchenwald, which looks more like a capital city, but then, the two camps will never be similar, so it isn't a question of comparing them. Still, Dora now possesses most of the elements necessary to allow a satellite camp to become self-contained first and then a large, independent camp.

Not so long ago, roll call square was a low-grade field strewn with frozen, rotted lumps. Now it's well paved, complete with expansion joints. It starts at the entrance gate and spreads out majestically, surrounded by new barracks on all the level areas. The tree-felling on the hill and beyond is done, and concrete walkways lead to each new barracks. Electrical and water lines have been installed. Every barracks has a Waschraum (washroom), with two fountains of water under pressure, and its own WC, with latrines of enameled porcelain. Used water is collected in a drain. Many from the depths of Europe and Asia have never seen such marvels. All installations are kept perfectly clean. It is only camouflage, so that an unexpected visitor, Red Cross or otherwise, to the new section would have only flattering things to report to the outside world.

The SS go further. They have barracks chiefs in a preecological wave sowing flowers and plant cuttings around the barracks. Next they acquire some pots of paint so as to add some very ravishing pastel shades of color to the refectories. The Stubendienst, equipped with big, rubber-bladed scrapers, sweep away the dust and mud in the barracks. In areas reserved for prisoners, everything is perfectly lined up. The barracks chief has his own room, well furnished with a bed and two blankets, a table, a bedside table, a lamp, and a wardrobe for his clothes and belongings.

A new infirmary has been built, with an X-ray room, a dentist's area, and an operating theater. Another new building takes in hospital patients. The kitchen and Effektenkammer haven't changed, but the kitchen has been built and fitted for permanent use.

The biggest change is the crematorium, finished and magnificent with its squared brick chimney and flaming new furnaces. Factory fresh, it throws glorious puffs of smoke into the sky. Dora no longer has to beg Buchenwald to treat its bodies; it's now handled in situ. Besides, this crematorium has lots to do, for the brutal work speedup is decimating the prisoners' ranks. The tunnel must be finished quickly, regardless of the cost in human lives. Kommandos working underground see their numbers melt away. Long lines of men, their lungs eaten away by the dust and humidity, struggle to the infirmary, only to go up in smoke a few days later.

The Peenemünde factory was destroyed in the summer of 1943. Since then, none of the new weapons that could change the course of the war have been built. The German general headquarters, OKW, is well aware that, against the enormous Russian potential in weapons and men, on the one hand, and, on the other, the fantastic American technological power now in England twenty miles from the French coast, Germany can no longer count on its once great military science. In but three weeks, German power had blasted the French army apart, an army considered the best in the world since 1918. The rest of Europe had then been swallowed up like a loaf of bread.

With Russia, Germany faced something incomprehensible, an army in full rout but with people who took up arms and fought, regardless of the consequences, in a visceral, irrational refusal to give up their homeland to the Hun invader.

Now the Nazis complain that Italians, Poles, Jews, "niggers," all these "outcasts" from Europe and Africa, with their crushing power, are preparing to invade Hitler's "Fortress Europe." Millions of French, humiliated by the abandoning of their *"mère patrie,"* along with the Dutch and Belgians, hopefully await the hour. The magnificent English, who have quietly endured everything, also await their hour of revenge. You cannot touch England without one day having to regret it.

Against these dangers, Germany has two trump cards. The V-1 is an amusing little kerosene-burner but not too efficient. It doesn't have much speed, and the RAF knocks it out with a burst of gunfire. Sometimes, pilots even save the cost of ammunition by flying alongside and throwing the V-1 off course with a touch of one wingtip to another. But the V-2 is something else; it soars to fantastic altitudes, then drops, faster than the speed of sound, to destroy its target before anyone can even hear it coming! This is the weapon that is supposed to change the course of the war.

Since the V-2 will be built here, this model facility must become operational quickly, no matter the cost in prisoners' lives. Emerging from nothing, with its little potted flowers, enameled tables, and other cosmetics, Dora presents a deceptively misleading image.

The reality is murderous. Prisoners work twelve hours a day to satisfy the SS. They stand two or three hours of roll call, plus their marches, the "lice control" bits, and other good things. There are the TBs (tuberculosis cases) and the shitters, both of whom drop like flies. That's fine, but it's imperative that they work, for the life or death of Germany now depends upon them. Churchill, speaking of the RAF,

said words to the effect that "never before has so much been owed by
so many to so few," and now, in effect, Germany was implying the
same about the doomed souls at Dora. What an irony. Never has Germany had such a desperate need of non-Germans—in fact, of anti-
Nazis seized from the four corners of Europe—to save its precious
Third Reich!

So things will be speeded up. The tunnel, originally planned for V-2
construction, will also build the V-1 and Junkers engines. Dora will
also have extensions on the other side of the hill, to be known as Ellrich and Harzungen. The prisoners will be driven like demons, no
matter the consequences. There will be thousands of dead, of course,
but that doesn't matter. The important thing is to remain in advance
of the formidable assault that is being prepared.

The project directors are here. First, there is Wernher von Braun, the
same chap who, after the war, will be venerated and shown as a fine
example to young generations of the West. There is also Gen. Walter
Dornberger, who shares responsibility with von Braun for building the
new weapons. Their objective is to get full-scale production going
immediately.

The galleries must be finished as quickly as possible, eliminating
such wasteful use of space as the four dormitory areas. This presumes,
of course, completion of the surface camps. A special effort must be
made, and the barracks will be finished at a man-killing pace. At the
same time, the surface worksite, extremely vulnerable to bombing
raids, will become a transit site. Material will only be there for minimal
periods before being transferred into the tunnel in huge stores. In order
to achieve this dual goal, the prisoners will be driven harder. If all goes
well, the factory will be up to cruising speed by the month of August.

Beyond this, the drilling under the mountain at Ellrich and Harzungen is being pushed at a severely forced pace. German war production is
going to go deep underground, and even if the Anglo-American bombers
increase their raids, they'll only destroy a minute portion of supplies.
The factories beneath the mountain will be impervious to attack.

Enlisted personnel, that is, club-swinging lackeys, might be insufficient in numbers. New Kapos are needed and new Vorarbeiter and barracks chiefs. Buchenwald will be asked for some. It is a camp where
the administrative posts are held by Communists. A few years earlier,
a pitiless internal war had pitted the Greens, or criminal prisoners
who were masters of the place, against the Communists, who not only
won the battle but went on to set up a bloody repression that decimated the losers. Those surviving were sent off to other camps, especially Dora, where they were once more preeminent and held a strong
grip on the camp.

Buchenwald Communists are not keen on going to Dora, which has a detestable reputation even for people sheltered from major dangers by their positions. However, big as it may be, Buchenwald can't provide all of its Communist party members with interesting jobs, and in any case, Dora must be conquered. The policy of the Communists is to oust the Greens and take their places. So Buchenwald sends trusty party members to Dora, an armband in each pocket and truncheons in hand. It isn't a question of turning Dora into a Salvation Army post, just a question of conquering the camp. That's all.

The SS favor this change in the prisoner hierarchy. From experience, they know that the Greens only instill a bloody, sterile mess. And the SS have known the Communists for years, since the street fights that brought them face to face in Hamburg, Berlin, and all the large towns in Germany before Hitler came to power. Their two parties have a complex structuring and are tightly disciplined. Therefore, the Greens will be ousted from any important jobs, and the SS will no longer need to worry about administrative duties.

The pneumatic drills will soon reach Point Zero, where Hall 1 is located. Thousands of bags of cement arrive daily to concrete the floor, and the two normal-gauge railroads are laid as the work progresses. Huge ventilation ducts are extended little by little toward the far end of the tunnel, secured in place by attachments overhead and along the walls. Electricity and compressed air are beginning to animate the assembly halls.

Huge machine presses await the moment of arrival in their new homes, and hundreds of electric welding rigs have been piled up in the galleries. Mills and frames, welders' masks, hammers, and files all locked in cases are arriving day and night in what appears to be an endless chain of trains. But we must all work more quickly, always more quickly! No V-2s have been built for several months, and the invading Russian armies are there at the very doors of Germany. The assault could begin this year or perhaps soon afterward, but no one knows.

Although the German army has been humbled in North Africa and Russia, it is still formidable. Face to face with an equal force, it fears no one. If, as well, it has new weapons no one else possesses, able to crush concentrations of men and matériel on the spot, then the Wehrmacht will win. And these new weapons are already potentially here at Dora. They'll be built as soon as the factory is finished. Around the clock, day after day, the V-2s will fly, spreading destruction and terror among the Allied armies. There will be no warning alert; fire and death will strike from above. So the order is to work more quickly, always more quickly, even though you die, prisoners; the salvation of the Reich is in your hands.

★   ★   ★

All night long, Didier has been spying out the place to see whether he can find a safe place to hide and sleep. Every Sunday brings the same worry: how to manage not to leave the tunnel for the dreaded roll call. He has already tried many hiding places but felt so insecure in each that he didn't use it again. Already he has slept in an unlit hall behind a pile of gravel, but during the day, a group of engineers came and he only barely avoided being caught there. Another time, he had tried to rest his aching body in a hopper that was located in a dark, restful-looking corner. The hopper had been derailed, and it seemed a perfect shelter. He had drawn back the panels covering the sanctuary but then had been almost unable to get out again! He had also used holes that for the moment were not being used and even a kind of nest he'd found behind a stack of barrels.

One day, things had turned out badly. Didier had stretched out along a ventilation duct that was the beginning of a section to be laid out through the main gallery. Ironface had appeared out of nowhere, spotted him, then chased him, firing a fusillade of 9mm slugs at him. It had become a wild chase, and Didier escaped only because of the one advantage he had over the SS man. For while the murderous Ironface had to zigzag over and around the obstacles between them, his very fury interfering with the accuracy of his shots, Didier dashed wildly off like a maddened creature and so made headway on his would-be killer. He came upon a dark area and jumped downward, his heart in his mouth. He found he had crossed a transverse hall, darted into its welcome darkness, and so eluded his SS pursuer.

Now he must find something else, a safer place; he doesn't yet know where or what it may be. At any rate, he won't go outside. He prefers to die at once, no matter how, but so long as he can, he will stay in the tunnel. He has not seen daylight, the earth outside, a tree, or a blade of grass for a month, but he doesn't mind. He has become a mole, knowing that his only chance for survival lies in remaining inside the mountain. He knows the tunnel is eating away at his body, but he feels up to fighting and playing as to who'll become fed up first, the tunnel or he himself.

His wife was arrested at the same time as he, and he doesn't kid himself: Her fate must be the same as his. He feels close to her and wants to shout out, "It's my fault; I didn't do what I should have done to save you from this monstrosity, this living bestiality, this hellhole. But I'll come back, I promise you. I swear it, I'll do everything possi-ble. All the unearthly things that happen to you, send them to me, and I'll bear them on my shoulders; I'm strong enough, and we will get out, the both of us. That's why I don't want to go outside, for outside I'll die—that's a certainty. I can fight on for days and nights without end in this tunnel; I'm used to it now. But outside, I'll collapse and die, like a fish out of water."

Every Sunday, the Zawatsky kommandos come out of the tunnel for a roll call and ration handout, sometimes for a cleanup and shower. Roll call lasts for hours in the open air, and the poor sods, their eyes hurt by the light outside, shiver in a world they have forgotten. Their bodies have become so used to marching, running, and galloping that they no longer know how to remain stationary on command; it has become almost impossible to hold themselves immobile, lined up in the snow and rain against bitter winds. The effort destroys them; their meager strength melts away in the desperate wait for the end of roll call, for the end of the delousing, the end of disinfection. And they know that tomorrow, if not this very night, they'll have to go back to the tunnel.

Didier has just finished eighteen hours of hectic work, running from nine P.M. Saturday until three o'clock Sunday afternoon. The tunnel work must run nonstop. However, once each month, there is a general roll call at which both shifts are brought to the surface outside for an overall census. It is only on this occasion that the SS know the exact number of prisoners in the camp. Between two general roll calls, they only know the number coming out, which must coincide with the number going back, after having deducted the number of dead plus the admissions to the infirmary. Didier cannot avoid the monthly exits because at these times, the tunnel is searched from top to bottom. During all the other weeks, he will find a way to stay inside. Of course, this means he won't have eaten anything from Saturday through Monday, but that doesn't matter; he has made his choice and will stick to it until the end.

The kommandos file their exhausted way in long lines toward the exit guarded by the machine gun that, perhaps one day, will end whatever is left of their lives.

The Kapos bark, count them, and do it again. The figures are never the same from one day to the next, but the only thing that interests them is that the number coming out is the same as that going back in. *Stimmt!* Exact, the only word that comes to mind for the moment. The columns move forward, one after the other. Picking his moment, Didier dives into the darkness.

*   *   *

You could say that spring has arrived one day at Dora. No, not the spring of poets, with birds, flowers, and the return of forgotten desires.

More exactly, it is the almost certain end of winter. Snow no longer falls. There are no more of these brutal turnarounds when rain turns to icy crystals and wet winds escalate into shrieking blizzards.

The hills of the Harz, so far from the Wagnerian setting of Buchenwald, seem ready for a renewal that can wait no longer. The few wild bushes remaining here and there have begun growing their 1944 plumage. The beech trees and pines along the crest of the hill are ready for the big moment. The vast plain, stretching as far as Nordhausen, seems to be waiting for the plowing to commence. All during the winter, only the SS could be seen with their dogs, but this immense space can be broken by the plow.

Even the camp has grown a new skin. The roll call square, now magnificently paved, waits for the crowds to push forward in perfect squares. Little by little, the muddy pathways are replaced by cemented walkways leading to the freshly built barracks. Everything that was of a temporary, makeshift nature has disappeared. Gone is the primitive crematorium, whose measures have been used for the masonry of the grand crematorium that is now finished and bordered with new plants and fresh cuttings.

Gone, too, is the single gallows of the Holzhof, now replaced with the improved gallows for six people, six Stücke (pieces, a term of contempt), that crowns the roll call square.

Even the prisoners have changed. The disorganized, frightened mass of men, galloping, moaning, maddened, and crying under the constant beatings, have gone through their own metamorphosis. They have become a conscientious, organized crowd of prisoners, knowing how to take blows or ward them off, how to live or die under the insane conditions of this life. The word *warum* (why) has disappeared from their very rich vocabulary. The "why" of it is finished; we're real detainees. We're going to play the game, and we'll play it to the last. The weakest among us—that is to say, the youngest and the oldest, those who had family worries or problems—have almost all disappeared, swept away in a matter of those first few days or weeks. A well-aimed blow from a Kapo or SS man, an extraintense tuberculosis, or simple ignorance of their new living conditions expedited them quickly to the crematorium. In a sense, they never belonged to Dora, for all those who could not manage an objective view of their new existence were swiftly eliminated.

Then, one after another, the kommandos began coming out of the tunnel. For weeks, for months that might have been centuries, they had only had quick glimpses of the outside. Their world was one of explosions deep in the mine, of brisk, often-hurtling clouds of thick dust. They were gray, filthy, and bearded; their skins were lizardlike, and they had all but forgotten that any world existed but their own. Their troglodyte eyes blinked with initial discomfort at the daylight, then widened with astonishment at this town that had sprung up out of nothing—this space that they didn't recognize.

At the same time, the emerging prisoners discovered the existence of a new race, called officials. In their minds, which sought only a means of survival, these poor wretched gladiators had but two conceptions of Dora's inhabitants: those equipped with truncheons, gummis, and guns and those without; those armed with the right to kill and those with only the right to be killed.

Suddenly now, they saw prisoners whose striped uniforms were clean, were well tailored and freshly ironed. A fearful shyness told them not to go too near these strangers. Even had they wanted to approach such folk, their own filth, their miserable appearance in dirty, torn rags would have dissuaded them.

You can't run a sound operation using a city of 15,000 inhabitants on work essential to Germany by employing only the stick as a deterrent. Some of the officials who had emerged through the force of circumstances had been recruited from French prisoners who opened the camp, survivors from the first transfer. Their living conditions were far superior to those of a mob; however, an inner uncertainty worried them. Because they were in touch with the SS and their secrets, they had become extremely vulnerable; the slightest false step could have them choking at the end of a rope or, worse, cut up in small pieces in the silence of the bunker. Ah, well, the final aim of the SS was to eliminate them as well. Dead men tell no tales, do they? And old-age retirement didn't exist in the camps.

In the beginning, the witches' brew that was Dora made it impossible for prisoners to know each other. After a while, you more or less knew that so-and-so was a farmer in Sarthe, another a craftsman on the outskirts of Paris, this one a police employee, and that one a student.

As for other nationalities, for the French they were Russian, Polish, Czechs, and nothing more. As weeks and months passed, the men began noticing one another more closely, and gradually, they began to form new groups—not by their former social standings, for these made no sense in Dora, but rather by affinities. Those who had been active with Resistance groups recognized each other through little mannerisms, perhaps a way of being, by the way they acted. They were quite distinct and discreet as to the reasons for their imprisonment, as opposed to "those who had done nothing, yet cried over their fate," which inspired the retort, "Well, it serves you right, you should have done something!"

Purely political deportees, arrested solely for their opinions or affiliation to a party, were quite rare. Those who were very young, the students and collegians who managed to survive, had a very hard time. Since they were unable to speak of wives or of children they did not have, nor of food, for they had never experienced these enormous banquets of another age that were the basis of so many conversations, they often found themselves off at the outer edge of the older group, left to fall back upon themselves. Since the war and its related problems were considered men's business, the younger men were treated with a compassion mixed with remorse and doubt as to what reasons could have brought them to this charnel house of madness and death. Faced with this involuntary yet hurtful oversight, the younger people shut themselves up in their shells—and never complained.

The very rare French criminal prisoners, included with the others when the Nazis emptied the prisons, stayed quiet, prudently melting into the mass. Existence at Dora was a far cry from the ostentatious display of tattoos common to Buchenwald, where necks marked in a blue dotted line showed the area to be cut, along with dotted lines around the sexual areas of the "wahines."

The criminals were quick to learn two things. First, they found that the tattoos impressed no one. What was worse, they had a great market value with SS collectors of rare lampshades made of human skin. Ilse Koch, the vicious "Bitch of Buchenwald," earned international infamy for her own unique collection. Thus, a tattoo was not something to ensure long life. The second thing the criminals learned concerned their ridiculous position. As gangsters, they had known both advantages and inconveniences. What they considered as advantages had been the easy money, silk shirts, well-tailored suits, and, of course, plenty of women. But now if they reminisced about these elements of their former lifestyle, it would only bring on gales of laughter from among the "suckers." So the gangsters found it more prudent to start off by attributing their presence at Dora to reasons more in line with the general population. It must be recognized that, for the most part, our gangster fellow prisoners behaved normally and were well integrated with the rest.

The French, considering their almost disorderly temperament, their fiercely nationalistic Gallic egocentricity, and their constant love of argument, began to form a homogeneous group. The frightening losses of life during the winter and spring taught them that the best chance of survival for each of them depended upon a continuous group solidarity. As a result, the company directors handled those they selected like professional laborers, and the fitters lifted the spirits of the shopkeepers. In an inexplicable paradox, amid living conditions that should have broken the French colony to pieces, our compatriots came to forget all their dissensions and to rediscover one another.

The Poles, at this beginning of spring, noticed that they no longer had a monopoly on the secondary but really powerful positions. French Schreiber (secretaries) appeared in the new barracks and different cogs of the administrative machinery. Still, the Poles kept such solid bastions as the kitchen, as well as the infirmary where the orderlies gave the decisive "thumbs up"—or down—on the fate of those who wanted to live, but their positions were not safe; they suffered some setbacks, having been the first foreigners, with the Czechs, to penetrate the camp secrets. Their decline was partly due to the fact that the elite among the Poles had been liquidated as early as 1939, even before those who survived them went to the camps. Beyond this, they only represented the large proletariat without any real chance of promotion aside from that secured through friends. Poles who had emigrated to France had fueled the fire by systematically criticizing their new homeland's welcome. This created a hatred, often quiet but often violent, between the two communities. As for the Czechs, who were the oldest foreign inmates, they kept a holy but upright mistrust for all the others. Their standpoints, rare but solid, didn't seem to have to be questioned.

The Russians noted no change in what concerned them. Their large, undefinable mass stayed the same, a colossal, devilish, unpredictable magma. One could not even judge their seniority from their roll numbers. The French were numbered according to their arrival (which "thousand"), so that one could say, "You arrived at such and such a date." But for the Russians, everything was incoherent. Their group numbers never followed each other enough so that they could catalog their order of arrival. But their social status remained firmly fixed—forever at the bottom of the ladder. The poor devils represented the lumpen proletariat, the lowest of the low, the very scum of the Earth.

The Russians frightened everyone. Certain Western aesthetes tinted with a genuine Marxism reviewed and corrected in the shadow of Pernod and the Popular Front tried to explain that this group wasn't composed of Russians but Ukrainians, or Chinese, or Mongols. Where, then, were the Russians? These masses have always fought, fangs showing, trying to survive.

The only thing that could have elevated the status of the Russians would have been the massive arrival of a group of Jews, with their yellow Stars of David and guaranteed abuse and death at the hands of the SS and murderous Kapos. The Russians would then have gone up a rung in the scale of values—that is, from absolute zero to almost nothing. But no Jews came over the horizon, and the Russians stayed where they were, at the very bottom of life in hell.

"Society" in Dora—if one can use such a term to describe such a living obscenity—began to become organized upon these weird basic ideas. The Anglo-American landing in Normandy was talked about, furtively, of course, and men spoke of the end of the war that would arrive one of these days. But time doesn't have the same meaning for a soldier as for a concentration camp prisoner. It was something like wondering about someone who had been poisoned and would travel by train to the hospital. Which would arrive first, the train or the poison traveling to the man's heart?

The answer to the question seemed quite clear. You had to use the means you had available to stay alive; you had to make do with whatever you had.

The transformation of Dora was accompanied by a change in its lifestyle. Until then, the tunnel people had given their all, nightmarish and deadly though it was. In theory, of course, they had no roll calls and no fatigue duties. In fact, they had no greater worry than each man's personal fight for survival. Besides, self-defense groups had been set up to assure their protection against adverse clans.

On the surface, it would be different. Daily roll call was inevitable, with its hours of waiting on the square in every extreme of weather while block chiefs clubbed the prisoners to straighten their ranks. Then followed the gardening duties, consisting of weeding the planted areas around each barracks to perfection and filling in the ravines that had formed in the sub-basements of the barracks. After this, the soles of each man's clogs had to be washed, so that no mud whatsoever would be carried into the building. Then each man had to go to the washroom to wash himself quickly, his clothing held tightly between his knees so that it would not be stolen.

Once each week, after the watery ration of soup, the barber came. A long line would form, the shaving brush would go from hand to hand, and, in three quick cuts, the barber removed superfluous hairs. There was also a regular flea count, where male nurses came to check the penises, the pubic areas, bottoms of trousers, and shirt seams. The barracks chief controlled these activities, and if he was in a bad mood, there would be organized sessions of twenty-five thrashes across some victim's ass. It was his usual way of demonstrating his authority.

Faced with this new way of life, the prisoners had to adapt quickly. Firstly, they were no longer anonymous. Although a number was still one's only official identity, each barracks chief knew the faces of every man. Once you'd been spotted, there was no way in which you could melt away into the crowd.

Such relative comforts as a wood-slatted bunk for two, a blanket for each prisoner, a table for eating, and a bowl you no longer had to carry on your person also carried sinister aspects—closer surveillance and a systematic spying by the orderlies. Despite this, however, a tranquillity took over since there were no longer any mad gallopings-around, nor attacks in the style of stagecoach robberies such as happened in the tunnel blocks. Robberies were still just as frequent, but they had become more subtle and were pulled off in the quiet darkness of the dormitory.

Highway robbery, as such, thus seemed to be disappearing, and the settling of scores was put off until men got into the tunnel. This new way of existing gave a far better chance for survival for the weakest, those who were helpless against the brutal savagery of the camps. Now they could at last speak to people, get to know their compatriots, and mix in among a group. An embryo of solidarity that had been unthinkable before began to emerge. Even the lame ducks, those men at the end of their days, found comfort before drifting away into nothingness.

It was unfortunate that the melting pot of populations disappeared at about the same time. In the world of the tunnel blocks, that incredible and marvelous thing had sometimes happened—a Russian and a Frenchman thrown together, sharing the same straw mattress on the off chance of when they arrived or helping each other, smiling and treating each other as "bum" and "lizopizdi," those flowers on a rotting hulk.

Now that the segregation was complete, the mistrusts flared up, and strict territorial limits were set out. A Russian going into the French zone was like a fox entering a henhouse; he was promptly chased away. The great theories of friendship among people that are so dear to our "thinkers" fly out the window when one has a slice of meat and the other does not. The fight for survival took on a tribal appearance. It was no longer each one for himself but rather: "I form part of a group that counts on me, and I count on it to try to survive." The fact of having a personal straw mattress was only a false security and didn't change the heart of things. "They're after my scalp, and without doubt they'll have it, but now I know some people, know their names; I have some buddies."

The prisoners had completely forgotten their past lives in their transformation to this obscenity of a Nazified existence. Enormous spaces opened up in the ranks, but there they were, the survivors, with an unbelievable capacity for assimilation. Many had arrived with a brother, a father, or a son who disappeared into the crematorium. They didn't speak about it, knowing their turn would come, too, for the SS would never let them out alive. But that wasn't the point; they had developed a turtle shell that would make them hold on as long as they had a breath of life.

★   ★   ★

The roll call square fills up little by little. Lined up in perfect ranks, the workers of several barracks have already taken their places. The recently cemented pathways now serving the camp are covered by the columns that converge on the square. Today is a general roll call, and the whole population of Dora will be present on the concrete square, except for patients in the infirmary. The sky is clear. A springlike sun warms bodies still aching from months of snow, rain, and wind. On the nearby hill, the few remaining trees are beginning to show a new growth of foliage.

The orders are barked in guttural tones. *"Abteilung, halt! Links um! Rechts um!"* (Section, halt! Left face! Right face!)

In response, the prisoner groups form into a *u*-shaped formation whose opening points toward the camp gate. The deluxe six-hooked gallows stands in the center of the quadrilateral.

The square is now full. The Lagerschutz (camp police) in light striped uniforms are at a slight distance. In the observation posts, where they are becoming bored, the machine gunners watch the show with interest whilst they amuse themselves by pointing their weapons here and there.

Fifteen thousand prisoners have been grouped on this enormous space. These detainees, so weak when you see them in their kommandos, now give an impression of strength, a force that could become savage and irresistible if just the right spark were to set it ablaze. Yet nothing will animate them. Here are the most desperate human beings of Europe and Asia, men who defend their lives with their claws and their teeth, who find themselves piled atop each other in a tiny space. They know what they want to do with the Nazis, but they are without hope, and yet, they obey their orders.

Among the fifteen thousand here assembled—still alive—from a hundred to a hundred and twenty will go up in smoke through the chimneys tomorrow and as many more the day after and in every day that follows. Within a year, the prisoner population of Dora will have been replaced nearly three times!

It is three in the afternoon. A bit of stirring about occurs near the gate, and a group of SS men appear. They are accompanied by the Lagerältester, "Big George," the Lagerdolmetscher, and the chiefs of the Arbeitsstatistik and the Politische Abteilung. All are carrying registers.

These SS are the Blockführer, not yet high dignitaries. Their uniform is more or less that of the army in action, the feldgrau (field gray), with only the black tab on the collar and cap. It is they who will check our numbers. They discuss the proceedings with the responsible detainees, who affect a compliant but relaxed attitude. A few laughs break out in the middle of the group. On the square, the barracks chiefs go to confer with their corresponding numbers, interrupting only to straighten out the lines of prisoners with the blows of their truncheons. This reminds one of cattle markets where breeders talk with their colleagues about the price of beef on the hoof, whilst keeping an eye on the herd. Shouts and orders are heard here and there, but they don't intrude upon the strange silence that rules the scene.

At the door to the infirmary, the service personnel stand in line. In the wards, even the patients in bed are at attention. In the mortuary, the bodies are neatly lined up, all on their backs and well arranged, their numbers marked in aniline appearing clearly on their stomachs.

"Achtung! Stillgestanden!"

Fifteen thousand pairs of clogs smack the concrete, and the silence becomes absolute. The Lagerführer, accompanied by his officers, arrives at the gate, which is immediately opened by a sentinel. They are wearing their officers' hats decorated with the feared skull-and-crossbones insignia, their long raincoats, and their boots shining like polished jet-black stone.

The group nears the assembled noncommissioned officers and officials, who are all standing at attention. The commandant asks some questions, which are transmitted downward through the hierarchy and returned via the same route. He seems satisfied. Then he lifts his eyes toward the sky, makes a joking remark that evokes servile laughs, and, with his officers, goes into the administrative building. The Blockführer, registers under their arms, then set off for the sections, where they will count the prisoners.

The other officials are together near the gate. They are well dressed, and most of them still have their hair. They are wearing waxed leather shoes, and their trousers are perfectly ironed. Further on, near the center, are the group of joiners, cooks, and intermediary services. Their uniforms and shoes are still in very good condition but lack the class of the others. These are off-the-rack, not tailor-made, outfits.

The farther you go from the center of the square, the more everything deteriorates. You pass quickly from mere poverty to the misery and then to the "slums." Here the prisoners are dirty and smelly and dressed in shreds. Their jackets are patched up with wire. Their trousers are either too short or too long, their openings without buttons, and they are held together by pieces of string.

Their faces are red, blotchy, and inflamed with erysipelas, their necks are deformed with swellings, and their hands are wasted with scabs. Dirty Russian socks or pieces of cement bags stick out from their clogs, which are worn out, broken, and without laces. The barracks chiefs, furious at the very idea of having to present such human trash, have relegated these scarecrows to the last rank.

"*Achtung! Mützen . . . ab!*" (Caps off!)

The prisoners, in one group movement, lift off their striped berets and stand at rigid attention, without breathing. The Blockältester rushes toward the SS man, who has just appeared. Bareheaded, quite stiff, he announces in a strong voice:

"*Block hundertfünfunddreissig, zweihundertundzehn Stücke!*" (Block one hundred and thirty-five, two hundred and ten bits!)

The SS man begins tapping on shoulders in tens with his cane as he counts: zehn, zwanzig, dreissig. The prisoners are motionless and completely devoid of expression, seeing nothing. They mustn't look at the SS man; you must never look at the SS man, it is forbidden. If he speaks to you, you must be at rigid attention, hat off, and not look at him but instead look completely blank.

The SS man continues, indifferent to their presence. Coming to the end of the column, he opens his register, notes the number of Stücke, and initials the Blockältester's book.

"*Mützen . . . auf! Ruht euch!*" (Caps on! At ease!)

The prisoners put their hats back on. They stand at ease.

The infirmary has already been checked, as well as the number of bodies about to be burned. In the sky, the birds fly about, chirping merrily. The sun brings them the joy of living. The Blockführer, having finished their checking, are beginning to come back down toward the gate to make their reports. Today, the commandant will know the exact number of prisoners living, dying, and dead. Only this morning, Jacky, while combing the tunnel from top to bottom, has managed to uncover two mummified corpses, which he has proudly carried to the mortuary.

The barracks chiefs, too, relaxed now, have gone back to their "friendly neighbor" visits. For even though they have armlets to wear now, with warm uniforms and boots, they know that, sooner or later, they are nothing more than crematorium meat themselves. Even after eight or ten years in the camps, they still know that gnawing worry, that inner fear that has never left them since the beginning.

The rank and file begin talking mezzo voce, about half the level of normal conversation. For a general roll call, it hasn't turned out too badly. It isn't raining, freezing, or snowing—for a change—and for once, there's no wind. The accursed muddy slime and quagmires of the earlier months have disappeared. On the ground, there is now beautiful concrete pavement, which is almost warm. Even the camp barbers have changed their hair-cutting style. The "autobahn" style is gone, meaning a simple cut in the middle from the forehead to the neck. This was alternated each month with the so-called Huron style, where everything was cut off except for the tuft that had grown along the middle. All that is now forgotten; each prisoner's hair is cut uniformly each month.

Today's only worry is that cursed gallows. The Lagerführer seems in a good mood, everything seems happy, flowers are growing, birds singing . . . but there is that damned noose, meaning that thousands will spend extra time waiting and watching while these Nazi slime execute another hapless wretch. If they enjoy it so much, why don't they hang the guys quietly in the bunker? If they must die, at least spare us these shows that only excite the SS.

"*Stimmt!*"

The word breaks over the loudspeaker. Stimmt, the count is exact. Everyone is in place, no one missing, dead or alive.

Even the crematorium kommando has been careful not to burn two bodies instead of one, which, given the scanty weight of the corpses, is something that could always happen. Come to think of it, how many of us are there? They don't tell us. Without a doubt, counting the recent arrivals, there must be about fifteen thousand. So many are guys from all over, with indecipherable numbers; nothing like the arrivals of Frenchmen freshly unloaded, men who could give us news from home. Anyhow, you must make do with what is sent.

In spite of hearing *stimmt*, nobody has moved. Everyone knows the second part of the program is going to take place; for the SS, it's the most interesting, most awaited event—the hanging.

There are already feverish movements by the gate. The registers have been put away, and the SS, forgetting all so-called protocol, start to raise their voices and let out great laughs. It's showtime.

"*Achtung!*"

The SS immediately snap into their proper positions, all according to rank, standing rigorously to attention. The Lagerführer solemnly emerges from his command post, followed by his officers.

At the head of the assembled SS, he congratulates them for their efficient running of the camp. Having complimented them, he lights up a flat oriental cigarette and, with all of his team, moves forward to the gallows. They relax; it isn't an official ceremony, just a show at which they'll be spectators.

The door of the bunker opens. Two SS men emerge. Each one has a Schmeisser machine gun loaded and ready in his hands. The eyes of fifteen thousand men turn toward them. Shrill orders are barked.

Now, one after another, twelve prisoners appear. They wear only shirts and trousers; they are bareheaded, and their hands have been tied behind their backs. Each man's mouth has been gagged by a lump of wood tied around and behind his neck, like a horse's bit but without the mercy accorded the so-called mere animal. These prisoners are now a pale yellow in complexion. They march in faltering steps toward their doom in the center of the square. You would look and have to say to yourself: "They are dead."

Big George awaits them at the foot of the gallows. Why, Big George is sociable as hell. He places the doomed men in two rows, six upon six, and he chats with them so smilingly, as if he were announcing some wonderful good news. The condemned men show no reaction to his sunshiny deportment.

Across the roll call square, fifteen thousand men watch. They are silent. Birds fly, seemingly playful, in the sky. The Lagerältester places the bench carefully vertical to the ropes, which are unusually thin, hardly as thick as a finger.

"First row. Forward!" Big George's voice is calm and satisfied.

The prisoners climb aboard the bench like so many robots. One misses his step and falls backwards. Big George belts him cruelly but then helps him up to where the rope is waiting.

The men who are about to die aren't all of the same height; some are big, others are medium, and some are small. However, that good chap the hangman has allowed for this by trimming the end of each rope into a piton set into the other end.

He moves from one to the next and pushes each prisoner's head into a slipknot, which he then tightens, just the right amount. Then he pulls on the ropes to tighten them up and fixes them, one by one, to the ring at the end of each piton. The executed men must not fall too brutally and die quickly from a rupture of the cervical vertebra; the SS feast of death would be too short. Each prisoner must perish slowly, strangled by his own weight.

Everything is in order. Big George turns toward the commandant, who lights up another cigarette and gives a sign with his stick. The executioner kicks away the bench.

At first, nothing happens; the bodies seem inert. The seconds pass by, then the hanged men begin stirring. Their legs move, as if looking for a foothold; then they come up, knees high, and come back down again. The movements increase, the bodies now waving about. Some touch and try to grip each other, to climb onto the neighbor, to loosen the rope. Then they break away, their bodies overwhelmed by frenzied spasms. The clogs drop from their feet, and their trousers fall down to their ankles. The hanged men seem to be caught in some violent wind as they bang against each other. They kick out in space, throwing their trousers to the ground. Little by little, this fury of bodily motion slows down. They return to the vertical. A trembling takes over from the furious motions of earlier minutes. Their heads are angled on their shoulders, and the ropes have cut deeply into their necks. One after another, the executed victims drift into the void.

"*Fertig!*" Big George pulls back the bench that lies under the gallows and frees the ropes. The bodies fall in a single mass. Men from the work party come to get them and throw them into a trolley with their shoes and trousers. It's intermission. The comments and laughter of the SS show their pleasure. Cigarettes are lit, and the tone of conversation mounts. Everyone has enjoyed the performances of the actors.

The six other condemned men have remained motionless. They have turned gray, but their legs still carry them. The bits tied in their mouths don't even make them dribble. They have pissed in their pants. George puts the ropes back into place in the correct order, the longest in the middle. He checks the slipknots; they have held perfectly. He puts the bench back under the gallows.

Intermission is at its end. The SS are hoping that the second part of the show will be as good as the first. The fact that the second batch of condemned men saw the first die may perhaps change their behavior and add a spicy supplement. Let the show restart, then. Big George nods to the second row. "Forward!"

The six men climb onto the bench.

★   ★   ★

Coming from the outside silos, the cartload of potatoes passes the gate and enters the camp. Like hyenas attracted by the smell of antelope, a group of young Russians prowl around the convoy. Sneering, they cross-examine the team doing the pushing and pulling. "*Eh, Micha, dawai kartochki.*" (Give us some potatoes.) The Vorarbeiter controlling the transfer is worried; he firmly sets his truncheon across the palm of his hand. The kitchens are less than a hundred yards away, but with this bunch of savages, you never know what's going to happen next. At any minute, the pack of them might attack and run everyone down. You can kill these Russians, but they just don't care. That cartload of potatoes represents the greatest wealth in the world, and it drives them mad.

"*Los, schnell, Mensch!*"

The men of the duty squad are afraid, too; they redouble their efforts, racing at full speed across the roll call square, turning the corner of the kitchen to arrive at the trapdoor. But two prisoners jump on the cart and stoke large shovelsful into the trapdoor. The hyenas are there, too, at a respectful distance, watching the work and waiting for their chance to pounce.

Shit! The potatoes haven't gone in far enough. The trapdoor is choked and won't close! And there are a good hundred pounds of potatoes piled up around the hole. In the name of God, what are those people inside fucking around at? This is all going to finish badly. The Vorarbeiter is white with rage. He grabs a prisoner by the sleeve. "You! Go and find Casimir! Tell him to come with an iron bar!" The prisoner dashes inside, returning in seconds with a giant sort of man holding a metal bar five feet long.

"Casimir, go over there and stand guard until we get the potatoes in and close the trapdoor. Hold those men back; they could get in and cut the throats of everyone. If any come near, you crush their skulls. *Rozoumich?*" (Understand?)

"OK," says Casimir.

The Vorarbeiter leads his whole team into the kitchen at full speed to clear the trapdoor. Casimir, well planted on his enormous legs, stands firm with the iron bar in his right hand. The Russians come and go—prudently—at a safe distance. They weigh the situation, seeking out a weak spot. *"Polski zaiobani"* (Polack, get fucked), they all laugh. Then they spread out a distance of five or six yards, forming a semicircle. Casimir feels the imminence of attack. He looks quickly around and gets ready. The Russians don't move; there are about twenty of them.

There is a movement on the right. A Mongol slowly moves forward. His narrow eyes have a humble look. In a moaning and beseeching voice, he pleads, *"Kamarad Polski, dawai kartochki."* (Polish comrade, give us some potatoes.) He takes a step forward, then another.

"Clear off, savage!" Casimir moves forward a little and with the steel bar takes a terrible swing toward the Russian, who throws himself back quickly. But at the same moment, on the other side of the semicircle, another Russian closes in swiftly, stuffs some potatoes into his shirt, and, with a kick, scatters the pile. The potatoes roll away from the trapdoor. Casimir charges in this new direction, swinging the bar but hitting only the air. The attack is now developed on the other side, where three Russians are bent down, filling up their shirts. Casimir rushes at them. Two take off at once, but the third steps on a potato, stumbles, and falls. The huge Pole is on him and beats him mercilessly. The Russian screams with pain, his ribs crushed and staved in by the steel bar. He rolls up in helpless agony on the ground.

Casimir turns around, his eyes flashing with rage. Nearly all of the potatoes have disappeared, and the Russians have vanished as well, weighed down with the booty that swells up their shirts.

The Vorarbeiter will not be happy about this.

★   ★   ★

All at once, insistent rumors fly among the prisoners as to the nature of projects on the other side of the hill. Now it seems that new tunnels are to be dug, to be known as Ellrich and Harzungen. These two names worry the prisoners, starting with the miners. There are still two or three veterans, men who struck the first blows into the tunnel with their picks and axes back in September 1943. All the others who were with them have long since gone up in smoke, to be replaced by new slave laborers who would soon vanish along the same route. With successive arrivals, however, the prisoner population has remained at a constant level.

Just a few days ago, the last charges were set in the rocky depths, and the mountain trembled for the last time. After finishing their work, the kommandos left for the tunnel entrance, where the blocks were already being dismantled. Here they must now dig down, no longer working horizontally. At this site, the V-2s will be set upright, so a vertical clearance of fifty feet from ground to ceiling is needed, for a length of a hundred and thirty yards.

The noise of pickaxes striking rock is frightening, worse than before. The two adjacent halls are still occupied by sleepers, but since they are exhausted by their day's work, the racket doesn't stop them from drifting into unconsciousness.

It's there, amid machines excavating what will be the floor, that the rumors start to break out. Firstly, the bottom won't be closed. Instead, a passage will be pierced to join other halls where the V-1 is built— that small robot gliding bomb now known as one of the "oldies" of Peenemünde. But who will be responsible for this factory and thus for its drilling, blasting, and digging? Another mystery. Perhaps it has already been started; nobody knows.

For the longest time, the miners had looked forward to the end of the cutting and blasting. Everyone said: "When we reach the end of this hellhole and when the last explosive charge is blown, I'll kiss the wall, and I'll go at once to declare myself as a turner, a driller, a welder ... anything. I'll set my ass on a stool, and I won't get off it until the end of time!"

Poor suckers! They dreamed of better times, of the forty-hour week, and of paid vacations at Dora-on-the-Sea.

But here's the reality of it, not obvious but instead insidious as it begins to show its deadly face. "Hey, guys, you're the champions of pneumatic drills and dynamite holes, so you're not going to end good careers so easily as that. You must keep going; you're specialists. The Führer needs you because without you he won't be able to make his filthy Third Reich last for a thousand years as he has claimed. So make a little more effort."

What frightens the men most is the transfer kommando. Staying in hell means starting all over to die a little with each day, but we're used to it. We no longer pay attention, and we no longer think about it. We know the Kapos and the SS; we know where they hide, waiting to leap out suddenly and strike like demons. Every corner of the darkness or light is known and memorized! Life and/or death become routine, simply daily events no longer arousing more horrified reactions. We've become completely passive.

To be transferred to another camp is to be thrown into a new and unknown world, one filled with traps. The SS and Kapos, embittered at having been sent to such a miserable place without the slightest hint of any comfort, become savage and ferocious. They massacre those whom they think are responsible for their lowered living standards. Everything must be learned anew; we begin at zero, and the losses of life are enormous.

The miners are well aware that they are like rats caught in a trap. There is no question of slowing the work to ease the pain. The shouts of those armed with truncheons, clubs, and pistols remind them of the urgency of their work, as well as the impatience of the authorities.

The veterans recall their arrival at Dora. They remember the bewilderment so swiftly stifled under the constant beatings, their incorporation into the kommando of miners—this twentieth-century version of the Phoenix, continually reborn from the cinders of the dead.

They've swept their minds clear of any recollection of earlier lives, of wives, children, parents, of streets and shopkeepers once familiar. They have dug like mad, have died without saying a word, and now that this tunnel is at an end, its survivors will be sent elsewhere to start all over again. It is certain that the kommandos won't be broken up. In columns of five, they will be sent to the other side of the hill with their materials. On the day when the engineers open a bottle of champagne on the tunnel wall, the slave laborers will be at attention on the roll call square, with tears in their throats.

The handling kommandos also worry. The narrow-gauge railroads have been dismantled, and the loaded wagons now enter and leave on standard-gauge track in the two big galleries. These other damned souls of Dora wonder what will be done with them. They are only useless, unskilled workers with no specialized knowledge, men who can be liquidated overnight without loss. There are millions like them across Europe, all unknowingly at risk as the potential "labor pool" out of which the Nazis draw to create new camps. Thus, the replacement of these unskilled wrecks poses no problem. The men who had timidly put out some feelers, smiled whenever they could at pals from Paris, Lyon, or Warsaw, hoping to manage to break out when things got better, suddenly feel their hearts gripped by a frozen hand. Hope melts away quickly as fear takes over.

On "rest" days, after they've worked all night, they prowl around the officials' barracks.

"Tell me, Stachek, listen, Maurice, we're from the same neck of the woods, can't you do something for me? Get me into a painters' or welders' kommando?" The pal in high places is kind and affectionate. He remembers the homeland, and he feels bad about lying because everyone comes to see him and he already fears for his own skin, which is worry enough. So he gives the standard replies: "OK, Antek, don't worry, Marcel, you can count on me. I'll do everything I can, but it won't be easy. Anyhow, nothing has been fixed yet. You can rest your head on your pillow. It's not even sure that there will be any transfers from Dora; perhaps everyone will come from Buchenwald. And don't you worry, we'll have a Pernod or a vodka in Rennes or Cracow in no time at all. The news is good; the Russians are still advancing, and the Americans will soon land in Europe. Look at the faces on the SS—it's as if they were already in our places. So, imagine your Uncle Stanislas or Cousin Robert, the state they'll be in when they see us come back. That will be great! Now, excuse me, but the barracks chief really doesn't like when there are visitors, even on the outside. So don't worry, and keep going like that. See you soon."

The Vorarbeiter are equally nervous. They have a quite ambiguous position, for it can't really be said that they are part of the hierarchy of the camp. They're a bit better dressed than ordinary prisoners but, in the end, not much better, and their armbands aren't really guarantees for a long life. Although a large number are Germans and criminal prisoners, there are amongst the group a lot of foreigners promoted by the run of circumstances.

The Vorarbeiter insignia is certainly something important, but this "something" can be lost at any moment, and its owner can find himself back at the very bottom of the ladder for nothing at all. Therefore, they feel pulled apart by dual worries and dual hopes. With a transfer, they can be promoted to Kapo; that's really the consecration, with all the advantages that go with it—warm clothes, leather boots, and as much food as they want. The great life, yes! But they can just as quickly, without knowing how or why, lose their badge and end up back among the Russians who are only waiting for the occasion to kill them. This perspective makes them tremble and brings about strange reactions. They even joke with prisoners and tell them "not to push the pace too much" when it is not too noticeable. They don't want to admit it, but they are dying with worry. If they beat up everyone in sight, perhaps that will earn them a marvelous promotion . . . but if, on the other hand, they are dismissed, within twenty-four hours they will have passed from life to death. If they are seen as obviously too lenient, they will be judged as not having the makings of a Kapo, and they'll rot in their status as a subaltern or even lose their armband, which brings back the first possibility. At those moments when an eventual transfer is confirmed, it is difficult being a Vorarbeiter.

★   ★   ★

Christian takes his small ration of margarine and puts it with the slice of sausage in a small metal box. He has managed to acquire two of the boxes, a real treasure. One is for the margarine, and the other is for his cigarettes. Then he takes his bread and cuts it into three thick slices—heavy, like the ones you bite into hungrily, not these thin slices made for pallid, skinny toast that, once eaten, leave only a sense of despair, as if one had eaten nothing, a feeling of having been cheated. Carefully, he puts the bread inside his shirt and leaves quickly. He calculates that he has just half an hour before assembly for the kommandos, so he must be quick.

Christian is continually tortured by the need to smoke. It began when he saw his pack of Gauloises, his last civilian cigarettes, placed on the Gestapo guy's table along with everything from his pockets. Following the Gestapo's first "cross-examination," which left him covered with blood, his nose broken, his ears torn, and missing a few teeth, he would have given anything for even the butt end of a Gauloise!

Afterwards, alone in his cell, he gathered the dregs of tea from the bottom of his mug and dried them out. Soon he had managed a good little heap. The old German soldier who acted as guard soon found it. "What's this?" he asked. Christian told him that he would very well smoke this dried-up tea if he had some paper and a light. The old reservist laughed noisily and gave him some papers. Christian quickly rolled one and lit it with the lighter held out to him. The effect was extraordinary and made him forget both his terrible hunger and his horrible condition for a moment. The smoke burned his lips, and his eyes swelled, but he thought that it might help heal his wounds. After a few drags, the hot ashes fell from the paper, scattered, and went out. Christian dived to the ground, trying to relight the butt ends, but it was too late.

He rolled some "cigarettes" with the tea-leaf dregs and paper that was left and hid them safely. Another two or three times, the old German gave him a light, and each time, Christian experienced an immense bliss, while his hunger waned temporarily. He had behaved like a free man and had felt a brief sort of inner pride.

Back among the prisoner population with his rations, Christian looks around. The thieves and the flea market aren't far. He puts a piece of bread in each trouser pocket, keeping the third in his shirt. He knows he must be very careful if he doesn't want to be thrashed and robbed without getting anything of value in exchange.

At the corner of the Effektenkammer, there is a small group. This is where business is done. The corner is poorly lit. Two young Gypsies approach him, offering a pair of leather shoes undoubtedly stolen from a sick patient unable to defend himself. Christian doesn't stop; shoes are far too expensive, and they're sure to be too small for him. A little further on, a toothless old Russian gives him a touting smile.

"Hey, Franzous, idi souda, papirossi. Du kleb!" (Hey, Frenchman, I got cigarettes. You got bread?)

He has a few cigarettes in his hand, but they are Makhorkovs, made from flower petals and a piece of cardboard, in the Russian style.

"Nein, Makhorkov Scheisserei." Christian doesn't want any of that shit. "Kein Makhorka!" (Do you have tobacco?)

"Oh, Franzous, lizopizdi." His tone is complaining, but from his pocket, the Russian takes a bit of newspaper in which there is a black ball. Christian sniffs. It really is tobacco. He takes the slice of bread out from hiding inside his shirt and shows it to the old man. The Russian pinches up a few leaves of tobacco and puts them on the edge of the paper. The bastard! There's not enough to roll a cigarette. A hot discussion follows, and Christian manages to trade the piece of bread for three cigarettes plus a piece of newspaper to roll them in.

While leaving, he is approached by three Russians who press against him.

"Franzous, dai pocourit!" (Frenchman, give us a smoke!)

"Fuck off, jackals!" he snaps.

Christian tries to shrug them off, but they jump him, with some vicious infighting. In the fracas, one of them pulls at a pocket, which tears. The bit of bread falls, at once picked up by the Russian, who runs off with his pals. "Smelly bastards," he mutters, "I'll find you another time."

Christian looks at his trousers. The leg is open almost to the bottom. He'll have to find some wire to repair them. Luckily, he thinks, he's saved the tobacco, the margarine, and his third bit of bread.

★   ★   ★

Charles arrives at the barracks with his face bloody and his clothing torn. He has the characteristic trembling of someone who has just finished fighting. Stani sees him and comes near. "What's happened to you? You're in bad shape."

Charles only stares at Stani as if looking at an enemy. His jawbone trembles nervously.

"Charles, come and wash your face at once. If the barracks chief sees you like that, he'll treat you like a dirty tramp and beat the crap out of you."

Stani drags Charles to the Waschraum and washes his face. He has a bruise on his cheek, and his lower lip is split, bloody, and swollen. Charles finds it hard to speak, and his lip hurts him. "It was those bastard friends of yours, the Polacks, who worked me over. This morning, I had a few words with one, and I flung my fist in his face. So this evening, there was a whole gang waiting for me after roll call, and they jumped me. I defended myself as well as I could, and I managed to get away."

"Look, Charles, first of all, the Polacks aren't my buddies." Stani didn't look happy. "My buddies I choose myself. And they're not my compatriots, OK? My father is Polish, but I'm a Frenchman, born in France. I've got a Polish name, and I can speak their language, but that's all. And believe you me, it's not always easy, to be in my position. And friends or not, those Polacks are real bastards. They give us French a rough time, almost as much as the damned Kapos. Just try going to the infirmary for a dressing when there's a Polish guard at the door. As soon as he sees your tab, he throws you outside with a beating. And in the kommando, he'll turn the Vorarbeiter against you and then laugh while you take a beating, not to mention the problems he can cause you on the block. And the soup: When the bowl arrives, you don't have any potatoes, nothing but slops. The Stubendienst, another Polack, of course, has given them all to his little buddies. You think that's normal? After all, we're all in the same boat here, and we haven't done anything to them."

"All right, Stani. At first, I asked myself the same question, and I asked my friends why, as you say."

Stani is watching the door. It wasn't wise to stay and discuss this any further in the Waschraum.

"I found that rotten, and I told them. That wasn't difficult; they explained it at once."

The Waschraum began to fill, and Charles attracted sly and indifferent looks. The two men distanced themselves from the other prisoners.

"Charles, when the war broke out in September '39, the Poles thought the French would eat the German army alive, but when it came to eating, it was Poland that was swallowed up in fifteen days. But they didn't despair; they thought we French weren't quite ready, that we were just waiting for the right moment to jump the *Boches* and eat them raw. You know that for the Poles, the French army was the finest in the world. Even when they saw the Germans' equipment, they said to themselves, 'Just imagine what the French must have!' They kept hoping, sure that everything would soon be set right; it was only a question of days or weeks. Then winter came, and guys were being sent off to concentration camps. Their morale wasn't quite so high, and their hope was transformed into a prayer that we'd come quickly, as quickly as possible. But we didn't budge; we just sat playing cards in the shelter. When it really started up, in May 1940, hope returned for the Poles. There they were; the French army would wipe out the *Chleuhs* (Krauts) and at top speed arrive in Warsaw. Well, you know how it ended. In six lousy weeks, our army, the most powerful in the world . . . the whole lot were in the Nazi Stalags, still playing cards but now prisoners. So for the Poles, their hopes were turned into hatred. They were finished with us."

"Yes, Stani, but that's all in the past. Now we're all in the same shit up to our necks. The very fact that we're here proves that we're not all so yellow."

"Perhaps, but don't forget one thing; most Polacks here aren't in their first camp. They've been to several. And it looks as if the first French who arrived in the camps in '42 were fairly mixed. There wasn't just the cream. Criminals were certainly few in number, but since they were the only ones to open their mouths, they made a bad impression. The Poles are mixed, too, but they don't care about that. All they can see is that we let them down and that we are not exactly as they imagined us to be."

"In any case, they can think whatever they like, but I don't intend to let them beat me up without doing anything."

"You're right, and besides, that won't change a thing. But I'm going to see the Polacks in your kommando and try to sort out this business. Otherwise, you risk finding yourself in the infirmary with a broken arm or leg, as sure as two and two make four. So avoid any trouble at work, and things should calm down."

Charles felt bad, but he knew that Stani was right.

★   ★   ★

Little Louis suddenly dropped his shovel, uncontrollably bending in two. He was livid. Martial rushed to his side.

"Something wrong, Louis? What's the matter?" Martial looked down and saw an enormous spittle of blood in Louis's hand. "Come with me, but pick up your shovel. Otherwise, the Vorarbeiter is going to smash his club across your back!"

They furtively entered a hall that was being fitted out. Immediately to the left, there was a sort of storage area for future spare parts, and here they hid themselves. Martial looked at Louis. He had a frightening look, the color of wax. The bags under his eyes gave him something of the appearance of a fetus, and he was trembling with fever.

Martial repeated his question: "There is something wrong. Tell me what it is?"

"Martial, I'm finished; I'm at the end of my rope. I don't want to start again tomorrow, I don't have any more strength. Tonight, I'll go to the infirmary."

"Oh, God, no, Louis; you mustn't go there. You know it's very bad. You never see anyone coming out again. Hold on, you'll see; you'll feel better tomorrow."

The two men couldn't fail to notice the slightly unreal noise in the gallery: the sound of trolleys rolling, the Vorarbeiter's hoarse shouting, the crashing of picks against stone, the scraping of shovels, the clanking of the clogs of the handling kommando, and, permeating the whole, the sound of gummis and truncheons striking human flesh.

"Better tomorrow, you're joking. Take a good look at me, and don't tell me a lot of rubbish. I'm spitting up my lungs; the fever is killing me. Yesterday, I looked at my legs. I was horrified; they're nothing but bones."

"But, Louis, we're all the same."

"Perhaps, Martial, but apparently you haven't got TB. Me, yes, and at the final degree. I vomit blood." Louis paused. The speaking tired him. "You know what will happen if I come back tomorrow? I'll either fall or lie down because I can't go on. So the Vorarbeiter or an SS man will see me. He'll break every bone in my body to make me get up. So you understand why I prefer to go to the infirmary."

Louis straightened himself a little, with great effort. "You tell me that if I go to the infirmary, I'll not come out alive. Well, I already know that; I'm not that stupid, and I couldn't care less. At least, perhaps there they'll let me die in peace—and horizontally."

Louis looked at Martial. He'd made up his mind and wouldn't change it. In two days, three at the most, he would have left Dora by way of the crematorium chimney. A little sooner, a little later, what difference could it make? "Come on, Martial, let's get busy; it's not worth getting another beating."

Louis was eighteen years old.

★　　　★　　　★

With the coming of spring, the invasion becomes one of the main topics of discussion. Will it come this year? Many think so, but there have been so many false alarms for months that no one really dares to believe it. So many "tips" have evaporated within a few hours, turning out to be no more than mythomaniac fantasies. And the Russians, advancing at a forced pace for more than a year, still have not been seen. In all that time of marching, they must have bypassed us without knowing we're here. Should we keep hoping or simply not think about it—think of nothing at all?

Guillaume is the great strategist among us. He had been a professional officer, so his opinion is straight. The men are gathered in front of the barracks, trying to catch the last rays of sunlight still sweeping across the plain. In half an hour, it will be roll call for the kommandos going down into the tunnel.

"I tell you," Guillaume begins, "there won't be any invasion in France, nor in Belgium or Holland or even directly in Germany. In military strategy, an army must strengthen its flanks, which are strongly anchored along one coast or along a frontier. A force stepping onto a beach will be annihilated immediately by the line of defense. That's the ABC of all high-command teachings."

"You mean the high command people who are in the prison camps?"

"Don't be stupid." Guillaume doesn't like such bizarre reflections. "The French and Germans each had a continuous front, and the German army attacked where we didn't have enough arms or men. They found our weak spot, and that's where they struck."

"So all in all," comes the sarcastic voice again, "all it takes is for one guy to go take a piss to weaken the line of defense and endanger the whole country?"

Everyone laughs, but Guillaume takes the ridicule personally. "If you use everything I say to make the 'gallery' laugh, it's not worth asking my opinions. Since you're so clever, you might as well go on believing in Father Christmas. He also lands every year, from what I'm told." Guillaume looks very hurt and appears to be leaving.

"Come on, don't get upset, Guillaume. I was only joking; I didn't want to upset you. But the Americans did land in North Africa, then in Sicily, and then in Italy."

"But it's not the same thing at all," replies Guillaume. "When they landed in North Africa, it was in a friendly country. OK, the French army was stupid enough to fire at them, but it was only a little fireworks, just to mark the occasion. Just for the beauty of it all. Two hours later, it was over and the African French forces were on the Allied side, at their service."

"And Sicily and Italy? They weren't allies after all."

"Well, there you misunderstand me. In Sicily, there was no defense, nothing at all. The few Italian units were only waiting for the chance to lay down their arms; the soldiers knew it was all over, and their officers weren't about to put up a fight just for Mussolini's pleasure. As for the landing at Calabria, that part of Italy is so narrow that it wasn't difficult to establish a continuous front, sheltered from sudden surprises. Moreover, there wasn't a hint of a German, which really made the job easy."

"But surely, Guillaume, all the American forces in England aren't there just to visit. They really mean to make a landing—but where?"

"That, my old buddy, is a secret I don't share. Perhaps they'll land in Italy or even make a series of diversions, but I don't see them landing anywhere and putting their equipment on a beach. They'd be massacred on the spot by Germans who have everything at hand and are waiting for them, their feet firmly planted on the ground. When you don't have safely secured supply lines and you have to depend on ships that not only might be sunk but will be sunk, then you're not just playing cowboys and Indians."

"Speaking of supplies," he goes on, "look what happened at Stalingrad. The Germans had stretched their front over hundreds of miles, and their flanks were extremely vulnerable. There's the danger. The Russians hit those vulnerable flanks and cut off their supplies. That flank attack trapped all those tens of thousands of Germans without food, water, clothing, or ammunition. They were finished."

"Then if I understand you, Guillaume, there won't be an invasion. So we'll be here forever."

"That I don't know. But I'm sure that if the English and Americans don't manage to establish a solid front with well-secured flanks, their effort will be lost. It's the basic ABC that they teach at the military college, and the teachers are experienced; they've studied all the modern and classic strategies."

"OK then, Guillaume, you give us all this talk about flanks and how smart they are at military college and continuous fronts. But everybody you talked about took a hell of a beating. I'm reassured to know that afterwards, they explained about how the Germans cheated, that they really didn't 'play the game.' So perhaps the Krauts didn't go to the same military college. So to be told we were clobbered by Germans who were ignorant of the art of war, I find that a bit vexing. Maybe our high command would have done better if they were offering candies to young ladies out of schools. But the cowboys, now, I'd trust them. I'm sure they have the guts, and one of these days, they'll jump the channel and stomp all over the damned *Chleuhs*' backs. Perhaps there'll be losses, but the cowboys have their own military college. They've come to have a go at it, and they'll do it, even if it's not in the Kraut military books or Aunt Bertha's recipes. And that's better because without it, if they knew your theories, they'd tell themselves they'd better go back home since they have no established flanks to protect them. But if they succeed, maybe we should get rid of our own old fogies and seek advice from the cowboys."

Guillaume, having heard this, gathers himself with as much dignity as he can and leaves the scene. His prestige has been blown to bits.

★   ★   ★

The Russian entity at Dora is a mad, unimaginable world apart from the rest. Other nationalities had arrived in the camps via transfers that were easily identified in time and space. The Russians, however, seem to have dropped onto the Planet Dora in one incomprehensible group—laughing, moaning, fighting, crying, a chaotic mass of men who die and don't care. They're a loose, uncontrollable body, warm, dangerous, brotherly, and also devilish. They're a jumble of temperaments and racial types spread everywhere that there are electrified fences.

Russia is forty times the size of France, covering 15 percent of the Earth's land surface. It contains an incredible mixture of peoples, many of whom have never heard of France, Belgium, or even Germany. There are tribes that don't understand each other at all, and the only Russian words they know are *"Nie ponimai"*—"I don't understand." They seem like biological strata that have ignored the passage of men and civilizations; for thousands of years, they have continued their lives, milking yaks and carrying their sour cheese to market.

Among them are Mongols who, in human memory, have always fought against the Chinese and the Russians. There are Cossacks whose ancestors charged their wiry little steeds as far as Paris and waged the endless pogroms of czarist Russia against its Jews. There are also descendants of the original Huns who, led by Attila, pushed as far as Châlons-sur-Marne and as far as the fields of Catalonia. But it doesn't end there. There are even Eskimos and Tartars, Kirghizes and Uzbeks, Siberians and men from the Ukraine.

One day in June 1941, this enormity of human types went to war. At Stalin's bidding from Moscow, men representing a tenth of mankind old enough to carry arms embarked on their march toward their Western Front. The initial battles were a disastrous nightmare, and a large part of European Russia was swallowed up by the German army, which closed its grip over millions of people. Since the Soviet government hadn't thought it useful to sign the Geneva Convention for the statutes protecting prisoners of war, all the Russians, civilian or military, found themselves at the mercy of the Germans, with no rights whatsoever. So millions died, but the Soviets, believing that all men owe their very lives to the state, decided that anyone taken prisoner was no more than a wretched dog who could rot away.

The Germans caught enormous numbers of civilians and soldiers in their campaigns. Without hesitation, the prisoners were sent to the concentration camps. Soldiers arrived in the camps still dressed in their long khaki coats, boots, and pointed hats with their red stars. They kept their military reflexes, obeyed their officers, and madly mocked the orders of the SS. In the big camps such as Buchenwald, they generally remained in unified groups, with frightening devastation. Lines of solidarity saved them; one deprived himself of a part of his rations to help others, but the result was the same: They died. Some, the last of them, were put into the striped uniforms and sent to camps such as Dora, but these only made up a small part of the huge Russian contribution to the camp system.

The civilians were the large majority of Dora's Russian contingent. They were a cross section of human groups—ranging from the big, white, typical European to the small, yellow man with narrow eyes—encompassing every possible human variation. The terrible conditions at Dora should have favored breakdowns into cleavages and tribal hatreds, but there was none of that. Instead, this strange mosaic of people became welded together by the absolute misery and destitution they suffered.

In the camps where there were no Jews specifically deported for "racial" reasons and categorized accordingly, the Russians were relegated to the slimiest bottoms of the "social structure," if such a term can be used amid such inconceivable conditions.

The Russians had nothing and wished for nothing. In Western-style societies, the "lower classes"—who have no inheritance or belongings to cherish—don't feel, contrary to what's said, any class "solidarity."

But the Russians don't even know about all this "social theory." Is one of them in trouble for having stolen a loaf of bread? Then the whole community is up in arms to defend him. Is another in danger for having committed a wild sabotage or threatening a Vorarbeiter? The sons of the immense Russia, the incredible empire of these ragged people, stand up together to accept the consequences, each one ready to give his right arm for one of his kind, even if he didn't know the man or really know what it was all about.

To touch a Russian is like attacking his brother, his father, or his son. Thousands of them have spent whole days standing up on the roll call square without protesting because one of them had rebelled.

On one occasion, there was a general roll call for the Russians for such a reason. In one barracks, young Aphanace had everyone's sympathy. He had the respect of the barracks chief because Aphanace painted quite well and had created decorations and pictures for the barracks. Prisoners liked him because he was a really good guy and was always laughing. They all wanted to hide him in the barracks so that he could avoid this terrible ordeal. But Aphanace refused and joined his compatriots without any speeches. With the others, he stood for twelve hours at attention and went to work the same night. That was Russian solidarity.

Where did these men come from? Who were they? For the Ukrainians, it was quite simple: They were already there, at home, when the German army advanced, then simply rounded them up and sent them off in the long convoys. The Asiatics had been brought west by the Soviet administration to work in the munitions factories and to build defenses.

They were all trapped in the Nazi sweep and constituted masses of the wandering and the unemployed, a vast well from which the Germans could draw in huge amounts. Many were sent as slave labor to the German factories, and many more found themselves on the roads to the camps.

Unlike Westerners, who were terrorized by what they discovered, who found it hard to adapt, and who thus died in enormous numbers, the Russians, with experience in their own system, were into the swim of things almost immediately. No settling in after a period of time; they integrated at once. If any of them had feelings to the contrary, no one ever noticed; they adjusted to the customs of this insane planet like fish in a pool.

The few parcels received by the French and Belgians caused the Russians to discover unknown and unsuspected treasures and brought about lust. Those who had never received anything organized regular gangs of thieves who attacked the happy recipients of tinned food and chocolate bars. Fights, which often became quite bloody, were the result and did nothing to engender understanding between peoples. A Russian prowling around the owner of a parcel represented an immediate danger, and help was called for. Considerable animosity was thus generated on both sides.

At work, the French created chaos without really trying, but it was the Russians who really organized it.

For example, take ten Russians with an object to be moved. It seems simple enough: Just hoist it to your shoulders and move it. But for them, it's different. This thing to be moved has nothing to do with them, so they get in a line, start to feel it, lift it up, and put it back down; then they discuss it. Then the Vorarbeiter arrives, cursing, beating his way into the group. The men scatter, dodging and squealing, and the chief finds himself there with the machine, which still hasn't moved. He prudently backs off, and the Russians come back. They finally pick up the machine and put it on their shoulders. They discuss it again. Some want to carry on their left shoulder, others on the right, and angry tones rise in volume. The Vorarbeiter becomes annoyed again and gives out bashings with his club—another mistake because those who take the beating want to rush off, and the others do not. The machine begins to list and threatens to fall. The prisoners put their load down. In the heat of his rage, the Vorarbeiter smashes in the skull of a Russian, who is laid out for the count, perhaps longer. Calm returns to the scene, but now the team is one man short. The chief orders them to restart, so they manage to lift the machine to their shoulders and advance. After only a few steps, though, they begin to stagger; their knees start to bend and their shoulders to give way. It's almost a catastrophe, with everyone pitching to one side. The machine is laid down amid a lot of screaming. The Vorarbeiter is overcome by events gone out of control. He no longer knows what to do and has already knocked out part of his team without any results; he cannot liquidate everyone. And if an SS man passes, he'll treat the Vorarbeiter as incompetent, strip off his armband, and send him to the furnace. So how is he to act with these guys who couldn't care less about dying and even seem to do everything they can to bring it on? The poor chief is having cold sweats; he can use his truncheon to kill, but that alone doesn't make these Russians work. So he takes a quick, furtive look to the left and right to see whether there are any authorities in sight, then he helps the gang to lift the machine. Once it is well seated on their shoulders, he steps aside and forwards the troop. They start off. Everything is fine for the moment, but the Vorarbeiter no longer has any illusions—it can all begin again at any second. What can one do with guys who mock death itself? Chaos in the work details was a hallmark contribution of the doomed Russians as they suffered and died in this insane world, the alien Planet Dora.

3

SUDDENLY, IN THE WEST

June 6, 1944

They have done it! They have landed!

Charles felt his legs trembling. He thought he was going to fall.

The news didn't merely fly, it exploded, rocketing to the far ends of the camp and to the bottom of the tunnel. THEY HAVE LANDED! The men were crying and laughing all at the same time. They had won! Who cared what would happen next? The biggest, most beautiful thing of all time had just happened. They have landed!

Never did any news race through any city so quickly, flying from barracks to kommando, briefly drowning the noise of the machines, climbing as far as those dying men in the infirmary, and penetrating to those men dug into the depths of the earth. Within seconds, it was translated into every language and all the dialects of Babel within the Harz Mountains. It literally flew along every route, sending its formidable tremor from the camp commandant to the lowest wretch still alive.

This time, the news was certain. It bore no relation to rumors, so quickly squashed, passed in secrecy, and welcomed with sarcastic jokes. It was soon known that the information came from French prisoners close to the Arbeitsstatistik and the SS command.

The invasion had begun that same morning in France, in Normandy, somewhere on the beaches between Le Havre and Cherbourg. An enormous Anglo-American armada had landed thousands of men and tanks, and the fighting was fierce.

All at once, throughout the kommandos and in the barracks, the Normans became important figures. "I'm from Bayeux," "I'm from Carentan," "I'm from Caen, on the coast. The beaches slope slightly, just right, so the guys will get ashore easy as a piece of cake. It's already won. You'll see, all the buddies who are still there, they'll really hit the Krauts. We're tough in our part of the country. I wouldn't like to be in the *Chleuhs'* shoes; they'll be rolled up like a bunch of tramps."

In the eyes of the Slavs, the French prisoners suddenly took on an importance they had never enjoyed before, and now they were looked upon with respect and consideration. The first question was usually, "What is this Normandy?"

Everyone tried to explain that this was a French province across the channel from England. "And the partisans, are there any?" And the answer would be, "Yes, there are lots, and the Allies are counting on them to disrupt the German lines of communication and railways."

The turnaround in the attitudes of the Russians and Poles was immediate. It was nothing like those early days and hours of hurtful sneers, of *"Franzousky, alle partisan."* The disgrace had vanished; the original sins of 1940, the mad flight of the French army, and the obscene armistice were washed away. These blemishes that the French prisoners had not deserved in themselves but that they bore in the view of the orientals were now swept away in the grand achievement of "The Invasion!"

The Kapos, Vorarbeiter, and barracks chiefs of differing grades didn't seem, from our viewpoint, to react in any way to news of the invasion. Certainly, they talked of it at other levels but remained careful so that neither their opinions nor their reactions would be noticeable to the eyes of the prisoners.

Despite the startling news, there was no change in the appearance of the SS that day, no apparent nervousness whatsoever. They were neither better nor worse than usual.

The roll call and assembly of kommandos almost trembled visibly with the fantastic news. Until now, the Russians and Americans had been like *Arlesienne* (French opera): spoken of daily but never seen. Today, however, something cataclysmic had happened, and all the prisoners felt it in their very skin. A surge of fever and pride swelled every heart. Their rows in formation were perfect, their positions irreproachable, and their pace more perfectly measured than ever before.

The arrival of the tunnel relief was welcomed by poor, dirty, unshaven faces with the skin hanging from their bones, transfigured by this new joy. They had rediscovered a hope that had disappeared for a long time, seemingly for centuries. "Perhaps we'll get out of here one day; there's reason to hold on! Perhaps in a few weeks, oh, God!" But for those who were at the end of their rope and knew it, those who hadn't the strength to begin the next day, it was now worth dying. Before life ended, the last thought in their minds would be—"We really got them!"

★   ★   ★

"Have you still got something to smoke? I'll even up with you when I have some. I'll buy some tobacco tomorrow in exchange for my margarine."

"I still have a little left in the bottom of my pocket, but I have no more newspaper. We'll use a bit of a cement bag."

Marcel opens his jacket. Underneath it is a cement bag with a hole cut for his head and two for his arms; it gives him a bit of protection from the cutting winds of the tunnel. He cuts out a bit of paper from the bottom of the bag, then soaks it well with saliva to make it more pliable and produce more smoke. Carefully, he rolls out a long, thin cigarette made of more paper than tobacco. A quick visit to the welders and he is back, hiding his smoke in the palm of his hand. Taking turns, the two men draw on the cigarette. The technique is well tested: You draw several puffs quickly, which you must not let escape, and swallow the lot, keeping it in your lungs as long as possible. The smoke is burning and slightly intoxicating. It is truly dizzying.

It's three in the morning as the tunnel crew begins its half-hour break. A strange silence fills the underground caverns, and the prisoners, having flopped wherever they found themselves, try to recover enough strength to hold out for another six hours before the relief arrives. The Kapos, Vorarbeiter, and SS have gone, and the tunnel seems dead, apart from a few whispers here and there. Marcel and Gilbert nurse the light on their cigarette. It's very delicate because they must wet it with saliva so that it doesn't open up—but not too much, or it will go out. It's all a question of proportion.

Marcel is worried. He has something on his mind and doesn't know how to mention it. Briskly, he broaches the subject. "I say, Gilbert, what do you think of transfers of invalids? What do you know about it?"

"Transfers of invalids? What are you talking about? You don't intend to go to the infirmary? If you're not ready to break, best you avoid it."

"No, it isn't that, but when I got here, I had my brother with me. He caught pneumonia and wound up in the infirmary. He was delirious. A few days later, all the infirm were led to the roll call, then loaded on a train. What do you make of that?"

Gilbert looks at Marcel discreetly. He sees his buddy, nineteen years old, returning home to hear his parents ask, "What have you done with your brother?" and Marcel replying, "I didn't know how to save him, and he wound up being roasted in one of their hellish crematoriums. It's my fault; I'm a bastard because I didn't know how to look after him."

Gilbert, aware of Marcel's keen feelings, knows he must be careful. Marcel's shoulders aren't broad enough to carry such an awful burden. He has asked the question only because it is torturing him. He knows the answer as well as Gilbert but wants to feel forgiven. Gilbert knows that if he can't find the right words, Marcel will be unable to support an unnecessary sense of guilt and will let himself go and die. His spirits must be pepped up and quickly.

"Listen, Marcel, I can't speak about things I don't know very well, but there's a Polack here who was in a transfer of the sick, and he's back from it. He's completely brutalized but not bad when you consider the alternative. I'll show him to you, given a chance, and you can talk with him yourself. He's real pudgy, with cheeks like my buttocks when I was at my peak. I don't know what he was sick with, but he was taken out and sent directly to another camp. I'm not sure of the name, but I think it was Bergen-Belsen. And now he's back, alive and kicking. He's renewed his lease on life, and it could be the same with your brother. So don't even think of it any other way!"

Marcel takes a drag on the cigarette. There is only paper left, but it does smoke; it turns your head, and that's good.

"You know, Gilbert, I didn't mention this so you could tell me a lot of rubbish, as if I'll find him all fresh and rosy after the war. But when you arrive at Dora as two brothers, you believe you're going to help each other and that you're going to leave the place together. Before we came, my brother didn't worry me too much, and we fought quite easily. He was older and used to muck me about with his stories about 'rights of the eldest.' But when we ended up here, we kept an eye on one another, and we didn't want to hurt our parents. We'd already done enough. You know, it was great when I saw him from time to time and I could say quickly as we passed, 'OK, poor cunt?' and he'd answer, 'You're gonna get it if this continues.' Then we went on our ways. Finally, I believe that in our thoughts, we were never apart. The day after the transfer, I went to the infirmary and managed to see a 'Doc'—a Dutchman. It wasn't easy, but I managed to get a word with him, a nice guy with hair. I asked about my brother. He didn't know him, of course, but he was kind and told me that nothing could be done for him here because Dora isn't a very hospitable place, so he'd been sent to a specialized camp where he'd be returned soon. Now, is that true, or is it rubbish? I don't know, and it torments me. Because, I'm going to tell you, I really think that my parents, if I go back alone, will never forgive me. I'll always feel their eyes on me as long as they live and even afterward. So if my brother dies, I'd like to die as well. That way, it will make room for the others, and I won't have to go before the family council.

"When my brother and I were caught, we were lucky, if you can say that, to see our parents. They're still young, but you'd have seen them as two oldsters, each supporting the other. We were surrounded by those nice thugs, the Gestapo, you see what I mean, guys who slavered with impatience at the idea of breaking us in two. And our two parents, who watched us being taken away in a Citroën car and who called after us desperately. We waved at them to stay clear because, you never know, they could have been picked up, too. I can still see them there, and it makes me feel bad. You know how it is here, we're dropping like flies, but my parents, I think they're having a rougher time."

It is almost time to go, but Gilbert is ready to wind it up. "Don't be upset, Toto, everything will turn out all right. If your brother is anything like you, he'll pull through, and you'll go to greet the family together. I'll take you to see the Polack from Bergen-Belsen, and he'll tell you about the transfer of the infirm. And now, for the tobacco, try to find some tomorrow but get Makhorka, none of that shitty Makhorkov; we'll roll a good one for tomorrow night."

The break ends. No siren blast, no whistle, nothing; you know it is finished and that you must start again. It is the castle of Sleeping Beauty, awakening again.

$$\star \qquad \star \qquad \star$$

The evening rations are handed out with unusual speed. Normally, the Stubendienst now has his great moment, his moment of power. The bowls are filled at the end of the table. The Stubendienst plunges his ladle into the soup tin. He knows his tin well and could describe the contents as if he had his nose inside. At the bottom, there are some delicious potatoes. Above, there is a thick layer of disgusting rutabagas that give you the runs. Then, two good thirds of starchy water and, finally, floating about, a few hints of meat. The operation is about to start, followed by anxious, hungry eyes.

The method is simple. All that would be needed is to stir up the ingredients so that the rations are equally shared. But the Stubendienst doesn't have an egalitarian mind; he has his friends and those he dislikes. He knows who will have this bowl, that bowl, and the next. He stirs the soup with seemingly big movements of the ladle, but within a few seconds, the potatoes fall back to the bottom of the pot and the slops float to the top. The handing-out of soup begins. For the buddies, the friends, the compatriots, the ladle plunges to the level of the potatoes, lifts up a good measure, passes quickly through the slops to finish, coming to the surface, and, with a quick wrist movement, picks up two or three bits of meat. But for the other prisoners, the ladle stops halfway and brings up slops. There's no question of protesting; that would put you permanently on the blacklist.

This evening, the ceremony is shortened; something is about to happen. The Stubendienst doles out the soup quickly, without the usual favored servings.

"And now, eat, you bunch of idiots. The barracks chief is coming in five minutes. I don't want to see anything left on the tables by then!"

What else are the Germans planning? The men are worried. It can't be a duty party; there isn't enough time. In half an hour, they must go back down into the tunnel. This new worry has its compensations for some in the rare pleasure of finding potatoes in their soup, which seldom happens. The soup is quickly devoured.

Heinz, the barracks chief, enters the refectory. He has a busy look, and his club is ready in his hand. He orders the prisoners into a semicircle around the room. Slowly, he looks around the group, pausing at some, passing others by. In a flash, he jumps on Lucien and throws him into the middle of the room.

"Your friend was in a fight today. It's verboten to fight in Dora; we are all friends. I'm your friend. But the French are undisciplined, and they don't understand where they are. So the Frenchman is going to get twenty-five blows . . . on the ass!"

He turns to Lucien. "Undress yourself!"

Lucien takes off his jacket and trousers and ends up in his shirt and long, striped underpants. He is very pale. The Stubendienst brings over a stool, which he places in the middle of the room. Lucien goes on all fours, his stomach across the stool. His position is grotesque.

Now Heinz rolls up his sleeves, holding the club firmly in his hand, and throws the first blow with a "wham." Lucien's body bounces against the stool, and a groan is heard. The second blow falls, hitting the bottom of his spinal column. Lucien cries out. Heinz turns red and strikes like a madman from Lucien's back to the cheeks of his buttocks. The moaning becomes continuous, peaking with each new blow. Lucien's mouth begins to foam. Now he seems half-conscious. The Stubendienst is counting the blows.

"Twenty-five, Heinz. That's it."

Heinz straightens up. Sweat is pouring profusely down his neck. He is panting, and his hitting arm is shaking all over.

"Good. OK, get up, swine." And everyone assembles.

Two men take Lucien by the shoulders, carry him to the Waschraum, and stick his head under the tap.

"Wake up, old buddy, we're going down to the tunnel. Hold on, here are your clothes. Put them on quick. OK?"

"I'll be fine, but you'll have to help me. I can't stand up."

"Don't worry about that, Lucien. We're here, and you can rely on us."

★   ★   ★

Claude noticed Albert that night as he was pushing a wagonload of spare parts. Albert seemed to be a storeman in a metal depot near the middle of the tunnel. An easy number.

"I'll come and see you during the break."

"OK, Claude, see you soon."

They had not seen each other for months—since Buchenwald—but there is a degree of uneasiness between them, an impression of caution. Claude sensed this once again and became uneasy.

They are from the same town—in fact, from the same Resistance group. When Claude was arrested, he didn't have the time to say a word but found himself thrown into a car. For Albert, things happened differently and turned into a tragedy. The Gestapo and armed German soldiers raided his house in the early hours of the morning while all the family was there—a family full of hate for the Germans. A battle broke out immediately. His father was killed, his mother injured, and his two sisters and he had been tied up and deported.

His had been a tough family for whom the idea of country held deep meaning; for them, to give their blood for their country was considered a natural duty.

On the evening of their arrests, Albert and Claude found themselves in the same prison cell. Albert showed abrasions and contusions from the fight but nothing more serious. As for Claude, he had undergone what the Gestapo so lightly referred to as a "first questioning," which left him in a pitiful state. Albert tended him carefully like a brother, but the next day, they were separated.

They met later in Compiègne, and then came the departure for Buchenwald—those infamous railroad voyages of three nights and three days, one hundred men to a cattle car, that could only have been conceived by sadists.

On the night before, those leaving were undressed, searched completely, and then isolated in a special compound. The crafty thing to do was to hide things beforehand, hide the tools and knives in the grass at the spot where you were re-dressed after the search; these tools hopefully could be used in cutting openings in the wooden cattle cars in efforts to escape.

The next day, the long column crossed Compiègne, the men's hands chained. They were put into the cattle cars a hundred at a time and held there like rats in a cage.

In his corner, close to a side wall, Albert began working with some others. He dug a hole in the lining. He spotted Claude and said, "You are coming with us, of course. We are going to escape."

But Claude didn't have the courage to accept.

The escape attempt never took place, after all, because men were digging in all the cattle cars. As soon as the first prisoners jumped, the train stopped, and the fugitives were shot. It was, of course, suicidal, for the Germans knew it would happen, and they were waiting . . . but still, Claude felt infinitesimally small and was painfully aware of it.

"Pausa! Pausa!"

The cry rings out at three o'clock in the morning. Prisoners drop on the spot, trying to sleep during the thirty-minute stop. Claude jumps over the bodies and zigzags to the hall to see Albert.

"I say, then, Albert, I didn't know that you were at Dora. When did you arrive? I've been here since March."

"Me, too, Claude. We must have arrived together. Are there any other friends here?"

"I noticed Philippe one day, but that was months ago. I haven't seen him since."

"Well," ventures Albert, "you know, Dora is big. There are even more prisoners here than there are people back home. And with the night and day shifts, you could spend a lifetime without meeting someone."

Here we are, thinks Claude, look at us. We've just met up again; we should both jump for joy. Instead of that, we'll exchange gossip for fifteen minutes. Perhaps Albert isn't thinking of the same things as I am. Maybe he's never thought about them and couldn't care less. But maybe he is simply worrying about his mother and sisters because he knows that they're in the same mess as he. But then, how can he know?

"I say, Albert, it will soon be the end of the break. I must go."

"OK, Claude. See you soon. And take care of yourself."

Claude gets up and rushes into the tunnel.

★   ★   ★

After all the noise about the invasion, things seemed to drag out, and impatience intensified. According to the anonymous reporters of news, whose sources seemed credible, Bayeux was taken on the first day. If things had gone badly for the cowboys, the SS would have been only too happy to crow about it aloud. So the Allied attacks must be doing well.

The prisoners, though, can't be happy with a little war that has coffee breaks, tea breaks, a forty-hour week, and paid leave for the soldiers. These men have no time left. They know that they won't survive another winter. The Allies must break through the German defenses, rush across France, cross the Rhine, and get to Dora within the coming weeks in their tanks and trucks at top speed. The very lives of thirty thousand prisoners in the region depend on it. So come on, you guys, and don't worry about speed limits! We'll pay your speeding tickets, if need be, but let 'em roll!

Meanwhile, in the infirmary, the TBs compare the progress of their illness with that of the Americans, and they understand that Koch's bacillus will likely cross the finish line first.

The prisoners have to admit that the invasion of France and then of Germany is not a simple affair. If, as has been presumed, everything is ready in England, all set to hit the continent, then boats will be needed. The very number of ships needed for the transfer of tanks, cannon, trucks, arms, ammunition, fuel, and men by the tens and perhaps hundreds of thousands is, quite simply, fabulous and far beyond their ability to conceive.

The French officers in Dora have had no experience with this type of operation, nor do they have any conception of what the American army is really like. Is it a methodical army that seizes hold of a piece of ground, then cleans it and takes advantage before taking its next step forward to begin again on a new piece of ground, then likewise before a third? If the Americans operate like that, then the war could go on for months and years, and Dora will be no more than a huge columbarium, a massive underground crypt filled with the ashes of the dead.

On the other hand, if their spearheads blow a hole in the German defenses, then smash through on the double with their Sioux war cries as far as this shitty camp, without taking care as to what lies to their left and right—without worrying about their flanks, so dear to Guillaume's strategy—simply looking straight ahead with their eyes fixed upon the milestones . . . so many miles to Dora and squashing everything that moves in front of them, then the prisoners, or at least some of us, have a chance of seeing the liberating army arrive. But we can't last indefinitely, sticking our imaginary pins into dreamed-up maps. Here, believers and atheists meet in the same communion, begging God, even the devil, and all the genius that may come to the hearts of men to inject into the Americans that madness that will make them plunge forward enough to free us. Don't lose any time, guys, we're here and crying out for help, and you should hear us well.

You, Harry, even if you have an ache in your side, charge on in spite of it! And you, Joe, even if your tank runs out of gas, push it with every ounce of strength! Even if you're tired, keep on as if nothing had happened, without stopping, so long as you arrive here! You'll have all the time you want to sleep afterward!

★   ★   ★

Spirits are still good at Dora, but now the prisoners begin to notice that the German army has not collapsed under the first attack and that there will be large-scale battles before the Wehrmacht and Nazi legions are destroyed. Big battles take a lot of time, something the prisoners don't have. The ranks continue to diminish, but death has taken on a sort of cruising speed. It isn't so ostentatious, and many prisoners die "a good death" at forty-five to fifty years, which is a reasonable age for such an alien world.

The truncheons and gummis are just as busy but seem to have lost some of their efficiency. Is lassitude overtaking the truncheon-carriers, or is careful calculation going on within the thick skulls of Kapos and barracks chiefs? Certainly, the mad attacks and bloody executions have become rarer. Now exhaustion, malnutrition, TB, and diarrhea are the main suppliers for the crematorium, plus, of course, the gallows, although its score, on the order of a dozen or so per week, is insufficient to be of statistical interest.

Life proceeds. The carpenters assemble the last barracks halfway up the hill. They have become quite dexterous and are managing to build one each day. The mushrooming village, however, keeps its air of a large village without any grandeur. The commandant has had a sort of mini sports field laid out on the left side of the camp, reserved for use by well-fed higher-ups. It is even said that he has asked the Arbeitsstatistik to find some painters and sculptors, the idea being to transform the wooden town into a high point of Nazi Kultur.

While these glorious moments of Germanic refinement await, the SS lay down the first panels of the whorehouse that will soon open its doors to its first clients. But what clients? Surely not the basic concentration camp inmate, whose physical condition has erased any possibility of lust and who has even forgotten that such a thing ever existed. Will this place be reserved for officials? Or for the noble SS?

In the tunnel, they're taking down the last "dormitory" block, which will allow all of the doomed laborers a time to live cleanly, so to speak, and inhale the pure air of Thuringia. One of the last Doran curiosities, this "dormitory" underground in the caves of the "metropolis" is about to disappear. These shambles of shaky bedsteads and straw mattresses alive with billions of fleas and lice are quickly evacuated. Now laborers, masons, electricians, and plumbers occupy the hall that is so urgently to be fitted out. The enormous ventilation shafts now run from end to end to each of the main galleries. A host of transport kommandos heave the hundreds of machines that are to be fixed in place in the workshops. In the railyards, whole trainloads of materials are swallowed up within the underground.

The equipping of the factory progresses at an impressive pace, transforming the place with each passing day. They must work quickly, so the prisoners work at a racing pace. Hiding in a dark corner is finished; there aren't any dark corners left. The air is still heavy with deadly dust but no longer as bad as it was when mine blasts shook the mountain. Everything is visible, so you can no longer rest your loads in the shadow of a pile of gravel. Now you must walk and carry nonstop, and the prisoners feel their strength ebbing swiftly. From the incredible folly of earlier months, life has gone swiftly downward to a mournful exhaustion.

To make the factory operate, which is a joke considering the physical condition of the prisoners, the management has obtained from the SS the opening of a canteen and the sale of cigarettes. Money will be needed for this, of course, so the prisoners will receive notes marked "Konzentrationslager Mittelwerk." With these notes, they'll be able to get pickled cabbage, not to mention a kind of pickled sprats (fish) that inflame disordered stomachs and intestines and that men hesitate to eat despite their torturous hunger. They prefer to spend their meager notes in buying their ration of Makhorkov Russian cigarettes and especially Makhorka tobacco—thick, black, and extremely strong.

So life seems to go on as if nothing has happened, as if the invasion has never occurred. News filtering in from the outside is like signals received from Mars. There, somewhere on another planet, tremors shake the German order in Europe. Cracks are seen, and other fissures appear. In this lost Nazi extremity, men await the arrival of formidable forces that will deliver them from this deadly anguish; it's only a matter of days, perhaps even of hours.

But Dora knows nothing of it. Dora evolves and loses its adolescent acne with but one idea: to equal and, if possible, overtake the great concentration camp metropolis. What happens outside is of no importance; it isn't the business of the SS, the new gods of a strange world isolated from all else. Officially, Dora doesn't exist. Originally, the place was called "Block 17/3 Buchenwald." Now it has the name of "Mittelwerk," but the name "Dora" is unknown to the Germans. But why worry, after all, since the traffic is all one way: You arrive at Dora, but you never leave, except via the crematorium chimney.

In the tunnel, as on the surface, the work comes to an end. While the underground prisoners, the miners, laborers, and handling kommandos are wondering what will become of them now, the surface kommandos are asking themselves the same question. When everything is finished, few people will be needed for the upkeep. Satellite camps on the other side of the mountain begin haunting their minds. They know that, even if the war ends quickly, before winter, they need only to be transferred somewhere else for their ranks to be decimated within days. They would really like to know what the SS may be planning, but they know absolutely nothing.

So their minds follow a quite curious progress. They know the invasion has taken place. They know that, if the English and Americans have crossed the channel, it's with a firm intention to finish the war as quickly as possible, and they certainly have the means. But at the same time, they and their captors continue to live and react as if everything would stay as it is until the end of time.

So what do you do but become interested in the daily routine? The lump of bread that was shared by four men is now shared by three, which means an extra slice. Once a week, a slice of sausage is replaced by a tiny piece of boiled meat. Although they are slightly bigger, the rations are no less miserable, with no chance of improving the gaunt thinness of the prisoners. Summer has arrived, and the sun gives its warmth to their shabby bodies. The French collect the rare dandelions, which they devour despite the sarcastic remarks of the Russians. Leaves torn from trees and shrubs are carefully dried and, once rolled within a bit of cement bag, make very convenient cigarettes when there are no more Makhorkas. Now that it's warmer, you can take off your shirt and ferret out the fleas clustering in the seams. When you see one of your buddies half naked, you say to yourself, "How thin he is, the poor devil," without realizing that he's making the same remark to himself about you!

The invasion? Oh, yes. It's true. We nearly forgot it.

*　　　*　　　*

"You, Frenchman. Come here!"

The Kapo points straight at Victor, who feels a gulp in his throat. "My God, what's happened? What does he want from me?"

The handling column has been stopped near enormous frameworks that other prisoners are turning into a hall through a series of careful maneuvers. Shouts and curses fill the air, but there are no beatings. The minions of the "master race" don't want to use terror when it might result in causing the material to slip and be damaged, so for a change, the chiefs and Kapos work with their throats and not their clubs.

Victor's eyes follow the Kapo, who seems lost in his thoughts. The man is vaguely humming an old prewar song. His eyes are heavy, and he wears a red triangle—one of these German Communists who are slowly beginning to take over in Dora. It must be ironic, thinks Victor, when this Kapo meets an SS man against whom he brawled in the streets of Hamburg before being arrested and sent to jail.

In theory, the political Kapos are not so bad as the Greens, the criminals, but in reality, they sometimes react like madmen to the slightest stimuli, and their clubs sometimes break as easily as the necks of the hapless prisoners they attack. You'd be tragically mistaken not to be extremely wary of these men, for they have become completely perverted by their "social" surroundings.

Victor and his guardian angel arrive in a completely equipped hall. An impressive lineup of welders, perfectly aligned, take up the entire length of the hall, more than a hundred yards long. A forest of electric and pneumatic cables, lined in rubber, comes down from the roof.

Everything is ready to begin, but the workshop is quiet, not a soul is there. The electric lamps give a white, shadowless light. The Kapo, followed by Victor, goes into the spare parts room immediately on the left inside the entrance. There are two tattered humans—ageless, colorless detritus but with the je ne sais quoi of a joker. One man is big and skeletal, the other is little but possessed of an assured look, a souvenir of better days.

"You bunch of cunts," cries the Kapo, "I've brought you a Frenchman; that way, you won't do each other in. So do your job, and don't bother me. Otherwise, I'll break you up into small pieces before the night is out. Understand?"

"OK, Kapo. We'll work hard."

The Kapo goes off but tells Victor, "You're just here for the night, just to give them a hand. Tomorrow morning, you have to be with me at the exit of the kommando. OK?"

"Ponimaich, Kapo." The Kapo disappears, humming an old tune from the thirties. Victor looks into the storeroom, where he sees great numbers of tail booms and sectional irons impregnated in oil.

"I say, guys, are you going to build a new Eiffel Tower or what? What's all this bric-a-brac?"

"Don't worry, Toto, everything here goes into building the tail pieces for the big rockets. We're storemen. When construction is under way, the guys will stock up here. When they want a tail boom or finishing steel sheets, they'll give me a chit, and I'll furnish them with the goods. You understand the job? If they want to build an Eiffel Tower, that's their business, and I couldn't care less. They only have to give me the order slips, which I'll stick into the thing you see here. Everything is very well planned."

"But I say, guys, you've found a really easy number here!"

"You said it, chum, but we are a bit wary. You know what an easy job is at Dora. If it doesn't look as if you're overworked as hell, the Polacks start to get interested in your means of existence. They'll grab your job, and you find yourself behind the cement mixer getting the crap beaten out of you. So my buddy and I groaned to the engineer, and we asked for a helper. That's why you're here."

"Well, good! So what's to be done?"

"Easy, Toto, don't get all worked up. There's nothing to do as long as production hasn't started. We have enough material to crush the whole world several times, so it isn't worth getting upset. Have you already smoked some Stark? We're going to roll a cigarette."

Stark! Good God! Victor had heard about it. Stark is the flower of the Makhorka, the Havana of the concentration camps. Against everything else that is smoked, Stark is like 90-proof liquor being compared to mineral water. The big skinny man brought a lump wrapped in a piece of cement bag out of his pocket. Jesus, that's equivalent to the value of two whole loaves of bread, enough food for a week!

"You look at my tobacco and think I'm crazy," said Big Skinny, "but what do you think? Do you think they'll let us out of here alive? Poor cunt, you're kidding yourself. Nobody will ever leave Dora. So forget your wife and children, and do what you feel like doing before it's too late. Meanwhile, there's nobody in this shit of a hall, and we're gonna smoke a fine cigarette."

Big Skinny takes a piece of newspaper, rare and expensive stuff, on which there is doubtless regional news, dates of farming markets, and even obituaries. He licks it well to make it airproof and rolls a majestic cigarette. One last lick and it's perfectly sealed. There are at least two layers of paper, which will only add to the deliciousness of the smoke. He takes a homemade lighter from his pocket, with flint from the solderers and gas from some unknown source. It works. He lights the almost cigar-sized thing, takes in a deep drag, and drifts into his private paradise. Now Victor has it in his hand. He takes the huge cigarette up to his mouth, takes in a great puff, and crinkles the newspaper. He draws in a little air between drags to soften the effects of the tobacco and swallows the lot. His lungs suffer a terrible shock, and he feels as if he'll fall. His eyes roll. The hunger that tormented him has disappeared at the same time. Good God, he thinks, if I should have to get up now, I couldn't do it.

Big Skinny watches him with amusement. "I say, Toto, my cigarette shook you. It's really good, eh? I'll tell you, I was at the opening of Dora. I arrived here last September. I don't know how long this mess will go on, but I really think I won't manage to see the end of it. My lungs are eaten away. From time to time, I see Jacky the undertaker glance at me. He knows that one of these days, I'll be one of his clients. So you see, the first person who speaks to me about clean living, I'll just let him talk. You know what it is to live eight months in Dora? In my opinion, it's too long; it's almost indecent. I don't want to

break any records, it's all the same to me now. All I ask is no more
beatings. When I see a cunt with the triangle of a Communist or a
criminal, I don't worry; I change to the other side. All I'm looking for
is to stay as far as possible from his club. Here, have another draw on
the cigarette."

Once again, Victor feels the powerful shock of the unbelievable tobacco. His eyes become misty, and he feels the tunnel move. My God,
he thinks, I only hope I don't end up like these two cranks, especially
the little one who hasn't said a word, just laughing there in the corner.
I wouldn't even give them a month to live. But perhaps I'm no better
than they. If I looked at myself in a mirror naked, without a doubt I'd
be frightened. So what's the good of brushing my head? They're right,
they're going to die like men, the real guys of Dora.

Victor sits down, stretches his legs out, then inhales a large drag on
the cigarette, and he thinks, "Oh, shit. How well off we are in here!"

★   ★   ★

Work in the halls starts up as the halls are completed, one after another. Workers in selected areas began work much earlier, supplied
with material and elements saved from Peenemünde after the RAF destroyed the factory there. For months, tails of V-2s have been arriving.
They are huge with their four pointed fins already painted in wagon
green, each one numbered, with tanks of liquid fuel built in another
factory. They have long semicylindrical fuselages and heads in which
the electrical command instruments are located. Finished rockets
have been coming out for months but at a slow rate, consisting mainly
of production trials necessary to enhance the ideal conditions sought
in this massive underground factory.

Because of the destruction of Peenemünde, Hitler missed his best
chance of crushing the Allied invasion forces by sending a deluge of
rockets tearing into the English ports of embarkation. But now the situation has changed, and a large part of Normandy must be added to
the list of V-2 targets—an enormous task. Still another reason for act-
ing as quickly as possible is to mass-produce these vehicles while they
still have strategic importance, for they can only reach maximum ef-
fectiveness when fired on fixed concentrations of troops and materials. If the Allied armies make a successful breakthrough and spread
their advance all over French territory, the V-2 will no longer have any
really efficient role.

The Zawatsky Company is responsible for the construction of the
huge rockets. They are looking for mechanics, locksmiths, welders,
and electrical fitters. What a miracle that Dora is filled with such talents. To think that the best workers from Citroën, Renault, Skoda,
and other factories have come together here in the hills of Harz!

The erstwhile farmers, shopkeepers, teachers, and public employees swear, by God, that they were weaned at Levallois or at l'Ile Seguin and that if the Gestapo now can motor in front-wheel drive, it's thanks to them. Of course, the fact is, they are making their second or third "declaration of profession" since arriving in the camps, but that isn't important; nobody checks.

The myth of "security of work," so dear to public employees and for which the world supposedly envies the French, is found in Dora but in a slightly different form—"working for security"!

Each prisoner's mind, if he has the strength, is bent upon survival against all the odds. The future of the species itself now lies in the rank and file of humanity. Intellectuals, for once in accord with their social preachments, suddenly leap at the chance to work on machines that they once despised but now regard with ecstasy. Civil servants who once scorned the populace at large now roll up their sleeves to exercise biceps made flabby by rubber stamps and Parker pens. As for the farmers and shopkeepers, well used to hours unacceptable to other social groups, these men are the first to volunteer for every opportunity.

Now, strangely enough, the Poles and Russians begin to feel the weight of the French presence, as they find it more difficult to find places in the workshops. Thus, the French succeed in their first breakthrough on the Planet Dora. They are no longer simply considered as miserable producers of perfume and beauty products or as ridiculous puppets asking by what right their captors are allowed to smash in the skulls of men who invented human rights and the rights of the citizen? Without knowing it, Andre Citroën, in constructing the famous 11 CV front-wheel drive, did more for the prisoners than all the bearded thinkers who ever lived!

So we rush to the workshops as quickly as they are finished and ready. Some are impressive, such as the areas for assembly of the tails or fuselages of the V-2. Huge frameworks, firmly fixed in the ground, hold slabs of sheet metal, fins, and profiles in place, and the welders come in to fuse them all together. Though it seems complicated at first, it is, in fact, the birth of a new art.

The sheet metal has to be cleaned well to remove any traces of paint or grease at its welding points. However, you must watch to be certain that the jaws do not touch any other part of the metal at the same time, which would result in an unwanted hole and a lot of telltale smoke. Meister, who are German civilian foremen, survey all the work without letup. Most of them are disabled Wehrmacht vets who have left a pound or two of flesh on the Russian front. Most of these guys are completely indifferent to the prisoners' lot, as well as their often-skeletal appearance. They don't even seem to see the prisoners when they give orders, shouted out in the German fashion. When they do speak to individual prisoners, it's to treat them as Drecksack (shit-bags), but it rarely goes beyond that. They are on hand just to give orders and stay within the limits given them. It's all too obvious that, in their eyes, the prisoners are no more than castoffs of a subhuman level who don't deserve even to be seen.

Some prisoners are unlucky. Imprudently having declared themselves to be painters, arc welders, or plumbers, they end up in front of machines or tools they've never seen in their lives, which they are totally incapable of operating.

Amateur arc welders see their electrodes melt away in a flash or, at the other extreme, stick to the metal and break off a bit of it. Would-be painters, not knowing anything about the correct proportions of thinner to paint, fearfully see their inept mixtures slide off in lumps onto the floor or, if the mix is too thick, leave telltale blotches on the metal.

As for many who declared themselves plumbers, the whistling of compressed air where their solders fail brings them the attention of all. These imperfections immediately set off the Meister's outraged howling, an incomprehensible mixture of cursing and threats from which the dangerous word *sabotage* emerges. The imprudent novice is almost immediately attacked by a Kapo, who thrashes him with his club first and afterward notes his prisoner number. Either that or an SS man passing through the area will march off the unfortunate man to the guard room at the tunnel entrance. At best, these prisoners leave the guard room beaten into unconsciousness and end their days in the handling kommandos they should never have left. At worst, they're dropped at the end of a hangman's noose the following Sunday at the roll call square.

Some men, however, have better luck. Declaring themselves, in a moment of madness, to be electricians, they are assigned to the changing of lightbulbs. With large aluminum ladders, they visit the galleries and workshops during their twelve-hour stints, replacing blown-out bulbs.

The storemen also have a coveted job but one largely reserved to professionals. When you're presented with an order for something specific, you have to know what it is, especially if the orderer is a Meister. For the basic materials, such as sheeting, fins, and profiles, these are quickly picked up and don't present a problem. But for tools, it's another business entirely. The size of electrodes, the thread of mills, the amperage of fuses, and the grain size for files are all vital. The simple hammer is categorized in relationship to its weight and use—all in German, of course. So to declare yourself to be a storeman is to flip a coin with your life, heads or tails—relative relief . . . or definite disaster.

Life organizes itself slowly in the tunnel. The bloody delirium of the first months gives way to an absurd atmosphere, a frozen and illogical

world. Men from the outside—civilians, engineers, Meister, good hus-
bands and fathers, men who respect law and order, who wouldn't hurt
a fly, who bring up their families as their ancestors did—now live,
count their retirement points, and carry out their professional careers
among beings who suffer daily and die, one after another. What can
these civilians talk about when they meet together after work? It's a
mystery. The children must ask their fathers what happens in the secret caves they can never see on a school visit because it is strictly forbidden. However, it must be extremely interesting to see the prisoners
from close up, these Untermenschen (subhumans) of whom they have,
quite by chance, seen a few specimens on outside working parties.
They must be very bad men to be treated like this. Tell me, Daddy.
Does Daddy tell?

And their mother, the "Mutti," almost the Italian "Mama," does
she ask any questions? The husband might, in relaxed and confiden-
tial moments, allow himself to mention tattered human beings, cries
and beatings, and even the gallows. One can almost hear the Mutti
saying, "My God, all these horrible creatures scare me. Why not kill
them at once, before they come and kill us? It's too dangerous to have
that scum nearby. I can't sleep anymore. How many did you say there
are, more than fifteen thousand? I don't understand why they keep
such men so close to us. One day, they'll come and cut the throats of
our children."

Probably the head of the family reassures her. "Don't worry, Mom.
They're well guarded. There are machine guns everywhere. And anyhow, they won't have the strength to reach us. If you saw them,
they're so tattered, they couldn't do a thing, and everything is seen to
in that line. You can sleep soundly; our children risk nothing."

Along with the male civilians, female secretaries begin to appear in
this alien world. They arrive in the morning in their neat little suits,
topped with woolly sweaters since the tunnel is damp and the poor
dears might catch cold. The fashion of the day is to wear their stock-
ings inside-out, with the seams on the outside. As soon as they pass
the SS control at the tunnel entrance, they hurry quickly to their office, which is above floor level in the halls.

They pass the prisoners—whom they avoid looking at—their high
heels clacking all the while on the concrete. Once in their office, they
straighten their hair, check their nail polish, and do the necessary
feminine touches. Then a last glance to be sure that the typewriter,
paper, and carbons are in place, and everything is ready for the arrival
of the boss.

There are terrible moments when prisoner-engineers or technicians
come in for orders. They are not only filthy, they also smell sicken-
ingly foul. These well-dressed and very healthy girls feel their flesh re-

volt at the sight of such Untermenschen, who discreetly come to receive their orders. Happily, bottles of eau de cologne are near at hand, and their contents create an air of protection between refinement and such bestiality. *Mein Gott*, what we must suffer for the Fatherland!

Other groups, too, appear from time to time in the tunnel. There are engineers and technicians sent by the firms that contribute to the construction of the V-2 rockets. Zawatsky has subcontracted with many enterprises that come to check on the site. They wear loden and feathered hats, and they also have a selective look. Are they merely blasé? Or have they had orders? "See nothing, hear nothing, say nothing." They move among us as if there were nothing unusual about us or them. They could take photos. It would be interesting and guaranteed to excite lively evening conversations among friends and people they know. But they take no pictures. They remain serious and efficient. Occasionally, they'll share a big collective laugh at some coarse joke, bringing about the good feeling necessary in all work groups.

One type of visitor is much more worrisome: the Gestapo. Since the prisoners left France, the Gestapo hadn't been seen. Of course, they come to Dora regularly, for they never abandon their prey, but they hadn't crossed the camp gateway. Now we see them from time to time in their long raincoats. The mere sight injects a chill of dread into your spine. They don't go into the tunnel; that isn't their concern. Rather, they stop at the office at the entrance. When they're present, it isn't to check on some old arrest; it's to check on discipline and search out sabotages, which have begun to occur. When it comes to interrogating and cross-examining suspects, these inhuman monsters are far more fearful and painful than the savagely brutal SS. Their work is sought by many German firms responsible for efficient running of the factory, and their arrival inspires not only worry but deadly fear among the prisoners. I only hope that my machine doesn't quit, that the fuses don't blow while they're here. If that should happen, I'd likely be taken. When I was still a human being, they cut me to pieces, but now that I'm a remnant of my former self, I wouldn't stand a chance to survive.

Now that it shelters this new population, the tunnel has become an incredibly clean place, almost sterile. The only unsavory parts are the prisoners, still filthy and fleshless.

The veterans recall what they found on arrival. It had been a sort of cave that had been used as a fuel depot. The air was thick with gas fumes, and there was a high risk of explosion. After a short roll call at the entrance, the work had started. In the country air, the first sound of a man being beaten was heard, and thereafter, the beatings never stopped.

Ten months later, the eighth wonder of the world was completed. It was a perfect network of bombproof galleries, ready to produce the secret weapons of the Reich. How many men's lives did this wonder cost? It is difficult, if not impossible, to say, but something on the order of a few thousand should be conservatively correct, given the constant beatings, the executions, and the criminal maltreatment in the infirmary.

The prisoner reinforcements arrive at a regular rate, and the crematorium burns at full blast. The older men search each other out and take a rough body count, only to realize that they are now all that is left, no more than a few dozen still alive out of the thousands who first began swinging picks at Dora. Now they will turn in their mining tools; they are going to change jobs. But the SS are still in charge and still carry the same orders direct from Reichsführer-SS Himmler: Liquidate all the prisoners. So don't imagine any better days, guys. You'll never see another view; this is the last one.

★   ★   ★

Dora's camp commandant has just lost one of his numerous inferiority complexes vis-à-vis Buchenwald. Now he has an orchestra of Gypsies. He should have celebrated this great moment of success—the beginning of rocket production—with his high command. Doubtless, he should have made a speech, promising that Dora would last as long as the Thousand Year Reich and that it would be seen by history as one of the greatest achievements of human genius.

The Buchenwald orchestra was something worth a trip. Considering the Wagnerian aspect of the site, its entry gate and buildings, and particularly the fact that the "tree of Goethe," under which the revered poet and dramatist came to meditate, was inside the camp, you couldn't put just any orchestra in such a setting. No, it had to be special. The stroke of genius of Buchenwald's commandant had been to locate and acquire a truckload of circus uniforms—magnificent red dolman sleeves, black jodhpurs, and shiny high boots. Above all, there had to be brass and percussion instruments. He got them. The musicians became the spoiled children of the camp. They enjoyed good food and good quarters and spent whole days in rehearsal. The role of this orchestra—or call it more of a fanfare—was based upon its blaring out the departures and arrivals of the kommandos—to which another performance was added for the hangings. All in all, it was a life of ease for the instrumentalists, who went through a vigorous selection to play cheap music—and live a bit longer.

Although Dora's commandant couldn't duplicate the acquisition of the uniforms, he recalled that, among his prisoners, there were a number of Gypsies who, through some administrative logic of the SS, ended up at Dora. Gypsies play music; everyone knows that. So he will have them play "La Grande Berezina" and "Les Yeux Noirs."

The most difficult step, then, is to find and assemble the instruments. Violins, accordions, bandoneons, flutes, balalaikas, and the rest are difficult to find, especially when their owners have already been through several camps and stripped of everything in those larger prisons in the east. Dora receives only tattered men wearing the strict concentration camp minimums: jacket, trousers, shirt, long underpants, Russian socks, and clogs. Not even a spoon.

The commandant made a hell of an effort to get instruments transferred to Dora from the fabulous stores gathered at Auschwitz and Buchenwald. It took incredible bartering and much added bargaining to collect the marvelous instruments and then assign them to Gypsies, who were nasty, as everyone knew, but who were able to play such beautiful, decadent music.

How difficult the poor commandant's disappointment and anguishes must have been. Desperate hopes followed sleepless nights, with endless falsely casual but frantic phone calls, begging with good-humored laughter for the violins he so craved and desired. How many calls had seemed on the edge of success, only to be cut off by some stupid telephone operator in a mousy gray uniform? "Sorry, commandant, but I have a priority call from the Eastern Front that must go through. Please call later. *Sakrament!*"

The commandant was furious. "These bitches understand nothing! They'll finish us for sure, cutting off our phone calls. And now that filthy bastard at Auschwitz—who was all ready to give me the instruments—is going to wake up and ask me for things I can't give him. Tramps, that's what I have under my control. Tramps who have brought me nothing but their unworthy, rotten carcasses. When I think of having to call back to that beggar of a commandant and be obsequious all over again, it makes me sick!"

One marvelous day, everything has been gathered at Dora; the instruments are all lined up in the offices at the gate. Now the Gypsies are summoned.

They are greasy, filthy men whose servile smiles scarcely hide their fear of death. Now they, the last of their tribe, are going to be eliminated, those who have survived massive genocides. Now the "traveling people," the last free men in a heavily policed Europe, the men who have followed their caravans wherever they wanted to go, suddenly have to think about the rope that will cut off their breathing and send their bodies into another world of shit.

But now a miracle. They are given musical instruments, and they will be able to play them in Dora. They can walk where they want and when they want; all that's asked of them is to play music. Play music in Dora! What a laugh. They don't dare think about it. They were waiting for the big jump into eternity, and here they have been given bandoneons instead. Does this really mean that they are not going to be liquidated at once? That they will be relied upon to amuse the masters and their slaves? Many are so relieved that they'd like to laugh but dare not. Instruments are passed from one to another, and soon it all begins. "Les Yeux Noirs," they hear. Well, if the Krauts want "Les Yeux Noirs," we'll give them "Les Yeux Noirs" until the end of time!

In the tunnel, now being finished off, the orchestra goes from hall to hall playing "Les Yeux Noirs" and "La Grande Berezina." The show is so unexpected that prisoners stand with their mouths open. Suddenly, there is laughing and clapping. The musicians, with the ecstasy of fulfillment in their eyes, play the remembered songs of another world. Within the audience, however, you can feel the softening of faces, throats that dry up, shells that crack. Memories come flooding back, marvelous memories from a lost planet.

★   ★   ★

"Henri, is it really you, Henri?" The voice is hesitant, as if looking for its words. Henri looks at the other prisoner, noticing that the man's pupils are very large and no longer adjust. The man is terribly thin, his mouth with a grin showing his teeth, and his clothes floating as if on a skeleton. His feet seem enormous, and his silhouette staggers. Within his skull under that parchment of skin, only a shred of life remains, and this will soon be extinguished. He is almost a zombie about to die. How soon? In a day or two, more than likely. The prisoner will drift off at a slow pace, leaving the column without being aware of it. The furious Kapo will rush at him, cursing. One infamous blow of the truncheon across his head, and the remains of a human being will go down, never to rise again. This is how so many of the Moslems (camp term for men at the lowest level of decay) are pushed into the great beyond.

"Hi, chum, I'm glad to see you."

Henri wonders who in the world this near-zombie might be. It could be anyone; they all looked alike.

"Prison," says the specter. "You remember, we were there together. What was its name, that prison?"

"The Pré-Pigeon, Angers Prison."

"Oh, yes, that's it," says the specter. "That's it. We shared the same cell that last night, and we left together for Compiègne."

"Good God," thinks Henri. "It's not Laurent, but it can't be anyone else. That head, those scattered whiskers all turned gray; it's really him." Now he recalls the man he met during their last hours in that prison. He remembers this man with the gray hair, now so wasted away from lack of food but who had given off such an impression of physical and moral strength. How old can he be? Forty? Perhaps fifty. This man once had the indestructible look of someone who could go through everything and yet survive, never a crybaby sobbing about his lot or a phony who would be crushed at the first blow. Laurent had been a man of steel, as only a few could be.

"But what are you doing here, Laurent? Are you on a working party all by yourself? Where is your kommando?"

"I don't know, Henri. I was with the guys a little while ago, but I lost track of them. I must find them again."

Now Henri understands. This poor soul was with some Russians who dumped him because Moslems attract beatings for everyone. So they got rid of him. Like pitiless fledglings who throw their weakest brother from the nest, the Russians have thrown him out to die alone. Life has little value in Dora, and death even less.

"Listen, Laurent," he tells the man, "sit down here. I'll go and find your kommando, and then I'll take you back."

Laurent sits down without a word, indifferent, far away. His grin grows large and fixed. Since their meeting minutes ago, he has slipped lower in physical and mental decay. He mutters to himself.

Henri moves away sadly, with a lump in his throat. He doesn't flee. He does the only reasonable thing left: He leaves his friend to his fate. If only the Kapo or SS man who finds him can kill him with the first crushing blow to the skull, it will save Laurent useless torture and pain. With a little luck, within a few minutes, he will have finished with Dora.

★   ★   ★

Karl made a remarkable entrance into the surgical room at the infirmary. His left elbow was enormous, covered with vicious spots. Dressed only in a shirt that reached downward to a point just above his belly button, he paused a moment at the doorway, glanced around the ward, and, with wavy, effeminate steps, reached the bed just assigned him. All that was lacking for a perfect entrance were the three customary blows from the "stage manager." With a gracious movement, he lifted up the blanket, stretched out, and relaxed with a deep, throaty laugh.

Karl was one of countless German homosexuals arrested as such by the regime and thrown into concentration camps. Pink triangles sewn to their clothing showed the reason for their internment.

At the same time, homosexuality was very widespread in Nazi circles, reaching even into the origins of the Nazi movement. The leader of the SA (Brownshirts), Ernst Röhm, was himself a notorious homosexual. During the SA purge, he was arrested in his bed laden with like-minded young men. He was shot soon thereafter. The SS then took over from the SA as the power elite of the Nazi machine.

Within the SS, however, the homosexual "corporation" continued to hold powerful positions in the Third Reich. It displeased the Führer, and he ordered draconian punishments against anyone caught in flagrante delicto. Thus, poor Karl, onetime chorist at the Berlin Opera, found himself in the shadows of Dora's electrified fencing. It was a sad fate for a young man once so full of promise, whose lyrical career was also broken.

Now in his thirties, Karl yet retained a certain allure. His eyes were a brilliant blue, his complexion still more pink than gray; yet Dora was anything but easy on the aging homos. A few years ago, he must have brightened the night of the Kapos and barracks chiefs, but the years advance at Dora even more quickly than elsewhere. The arrival of the Russians marked the end of Karl's reign.

The young Slavs, with their still-tender flesh and satin skin, were poured by the hundreds into the camps, provoking sudden tidal waves of desire among the chiefs. Thus it was that Karl found himself in a killer of a kommando, which revealed one quality he had never suspected within himself. He was amazed to find that he had a strength of character. Finding himself subjected to the pitiless violence of the place and his fellow prisoners' sarcasm, he kept an eternal smile on his face, which allowed him to hold on until his seniority, his nationality, and some vague pushing enabled him to become assigned to a job that was a bit less exposed. He managed to acquire, here and there, an extra pint of soup or a lump of bread, which kept up his high spirits.

Once in bed, he suffered a moment of relapse. His elbow pained him devilishly, and the thought of an operation with no anesthetic wasn't a joyous prospect. Karl was experienced enough as a prisoner to know that at the infirmary, things were not done delicately. Even though amputations were seldom done, there was a pretty fair chance that his arm would be fucked up forever, even if the gangrene didn't consume his entire body. Bah! Nothing to do but wait and see.

"Well, it's you, Karl, old queer. Let's see your elbow. Oh, that isn't very pretty. We're going to have to cut up your arm a bit, that's for sure."

It was the ward orderlies, interested and mocking, who approached his bed for the sole purpose of doing their number. Those patients in the ward who were most able managed to turn to face Karl's bed, hoping for some amusement to help them forget their own anguish.

The Stubendienst felt that the crowd was ready; however, they would have to be careful not to go too far. Karl was an old prisoner and a German, above all else, and this necessitated a certain degree of prudence. There was no question of brutality disguised as fun; Karl was certain to have some supporters who could make trouble for the fools who went too far.

"I say, your clients are going to get bored without you, Karl," murmured an orderly. "It's bad to leave them unserviced. First thing you know, they'll look elsewhere. There aren't any good deals here; nothing but tramps who'll give in within three days."

"Don't you guys worry about me," responded Karl. "I'll still be here when you've all gone up the chimney. Now, am I going to have the diet?"

The "diet" was the camp's white and sugared soup, a marvelous thing especially noted for moistening the lips of those who couldn't have it.

"Well, it may not be easy to get, but we can see," said the orderly. "By the way, weren't you a singer at one time?"

"Yes. At the Berlin Opera."

"So? Then you should sing something. Sing us 'Lili Marlene.'"

Attracted by the idea, Karl sat up in his bed and began the song. His voice was warm and in perfect pitch, and he rolled his *R*s with the professionalism of the classical singers. The Stubendienst, their arms crossed, took up the chorus even while adding effects with their sleeves. Then they left with a great roar of laughter.

"OK for the diet request, Karl. We'll ask about it. Maybe you'll get it."

Karl laughs loudly and goes back into bed. *"So ist das Leben."* (That's life.) You have to know how to get through it. Tomorrow, he knows, they'll make meat out of him, but there will be time to think about it.

*   *   *

The news comes early in the morning. The Allies have attacked in Normandy with an overwhelming offensive. The English and Americans have smashed through the German defenses and are now spreading out toward the Mayenne, Sarthe, and Brittany. Information about the landing spreads throughout the surface camp with incredible speed. The reports are clear that one column is spearheading toward Le Mans, another toward the north of Normandy, while a third is preparing to penetrate in the direction of Rennes and St. Malô.

The official German radio speaks of very heavy battles and thousands of dead among the Allied invasion forces, but parallel reports from other mysterious sources give correct details, with the names of towns that have been captured. Hope, mad hope, comes back to the prisoners, who had feared that the Allies would be held back in the Normandy pocket for months. But now they've done it! The Allies are rolling and won't be stopped.

Once again, the French become the center of interest. The names of Russian towns, repeatedly scrutinized, are forgotten; they are replaced in all languages by Avranches, Le Mans, and Rennes. During the night, men who should be sleeping are feverish and restless. They leave their barracks to hold whispered conversations with friends. The guys from Sarthe talk about the important road junctions where the Allies must push at full speed.

Reason alone indicates that sleeping will be difficult in the tunnel, but who can think about sleeping when the liberators are on the way to Dora?

New discussions on strategy ensue. While the German army is extremely powerful and well manned, it is not inexhaustible. From the far side of the stretched-out Russian front, Hitler has sent all he can to the west, and if the front has been broken through, perhaps there are no more reserves to stop the Anglo-Americans. And as to crossing the Rhine, bah! What's that? After the English Channel, the Rhine is nothing at all!

Yet before encountering the Rhine, there is Paris to think of. Just to speak that name is to bring warmth and hope to spirits too long starved. Thoughts rush onward; yes, now Paris will be free, it is only a matter of days. The Germans are all but finished, no doubt about that. Soon we'll go back. We will go home!

How can anyone reason with these poor devils whose lives dangle by tattered strings, wretched and helpless to influence their own or their fellow prisoners' collective fate in any direction other than toward the crematorium of Dora?

In the high levels of Allied and Nazi camps, commanders are studying maps and working out strategies—some to effect quick thrusts forward, their opposites to halt the advancing Allied legions.

And the doomed of Dora are all but unknown. No one thinks of them, and they are certainly not included in the input to the problems of advancing through the Third Reich. Few living men even suspect that they exist, and those who may know something are in no position to do anything.

So the prisoners are alone in worrying, hoping, or thinking about their own case. How fervently they would like to get a direct contact with Allied GHQ and give them the shortest route to Dora!

Since none of the prisoners can help out in the actual running of Allied operations, their Kriegspiel (war game) conversations take place on doorsteps and in the toilets. The competent people, like soldiers, are not given much respect. The Sunday gatherings, with their loud voices and simplistic arguments, are the most successful forums.

The men who had always most loudly doubted any possibility of a landing are suddenly the first to claim, "I told you so!" And, indeed, we are so desperate for hope that all of us are ready to believe the wildest theories imaginable.

More thoughtful minds would like to counsel, "Careful, guys, don't pack up to leave just yet. An army can't just cover hundreds of miles in a flash without stopping and regrouping. Supplies have to be brought up. A modern army is heavy, and that includes an incredible amount of supplies, including fuel, bombs and ammunition, food, spare parts, communications gear, and medical supplies; all this stuff can't be moved at the speed of a racing car.

"But aside from the equipment, even the troops need to rest, recuperate, and get their wind for the next plunge. An offensive can be pushed a great distance, but there are limits depending upon so many variable factors that you just can't ignore them. So take it easy, guys; don't expect the Americans to arrive here in a fortnight."

Yes, that's what more thoughtful minds would like to say but cannot. The prisoners have so seldom had anything to raise their morale, so why break it? Soon enough, they'll come back to earth all by themselves.

Almost as if they know something, the Kapos and barracks chiefs become cautious again. If the war happens to end within a few weeks, they don't want these thousands of living skeletons upset with them. If they beat prisoners as they did in the good old days, the victims will remember, especially the Russians. Those Slavic animals, with their powerful reflexes, will massacre SS officers with fiendish sadism as soon as the first Allied helmet comes over the horizon.

There is an eerie quality to the strange looks and mocking laughs the Russians now have for those who wear armlets. With no excuse at all, they'll start a riot, so the truncheon of discipline is still needed, if only to be feared. Now, however, it must only be used with caution and in earnest. Such restraint is difficult for the club-wielders, of course, for they have derived such great pleasure in beating the lives out of these prisoner swine. But now these bastards realize that this is the time to think of the future. From now on, anything can happen . . . and at any moment.

But the SS—curse their perverted minds—see it all differently. They have become the basic structure of the German state. If the state disappears, they, too, will disappear. Thus, there is no question of changing their mission, which is to liquidate the tens of thousands of prisoners after having bled the last erg of effort out of them. They do not seem even to consider the possibility that these subhuman slaves might revolt. But then, that would be a circumstance without a chance of success. The machine guns are zeroed in to wreak absolute carnage at the first hint of rebellion. At that point, some fifteen thousand prisoners—the current population—will be massacred within two or three hours, give or take a few minutes.

Those in Dora who are now the most worried seem to be the German civilians working in the tunnel, the Meister, and the engineers. Most of these have known the doubtful joys of the Russian front, from which they have returned disabled, so they know what to think of the official bulletins! When they were immured in the snows among frightening losses and the hideous deaths of thousands and then read the bulletins from the Nazi GHQ describing "strategic" German withdrawal and the enemy forces being victoriously repelled, they had to try to laugh dryly even while choking down such crap.

Today, official news of the same type is arriving from the West, and this gives them food for thought. Obviously, they can't share their worries, but their faces are eloquent enough. So they continue working as if nothing has happened, the prisoners remaining, as always for them, the same transparent Schweinerei (subhuman pigs).

One by one, the halls open up again for production in the tunnel. The labor force grows unceasingly. Large-scale production of the huge V-2s will soon be under way. Even now, when the war is in the throes of devastating change and the end of the Reich has become foreseeable in the near future, Dora continues along its insane path, as if it were some other mad little planet.

★   ★   ★

What were once worries whispered to one another have now become cold realities. Now transfers are actually leaving for the new tunnel being dug into the other side of the mountain. It is called Ellrich. Now kommandos that have become useless or too numerous, such as the diggers or the laborers, are regularly held back after the roll call. The SS pass among them, noting the numbers of a certain percentage of prisoners, who are then isolated in the new barracks to await their departure. The selections become more frequent, and the anguish among the prisoners grows from day to day.

Among those chosen, morale is at its nadir. Some have survived working through the insane quarry at Buchenwald, a bloody slaughterhouse. Then they were transported to the terrible massacre known as Dora, and now they are being sent to Ellrich, just another way to spell *hell.* It seems that conditions at Ellrich are the same as they were at the beginning of Dora, and the loss of lives is just as frightening.

The Kapos sent to Ellrich are the very scum of their group, men so depraved that they have even managed to revolt their equals. Their own comrades have jumped at the chance to be rid of them. Their armlets are tightly sewn on, and their truncheons are of the extralarge size designed for heavy work.

The shouts and cursing on the roll call square bring to their minds the "good old days" of autumn and winter. The NCOs who have come to say "so long" to their buddies come back smiling and, to get into the mood of things, have a field day at the prisoners' expense.

The men who happen to be on hand for the departure of the pioneers of the new underground world feel lumps forming in their throats. They know that the men in this column soon to cross the camp gate are doomed to die. Within a few weeks, they will disappear, and truckloads of bodies will return each day to Dora's already overworked crematorium.

We, too, will fall apart, but at least we have a rough idea as to where it will happen. We have become domesticated, perhaps slightly "bourgeois," and familiarity with our surroundings lends a sort of peacefulness to the awareness of our fate.

Our attitude has become like a concession toward the life we live. In contrast, to leave for a new camp under construction is the worst of destinies. The Kapos, the Vorarbeiter, and the barracks chiefs as well as SS sent to the new site consider this transfer as a dismissal. This is, in fact, often the case, and these men take out their revenge on the prisoners. Until now, the poor devils have developed a sense of minimal comforts and security, of friends and familiar habits, but as of this moment, it is all gone. Everything will have to be painfully rebuilt again by the slaves, starting from zero. Enough brutality surrounds them to turn them bloody in an instant. To resist is death.

The older men, as they leave the camp in a column, realize that they risk an irreparable disaster. Although their lives were hardly worth much in Dora, now they have reached a new low in the scale of inverse values, quoted at zero in the camp "stock exchange."

As for the new men, who until now have known only quarantine— that is, isolation without work—their pill is bitter indeed. The brief comfort of the quarantine world where only the old died—since it was indecent for a prisoner of fifty to remain alive—that comfort is finished. Now the young men, tough fellows thirty and thirty-five years old, will die in their turn and at a quickened, brutal pace.

You look at these men and tell them in your thoughts, "You poor devils, you have no idea what is waiting for you this evening. If you did know, you'd hate your own mother for bringing you into this

world. You're going to learn all the joys of being tattered wretches at
the mercy of wild beasts. Those old prisoners by your side have known
a thousand deaths and are off on another course, without doubt their
last. Of course, you don't believe all that. You guys think you're martyrs just because you've taken a few beatings from the barracks chiefs
and a few slaps from the Stubendienst. You think the old-timers have
told you a bunch of fantastic lies just to make things interesting. Well,
you'll soon think again. Until now, you've been protected, but wait for
this evening. After your little walking tour in the Harz Mountains,
you'll suddenly fall right into hell—savage, unexpected hell, a terrifying madness that destroys, kills, and massacres.

"You'll experience the agonies of hell, courtesy of Hitler, Himmler,
and all their good buddies. It'll hit you so fast that you won't even
have time to wonder what's happening; suddenly, you'll become a disorganized gaggle of terrified animals. Because that's what we have
known, what we now know . . . and what you're going to know. A few
of you will hang on and, like us, become real prisoners. But most of
you won't be able to survive, and you'll soon disappear. Why? *Warum?*
Potchemou? Pourquoi? How the hell do I know?"

The slave laborers of Dora are afraid of Ellrich, afraid of Harzungen,
and afraid of all these fucking things that are beginning to proliferate
like an evil metastasis. You develop habits, become accustomed to
Dora and the tunnel; now suddenly, this bloody cosmic nightmare
looks like a delicious place where you'd like to end your days. So you
hold on by your teeth; you're fed up with the idea of moving anywhere
else. Each one has his turn, you think.

Throughout Europe, there are thousands, even millions of men just
right for and capable of digging out the new tunnels as we've already
done here. It's up to the SS to get organized and find them. We are only
asking for one thing, to stay right here until the end, the end of The End.

Dora's men watch the successive departures. They are unan-
nounced, having been concocted in the padded silence of the Arbeitsstatistik. One morning, the kommandos are on the roll call
square as usual. The columns leave, one after the other, but some
don't move. These represent the well from which the Nazi lords will
fish for new slaves to stoke the new witches' cauldron at Ellrich. The
SS and other officials arrive and draw from the pile at will.

Fucking life!

4

THE SUMMER MONTHS

The barracks is on the heights, almost at the limits of the camp. It has been empty for a few minutes but will fill up again in an hour when the night shift comes out of the tunnel. The Stubendienst are cleaning the refectory with buckets of water and broad, sweeping strokes of their mops and brushes. The place needs it because it looks like the aftermath of a full-scale battle. The walls are covered with lumps, streaks, and splotches of white cheese. The men's feet slip on spots of soup and on bread rations that have been crushed everywhere across the floor. The Stubendienst mutter bitterly while trying to sort out the disaster. This is Follette's block, for God's sake, and he is one of the most infamous Blockältester in Dora. The man is a terror, a devil.

At this moment, Follette is pacing back and forth, rapping his truncheon upon his palm in an extremely agitated state. The team that will soon arrive is going to be allowed a first-class "festival."

Follette had received an extraordinary chance. He could have spent his life in prison, pent up until the end of his days in first one cell, then another. In prison, one has to be strong to win respect, but this Follette could not do, for his small size and puny look exposed him to the sarcasm and brutality of fellow prisoners. Then he was sent, petrified with fear, to a concentration camp. Right from the beginning, it was horrifying, but somehow he managed to survive, and one day there he was at Dora, wearing a barracks chief armlet.

Now Follette has joyously discovered the formidable power he has over his fellow prisoners, power conferred by the armlet he wears, by his club, and by the right to kill. It is not the same right as that of gladiators, who were armed and equal to formidable opponents, each determined to defend his own skin and hit the other first. No, Follette's right as barracks chief is the right to brutalize, martyr, and beat poor, terrorized rags of men to their deaths, men who, their eyes wide with fright, can only watch as death comes raging at them. This is far more exciting to Follette. He loves bursting into a roomful of these tattered beings, shouting, cursing, stampeding them in all directions as he swings his club into the melee of fleeing bodies, driving them under the tables and behind the doors. It is especially satisfying to explode into the room when the meager rations have just been handed out, to see the food go flying as tables overturn amid the headless panic. In lunatic efforts to escape, the crowd will rush from left to right, split up, regroup, then scatter again, with feet crushing hands and heads alike. Bits of bread gathered up in jackets or shirts fall and are instantly reduced to crumbs. Slippery soup bowls will fly across the room, as prisoners' feet slip out from under them on lumps of slops, which are flung everywhere.

This would be Follette's big moment. He would block a dozen frightened creatures in a corner, stare at them, choose one, and make him realize that it's his turn. Then Follette would rush atop his victim like a madman, slashing, beating, and chopping with his club until the poor devil no longer moved. Ah, he would think, this is the great life, the real thing!

No need for a pretext to attack, besides which it would be difficult to find any. In his barracks, the prisoners are remarkably docile and clean. Before entering, they wash their shoes under the cold-water tap, then go through to the Waschraum and carefully wash themselves without spilling any water outside the bowls.

Why, these prisoners can even put down a shirt or jacket without looking; no one would steal them, for that might trigger some cries of indignation, upsetting Follette. In the refectory, one could literally hear a pin drop! The daily issue of rations is, if anything, less noisy than the taking of Holy Communion in a Sunday mass. In the case of doling out rations, the benches are moved with almost exquisite silence, and the soup bowls touch the tables as softly and gently as if they were made of the rarest, most delicate crystal of all.

But Follette is on watch in his room . . . having warned them that he is resting and doesn't want any noise! So the men must be very careful, even with such trivialities as a falling spoon, and, of course, with any discussions, even those in low voices. So the prisoners try to do the impossible, hoping to lull the madman into sleep so that he will forget his "healthy exercise" upon their heads and bodies. But then, catastrophe strikes. A man is seized by a fit of uncontrollable coughing, and that does it. The demented one rushes into the room wielding his club, striking out in every direction. Another scene of carnage, as if anyone were able to keep track.

Now as he awaits the arrival of the night shift, Follette paces back and forth in front of the barracks, quite worked up. He is worried and, in fact, has been worried ever since hearing the news that the Allied troops had landed in Normandy. He doesn't like the way things are going. Here at Dora, he is happy, a thousand times more so than when he was free. In this wonderful place, he has everything he needs: good warm clothes in winter, cool garments in summer, and assorted good food plus contraband alcohol. Beyond all these, he has a room with a comfortable bed; but above all, he has his formidable truncheon and four hundred walking skeletons to liquidate, stroke by delicious stroke! Where else could he find such happiness?

Should the Allies advance as far as Dora and liberate the camp, undoubtedly he will be exonerated by a tribunal of good folk and immediately released into the streets of Europe's big cities. Within days, he'll find himself back in jail for a murder he couldn't stop himself from committing.

Yes, but by that time, there will be no more Dora, and he will be locked up in some bottomless hole, without his protective insignia, without permission to kill at will, without his deadly truncheon . . . and without anyone to assassinate.

"Who are these goddamned Americans who are coming to muck us around?" he murmurs to himself. "I didn't ask them for anything. I'm fine just like this. Why don't they go fuck themselves and go back home to their own country? Am I going to stew about those bastards? I hope the Wehrmacht will beat the crap out of them, and they'll turn and run for safety!"

In spite of the humble demeanor of the prisoners, since the news of the Normandy landings he has noticed an air of excitement among the men. It is subdued, to be sure, but its very existence infuriates him. The atmosphere has changed subtly, although outwardly everything remains the same. The men bend their backs at work; their fear is permanent and total. No one dares look him in the face. It has been months since he has seen anyone look directly at him.

All the same, Follette senses that these swine are starting to count the days, that they are telling themselves they may now have a slight chance of passing across the Allied lines. For them, the countdown has begun. With each passing day, their hope grows. And if those filthy Americans break open the gates of Dora, all this scum will set upon him like a maddened mob and kill him. Follette imagines the sudden commotion of damned Yanks at the entrance and the uncontrollable horde surrounding him and tearing him into a thousand lifeless pieces.

"But, wait," he thinks, "you miserable pigs, you haven't got me yet. For the moment, I'm still the one who can wipe you out. I'll show you bastards what I'm capable of. When you return, I'll make you regret even thinking such thoughts of revenge!" Looking down, he notices a few weeds beginning to appear along the barracks foundation. He can organize a gardening detail. It's good exercise for the back, and his club will be handy to awaken any lazy spines. After that, there will be the usual delousing, and the barber can come and clip their newly cleaned heads. Then, too, the straw mattresses all stink, so they'll be taken out for an airing and shakedown. The dormitories will also have to be cleaned since they will be full of rubbish. And numbers, there are numbers missing on some trousers. These will all have to be restitched. After all this, he'll see if there isn't something else to do for these bastards who would turn the barracks into a pigsty if left to their own devices. And if Follette hears a single whimper because the soup is too cold, he who complained will regret ever having been born!

In the distance, Follette can make out the long gray column returning from the tunnel. The camp gate swings open, and the SS are in force as usual. One after another, the kommandos present themselves, banners held on high. In a single movement, on command, the prisoners remove their hats. In turn, the Kapos rush toward the SS to announce their numbers. Then the kommandos march by in ranks of five. On command, they put their hats back on in unison and start to follow the walkways that lead to their separate barracks. Follette scrutinizes the different groups and finally locates his own charges. He grips his truncheon in his right hand and nervously taps it against his boot tops.

★   ★   ★

The news that had been expected for several days and is now announced in both the official and clandestine circles of the camp nevertheless comes as a shock.

Paris has been LIBERATED!

It isn't necessary to draw a map for even the most primitive Asiatic to make him understand the importance of this event. Since Stalingrad, nothing so cataclysmic has hit the Nazi cause apart from D day in Normandy. Now they have been forced to flee from Paris!

Strategically, the routes from the French capital reach out in all directions, allowing for an infinite variety of maneuvers, but above all, the psychological significance of a free Paris brings worldwide prestige and elation. For the German Wehrmacht and Hitler's fellow criminals, the loss of the city reconfirms the fact of an immense defeat, one that is all but irreparable.

Just as when the Allied landings became known, the whole camp begins rejoicing in secret. The anguish and worry of the moment give way to fabulous but hidden hopes. After hearing about three weeks of driving advances, to know that the Allies have arrived and taken Paris is almost too much for the heart to contain. Doubtless, the liberators have driven onward, not stopping to taste the delights of a thankful city, and the very thought is even more than we had ever dared hope.

The clandestine radio adds that it was the French army that led the Allied advance into Paris. Across Dora, all at once, the Russians, Poles, Czechs, and Yugoslavs now congratulate the Frenchmen who had been the object of so much distrust on their part. A large part of the dishonor of 1940 is washed clean from the French prisoners. Suddenly, France is seen as a new and vital fighting force, and who knows, perhaps the French will arrive first at Dora's gates. So stunned with delight are the prisoners that the few Russian soldiers in the camp go so far as to congratulate the Frenchmen in their kommandos.

This time, it's the overall demeanor of the SS that reflects the extent of the debacle. The German armies must have lost enormous numbers of men in the battles, resulting in the breakup of their front. The dead and captured must be counted in the tens of thousands, and these must be replaced. Why shouldn't the Dora SS be chosen for the front?

It is, of course, much easier to assassinate helpless prisoners than to face the onslaught of oncoming Allied tanks. The once superb arrogance of the SS now gives way to a degree of nervousness that bodes ill for the prisoner population. There is static lighting in the very air. It is keenly sensed during roll calls when even the Kapos and barracks chiefs behave in a very reserved manner, almost like circumspect servants of their lordly masters, the all-powerful SS.

As always, the lowest of the prisoners pay for everything. They have to be extremely prudent, more so than ever, to escape the glances of the chiefs' eyes, to obey every nod and expression so as to avoid the unleashing of latent fears and furies.

The word *sabotage* is heard more and more, and now the multiple gallows has a permanent place on roll call square. The bunker suffers from overpopulation, and the hangings become a grisly, everyday spectacle.

Throughout the days, the weather is magnificent. The sun rises each morning in a deep blue sky, flooding the hills with its splendor. However, the camp is situated within a bowl that collects its rays, and the surface kommandos suffer under crushing heat. Tortured by thirst, they beg the Stubendienst for water, but he sneers and sends them packing. After the awful rigors of the cold, snow, and ice, the biting rain and chilling wind, now the sun becomes a new and dreaded tyrant. The roll call square is comparable to a hot plate that men hesitate to think of crossing. And no flasks or bottles are allowed the men, nothing that could be used to carry even the most meager supply of water. Now uniforms are no longer wet from the rain but from sweat.

Along with weakness from perpetual hunger, dehydration now causes the most feeble victims to drop like flies. The desperate need for something to drink becomes a fixed obsession born anew each morning, torturing men's minds and bodies until the brief respite of total exhaustion that comes with sleep at the end of the day.

In the tunnel, the German civilians, of course, don't mention any of their doubts as to the usefulness of the big V-2s. What purpose can these large rockets serve against armies in continual movement? Calculations and fixes on impact points would be outdated by launch time, when the advancing Allied target armies would be many miles ahead of the incoming rockets.

Meantime, the smells from the crematorium in the overheated air are unbearable. Unable to rise, the smoke comes back down, thick and black upon us, onto the roofs and throughout the square. It penetrates the infirmary through the wide-open windows, giving patients a foretaste of their own last passage up through the chimney.

At the tunnel entrance worksite, the sheet metal and machines become hot enough to burn flesh; you have to be very careful before touching anything. The Kapos, cowed by the intense heat, seek out shadowy corners, moving seldom except to shout a volley of obscene curses and lash out with a torrent of clubbings and then retire in search of the shade. The sentinels take turns in sheltering under the few odd trees, while their dogs let their tongues hang out and pant in the furnacelike heat.

On this cursed Planet Dora, everything becomes a torture for the prisoners; everything turns against them. The sun, rain, wind, and snow—all these elements from the beginning of time, which man had learned to domesticate—now become sources of primal suffering.

Even the extraordinary news of the war is not exempt. In the real world, it is echoed with heartfelt joy, but within Dora, it must be kept secret. It can only be whispered from one ear to another. Perhaps we will be free . . . if all goes well . . . if the Allies continue their onslaught . . .

But until that last day, until the exact moment when an Allied tank smashes through that gate, your life as a prisoner must be lived, and you must die your death.

Somewhere in France, big things are being prepared, to be sure. Rough decisions are being made that will send the liberating angels, the greatest men of all times, gods with guns in their hands, thrusting into the very heart of Germany.

For our part, there is nothing we can offer them except a hellish revelation they won't easily forget, but they will be welcomed as no other conquering force has ever been welcomed in all history! The Roman triumphs will be a Boy Scout parade compared to the reception of these young heroes from another planet, the Planet Earth. From the forgotten depths of Dora will emerge pitiful shadows who will break out with a smile and a sob.

My God, be quick, I pray. We can't hold out anymore.

★   ★   ★

July. A batch of new prisoners has arrived from France.

André and Michel climb back out of the tunnel this Sunday afternoon. They have just finished a week of all-night work, and now, after having worked eighteen hours on the run, they are allowed an eighteen-hour rest. They won't have to go back below until the next day at nine o'clock. Driven by hunger, they quickly consume their rations of bread, margarine, and white cheese, then hurry toward the heights of the camp, where the new prisoners await their assignment or transfer to Ellrich or Harzungen.

In fact, there are prisoners in new clothes around several of the barracks. The barracks chiefs have probably sent them outside after beatings, and they make up small, slightly nervous groups turning in circles because they don't dare move too far away.

"Look at that," says Michel, "did you see their numbers? In the 77,000 shipment. They've more than doubled since my arrival!"

Michel, who arrived in shipment 30,000, finds these numbers a bit dizzying. The new prisoners are also impressed. André and Michel are a 43,000 and a 30,000, respectively; they must have been in this place a hell of a long time. The new people are all impressed by our numbers and look cautiously at the two buddies.

André and Michel greet them. "Hi, guys, we're French, too. Where are you from?"

"Oh, we've come from Buchenwald," replies a new arrival. "We've just finished the quarantine."

"We couldn't care less if you come from Buchenwald," says Michel. "What part of France are you from? I'm from Quimper. Is there anybody from Quimper among you?"

Michel, being a bit quick-tempered, brushes aside all those who haven't had the chance or honor to be born in his district. There are people from all over but none from Quimper.

André and Michel examine the new arrivals. These men seem to be in relatively good health. They don't appear to have spent much time in the prisons, where a highly slimming diet prepares one for the joys of concentration camp life.

"Good God," thinks André, "beside these guys, I must look like death warmed over. There are big ones and little ones, thin ones and fat, but almost every one of them still has a bit of strength left, a little meat on his bones, not to mention healthier complexions than ours." He looks at his own dirty clothing, all gray, torn, and held together with bits of wire. Only his shoes are comparable. The new arrivals' clogs are like his, the wooden soles hollowed out and the cloth uppers now torn. Yet in spite of their muddy complexions and tattered rags, Michel and André must look like old veterans of the Empire, for they can feel the glances of admiration cast at them.

Michel, however, hasn't come to be admired. He quickly gets to the point.

"Right, then, guys, how is it going, the war in France?"

By now, the two veteran prisoners are surrounded by a large crowd with information to give as well as questions to ask. The new arrivals want to ask questions at once and know what to expect, what will happen to them in this place. They have been surprised and abused at Buchenwald; now they wonder what end awaits them at Dora. The answers to Michel's question come bursting from all directions.

"The war? It's practically won. The Allies are advancing everywhere, and there is no longer a German army to stop them."

A big, heavyset guy stuffed into a uniform much too small for him speaks up. "I was in Paris at La Santé prison. They rushed us off to the Gare de l'Est a few hours before the liberation. They pushed us into trucks, and we crossed Paris almost without touching the ground. We could even hear shots being fired in the streets."

Another new arrival speaks. "I come from Angers prison. The Germans emptied the cells in a big hurry and rushed us all to the railroad station. The trains couldn't operate because there was so much bombing. We saw Americans everywhere, and they were machine-gunning everything that moved. More than once, we thought the Boches would leave us aside."

Everyone speaks of German troops in confusion, of archives hastily burned in the prisons, of trains using the secondary tracks to make progress. In the towns evacuated at the last minute, panic had set in among the German troops.

André and Michel are all but drunk with excitement at hearing all this news from so many tongues. It's wonderful beyond words to hear from eyewitnesses. But Michel comes back to his basic idea, the only worthwhile question: "Good, all this is very well, but where are the armies, and is the war going to end?"

The hefty guy from La Santé takes up the initiative. Military commentary, that's his business. "The Allied armies? They are everywhere. The French have landed in the south, and now nearly all of France has been liberated. The troops are breaking through and encircling all of the Germans who haven't already surrendered. Tens of thousands of Fritz are caught and trapped as if in a net. The Americans, French, and English are everywhere. And the planes, it's fantastic, there are thousands filling the sky in nonstop operations. You see nothing else but them in the air. And on the roads, no road in France is safe for the Germans. They don't even have any more guns and try to save themselves by any means available. There is no one to stop the Allies at the frontier."

Michel studies the man for a moment. "And the Siegfried line?"

Without a pause comes the reply. "It will be like the Maginot line; it won't hold for more than three days. The Allies will roll right over it. I tell you, the Boches are finished; it's practically over."

André listens to all this heartening news yet cannot quite lower his instinctive defenses. He'd really like to believe all this, but he knows how easily it could get out of hand. If it continues, he thinks, all at once there will be some guy who will look toward the plain and start shouting, "Hey guys, there they are—I can see them!"

So André responds, "I hate to say it, but it seems to me that you're burying the German army a little quickly. Before saying it's finished, maybe we should wait and see what happens around here in the next few days or weeks. In any case, look around; the SS don't look as if they're about to start packing up to leave, do they?"

Another old-timer addresses André. "But, you poor cunt, you don't know anything. These guys were in France three weeks ago. They know what's happening there a lot better than you do."

Michel's expression shows his distaste. He had momentarily drifted into wonderful dreams of freedom, and now this idiot, André, has to come up with this rubbish about waiting to see. Why, if these new guys say that the Boches have been shriveled up, then it means that they've been shriveled up. We'll soon be able to pack up whatever we have and get the hell out of here.

Now the new arrivals, having greatly uplifted the morale of the veteran prisoners, want to have whatever information they can get about life in Dora.

"How are things here? In Buchenwald, they told us that Dora was ugly even without saying we'd wind up here. What are we supposed to think?"

"Well, obviously, you could be better off," André laughs. "Up until now, you've had life easy, playing with your thumbs in quarantine. But now you'll get blisters. They'll put you in kommandos or assign you to Ellrich or Harzungen, small camps near here. Let me give you one good hint. Stay among Frenchmen as much as it's humanly possible because you're going to meet some real beasts. And try like hell not to let the SS or Kapos or Vorarbeiter or even your barracks chiefs notice you because that brings on beatings in a hurry. Finally, we're not trying to break your morale, but you've never seen, let alone imagined, a place like this."

"OK then, guys," says a newcomer, "even so, we've already been through the prisons and Gestapo interrogations."

"Yes," replies André, "well, just try to forget the prisons and the Gestapo. Here, it's different; you'll see how different it is all too soon. So make yourselves small, as small as you can, and follow whatever's happening without making waves. It'll be a whole lot better for your health."

The Parisian André addressed doesn't seem too worried. He's seen the situation in France and feels sure he knows what he is talking about.

"Well, we're only going to be here for a few weeks at most."

★   ★   ★

An August morning. The sun is rising in a clear blue sky. At seven o'clock, Bertrand makes quickly for the assembly place of his kommando, the Barakenbau-Tischlerei. The day will be a scorcher, with the men driven by thirst until night. The kommando lines up on the slight hill leading to the joinery workshop. About a hundred old hands are waiting for the two Kapos, one for the joiners and one for the carpenters. There are a few Czechs, reserved and scornful joiners, some Poles who would like to be but can't, and a horde of Frenchmen and Russians who are the barracks fitters. Despite their differences, the group has acquired a sense of unity.

The waiting becomes longer than usual, and the prisoners begin to worry. What's happening now? It isn't normal to be standing around, just waiting here, when we should already be at work. The joinery Vorarbeiter, a crafty look in his eyes, walks around the group, looking like a man who knows something but is keeping it to himself. He tosses off a few jokes, and these bring out slavish laughter from the Poles. He picks up a small log near his feet and announces that he'll mill it down to make a good truncheon. The laughter doubles, and the flatterers say that will be something new since they've never seen him with a club.

Anxiously, the prisoners watch the camp gate, clearly visible from their position. The Kapos must be out there by now, taking their orders from the SS. But what orders? The men begin looking around and notice that they are not alone. The shoemakers and laborers have also been held back. Bad, it looks bad. Denis would say there is something very . . . but he does not dare voice the word that comes to mind, fearing lest he tempt fate. Standing beside him, Bertrand also seems preoccupied.

Bertrand turns to him. "Denis, what do you think of all this? What the hell are we waiting on?"

"Well, old man," begins Denis, "if you're thinking the same thing I am, it looks as if a transfer is being prepared."

Good God, that's it! The feared word has been spoken, and there's no doubt, it must be just that. Bertrand feels a cold sweat running down his back. He hears the word being whispered in frightened tones from row to row. It's been only a short while since Bertrand predicted a forthcoming catastrophe.

The kommando has analyzed and perfected their operation in the assembly of a barracks. Now that they're in the swing of it, they can assemble a barracks in a day. Recently, however, it has taken two or three days to do the same job since the men are physically unable to sustain the pace. The laborers drag their feet and tend to become like road workers. As for the shoemakers, these are little old men in their fifties or invalids from whom the Germans can draw to fill out the desired numbers in various transfers. If these men are on hand, then it really is a transfer getting under way. The obsession of Ellrich and Harzungen grows anew in their minds.

"Hey, Denis, do you think we're part of this transfer? They're not going to send everyone, are they?"

"Certainly not, Bertrand, but up against the Czechs, you don't make the weight. You couldn't even make a soapbox, and the Vorarbeiter knows it. The big queer hasn't bothered you because deep down, he's a good guy, but he'll send you down because he needs guys for the transfer. As for the Polacks, you can be sure that their friends in the Arbeitsstatistik have already been warned and will try to save them."

Suddenly, a group near the gate begins moving. There are SS and Kapos, those of the kommandos that have been held back. They speak for a moment near the guard post and then separate. The Kapos for the joiners and carpenters cross the square and, with an SS officer, climb the short walkway leading to the joinery shop.

"Stillgestanden! Mützen ab!"

As one man, the prisoners snap to attention, sweeping their berets off and to their sides. The SS officer passes in front of them but without counting. It is not a roll call. The two kommandos are separated by just a few yards. The SS officer speaks first to the joiners' Kapo, who immediately opens his register. With the approval of the SS man, he takes out all the Czechs, a few Poles, and one Frenchman. A good half of the workforce stays put.

They move on to the carpenters, and there the selection is more strict. Only a quarter of the prisoners are kept back and return to the workshop. Those who remain in front of the door are carefully noted in the registers. The SS officer, with a grunt of satisfaction, returns toward the gate.

"That's it. We are all set for Ellrich!"

Bertrand is pale. Mechanically, he glances toward the square. The shoemakers have taken a massive blow; there will be practically none left. It's the same with the laborers, from which nine out of ten have been taken. The SS will keep behind just enough men for the maintenance work of the camp. All the rest will breathe the poisonous underground air on the other side of the hill.

On an order, the groups march down to the roll call square. Several hundred other prisoners are already there, with different kommandos standing apart from each other and guarded by their respective Kapos. At this point, several officials emerge from the administrative buildings and come up to the groups.

"Bertrand, I have a feeling there will be some reshuffling on this detail, so let's keep our eyes and ears open; we might still have a little chance."

A well-dressed Polish minor official goes up to the Kapo and speaks with him. Denis quickly whispers again to Bertrand, "See, it's the last-minute pitch to save their friends. If the Kapo asks for specialists, get in there!"

Sure enough, after having listened to the minor official, the Kapo asks for some fitters, but Bertrand and Denis have hardly heard the end of the question before they have flung themselves forward. There is an immediate rush, which turns to a riot behind them. You can hear shouts in Polish and Russian, the Polish friends pushing with elbows and fists to get in front. The Kapo curses above the din and swings his truncheon into the crowd. Men who were well placed find themselves pushed to the rear and try to fight their way forward again where the prisoners, solid for once, hold firm. Quiet returns, and the numbers of the fitters and locksmiths are noted. Denis and Bertrand are always in front with a majority of Poles, French, and a few Russians. About fifty in all, they are separated from the others. Among the diggers, the proportion is a lot less, and it is zero among the shoemakers. The numbers are noted once again. Bertrand feels satisfied but doesn't know quite what to think.

"We've gotten ourselves into something, here, Denis, without knowing too much about it."

"Personally, I think we're going down into the tunnel. That could be a good thing."

"Well, I hope they're not going to make us take a test first, Denis. It could turn out badly. I've never been in a factory or workshop."

"It's never too late to start, my friend, and we'll see. In any case, if you want to go to Ellrich, there's still time; you only have to go back with the others. As for me, I'm ready to work at any odd job to stay at Dora. Here, at least, I know the place!"

★   ★   ★

In columns of five, the "saved" pass through the camp gate. At a measured pace, they cross the several hundred yards leading to the tunnel and, having crossed the stockyard, arrive directly in front of the entrance. The camouflage net is still in place, as are the two tanks half dug into the ground. "Halt!" Bertrand and Denis, who haven't been there for months since they managed to be sent to the surface, now contemplate the spectacle. They notice the heavy machine gun, which hasn't moved, but find that the mountains of debris are gone. The ground has been paved with concrete, and now a normal-gauge railroad has replaced the earlier narrow-gauge track.

A handling kommando enters the tunnel, the men carrying aluminum tanks on their shoulders. In front of the guard post, an SS officer counts the men, now and then tapping his supple whip against his boot. The Kapos of the new groups have pushed aside the former joiners, who have now become fitting specialists.

"Hey, Denis, have you seen our new Kapo? Looks like an old woman. If he keeps on like that, things won't be so bad."

The Kapo, a criminal prisoner, is as wrinkled as an old apple. Small, badly built, he doesn't seem to be much over forty-five. During the whole journey from the camp, he hasn't stopped barking at us, yet he never once swung his club on a single head or back. He must consider that truncheon more vital as a walking stick.

The handling kommando has entered; now it's our turn. Amongst us are old veterans who remember the tunnel in its hideous early days, filled with the deafening din, the shrill shouts, the endless processions, the great piles of debris, the explosions in half-darkness, and the yellow dust that coated the lungs and inflamed the eyes. Some men still live who have known the horrors and the beatings, the death and mutilation lurking each moment, the stones with razor-sharp edges that would slice men's legs open to the bone; men who have felt the mountain shudder under the mine blasts like some enormous, wakening beast. They have known the indescribable sleeping blocks where thousands of men slept, suffered, and died in the midst of the worst of thieves, cutthroats, and assassins under the endless din of explosions; these few who have survived on the planet of the mad.

Others who are here for the first time look worriedly at the giant earthen mouth about to swallow them up. The warnings about the tunnel that followed them from Buchenwald return to memory, and they regret having volunteered. The tunnel means death. How many times have they heard this warning? The outside kommando seems like a peaceful haven compared with this infernal hole, but it's too late to turn back. Now they have to go on.

In ranks of five, the men enter the tunnel and, to their surprise, find a clean, concrete-paved floor. The raw, rounded roof still shows traces of the drills that fashioned its surface. At the intersection of the wall and the roof overhead, large ventilation shafts loom beside electrical cables and ducts carrying water and compressed air. Like ants carrying exotic debris, hundreds of prisoners march by with parts of the V-2 on backs or shoulders. There is an enormous fuss going on, but for the moment, there are no more anguished shouts. The air is still cold and damp, but now it is at last free of the strangling dust of earlier days.

"Hey, Bertrand, look to your left!" The column arrives in front of the first hall, formerly one of the hellish dormitories. Now, however, it looks fantastic. The hall is deep and extremely well lighted. In the middle, a line of several rockets are set up on their tail fins. They are enormous, hemmed in by scaffolding, and prisoners are working busily on various levels. Through openings in the sides, you can see the reservoirs and piping, like the insides of metal whales. Men with screwdrivers and wrenches in their hands are fitting and tightening lugs, nuts, seals, and fittings in the stomachs of the beasts. The hall roof is lined with pulley blocks and rails. Amid the purring of motors, you can hear the orders that echo and ricochet off the walls as in some eerie cathedral.

The troop discovers other marvels as it moves along. Another hall also contains rockets, but these are horizontal and in sections and pieces. These are laid out upon workbenches mounted on rails, and the lot is in the process of being assembled. In other halls, they see only the torpedo heads into which men are soldering cable connections. A smell of burnt oil hangs in the air. At the far end of these halls, you can see the second gallery. Here, on another railroad, flatbed trucks circulate, carrying finished units.

Along the walls and at hall entrances, there are storage areas containing large quantities of supplies and spare parts. Some stand in groups, others are piled up, and all are shining and coated with grease. Machine tools are stocked by the dozens, awaiting only the completion of one workshop or another to be moved into position and bolted to the concrete floor. They carry inscriptions in German, French, Czech, and Russian. You'd think it was the cave of Ali Baba the mechanic.

"Halt!"

Bloody hell, we've arrived. This must be the place where they'll try out our abilities as "specialists." On the left, we see Hall 34, and just beyond the entrance, there is a spare parts store. There is also an electric welding plant as big as a cutting press, along with other smaller plants. At the top of the wall, a mezzanine holds an office, with windows for the engineer. To our right, neatly lined up one after the other, there is a series of chassis frameworks carrying glossy panels of sheet metal.

In the middle of the hall, there is a small room for the Kapo, a tool shop, and some more frameworks. At the far end, we can see an arc-welding room, a painting workshop, and various small spot welders and machines. Hall 34 stretches out for almost 400 feet, and aside from us, there isn't a living soul. The concrete floor is clean, and a network of lightbulbs fixed beneath the roof brightens the entire area quite well.

The Kapo asks if there is an arc welder. A young Frenchman volunteers and is immediately sent to the workshop at the far end. The Kapo asks nothing of the others; men are simply put in place as they arrive in front of a machine or chassis. The Meisters haven't arrived, and apparently, the orders to start working haven't been given. At the hall entrance, meanwhile, electricians are busy checking the different electrical junctions. The compressed-air circuit is also checked. *Prima!* It's perfect.

The Kapo begins hollering. Suddenly, he's annoyed as hell because his team is still unoccupied, and if an SS should come by, there will be bloody hell to pay. Then he has a flash of genius, if that's possible within a Kapo's mentality. At the least, it's a good idea, for all our sakes. Still hollering, he gives an order to the Vorarbeiter, who dashes to the tool shop and quickly returns with a packet of sandpaper. He hands out the pieces, and for the next twelve hours, we prisoners will busily rub, pounce on, and caress the same bits of sheet metal. At the end of the twelve hours, you could look at yourself in the surface.

"Not a bad start for this volunteering," thinks Denis.

*   *   *

Some badly beaten and battered prisoners have just arrived from Ellrich with disheartening news. We were already apprehensive when we saw the line of trucks loaded with dead bodies heading to the crematorium. The word is that Ellrich is beginning, like Dora, with a wave of obscene horror. The new Kapos, determined to justify their stripes, have flung themselves into wreaking mass slaughter upon the prisoners. The SS, once again in direct contact with their slave laborers, are indulging their desire to inflict ghastly cruelties upon the helpless. The reign of terror, Nazi-style, has swept through Ellrich, and the losses are considerable.

The veterans of Dora try to regain their old reflexes, but whatever hopes they entertained have vanished. They know they won't get out of this festering carbuncle on the asshole of hell.

The newcomers of the 77,000 convoy, who fancied that the Allied legions were right on their heels, have had a hideous awakening, and suddenly, they realize that time is not the same in all places.

With growing terror, they discover that in the concentration camp, life is counted in days, while, by comparison, the advance of the Allies is reckoned in centuries. Like trapped animals, they fight against death, but death laughs at them. The trap is tightly closed. No one can escape.

Ellrich and Harzungen will be part of an enormous underground complex for production of the secret V-1 and V-2 missiles and Messerschmitt fighter aircraft. There is enormous space under the hills of Harz, and you could dig within it for many years. All of Germany's military production, for that matter, could regroup and hide itself there, safe from the American bombs. The Buchenwald bombing that destroyed the Gustloff armaments factories showed that the only security was deep under the earth. A lesson well learned.

So the pneumatic drills reign again on the other side of the hill. Following the technique so effective at Dora, a magnificent tunnel will be carved and blasted far below the surface. Everything has been brought together to speed the work. Sadistic, bloodthirsty SS and Kapos are enjoying a killing frenzy, with an inexhaustible supply of manpower. What matter how many they kill? There are more where these came from. All the SS need do is fill out the request form, and new shipments of prisoners arrive. As for the materials, they are quite basic. A few compressors, masses of shovels, wheelbarrows, pickaxes, and electric wiring. Here is a factory that's not going to burden the subscribers' budgets!

If the Zawatsky Company, responsible for the factory at Dora, timidly complains to the SS that its so-called workers look too much like dying men and asks that their conditions be improved so as to make them a bit more usable, then that's one thing. At Ellrich, however, the SS know that they have no such worry. "There won't be any Zawatsky-type bleeding hearts to bother us with such weaseling considerations before the end of the tunneling," they think, "so we can amuse ourselves and crush these filthy Frenchmen, Poles, and Russians. It's a joy to begin it once again!"

The prisoners in that devil's cauldron no longer think about the war or news of its operations. It's past, something abstract, happening in some other part of the solar system. The only tangible reality is to know whether you will still be alive tonight. There is no other truth than to know whether, in the next minute, a crushing blow from a club will send you to join the heap of corpses that is growing higher. The only reality is also to know whether tons of rock are suddenly going to break away from the tunnel roof and crush you like a snuffed-out candle. Reality is also to know whether, at day's end, the masters will come up with some new vexation to keep you from crawling onto your filthy straw mattress.

Finally, reality is knowing whether this cough that has racked your lungs for several days is not a sign of galloping TB, which will soon liquidate you.

The stories told by Ellrich prisoners sent back to the infirmary are terrifying. They remind us of Dora a few months earlier, when the tunnel was being drilled. No one dares tell them, "You've been at Ellrich three weeks, and you're laid up, horrified by what has happened to you in that time. Well, things will only get worse. Right now, the hole isn't very deep, and a little fresh air still gets in. But the more you dig and the deeper you get into this bastard of a mountain, the less air you'll get. There will be nothing but dust to breathe and dripping water freezing on your shoulders. When you try to breathe, you'll feel as if you're swallowing dirt, until one day, you'll fall down and never get up again. The SS and the Kapo will come up to the wreckage that you have become, and one crushing blow of the Kapo's truncheon will put an end to all your worries. Then they'll take off your striped rags, mark your number on your naked stomach, and throw the corpse from which your soul has just fled into the truck with the others. And it'll be: Let's go! The direction? Dora's crematorium. And don't imagine that you'll have any chance of escaping your fate; this is an infallible diagnosis. When this shithole has become a beautiful tunnel, all shiny and new, out of the hundreds of guys you arrived with to swing that first pickax, there won't even be twenty still alive. It's only been a few weeks since they took you away from your wife, your kids, and your parents, but from now on, they wouldn't recognize you. You already look like a corpse. Remember the fuss you made when you saw us? Well, we may not be very crafty, but we could see that you took us for zombies. We couldn't care less; it's been a long time since we stopped looking at ourselves. When we got here, we, too, were young and handsome. We arrived in our thousands of good-looking guys; the 20,000s, the 21,000s, the 30,000s, the 31,000s, the 38,000 to 45,000s—that's a lot of young Apollos. Now, out of all those thousands, we're only a few hundred shabby veterans with deplorable-looking faces and bodies. And the work isn't finished; unemployment isn't chasing after us. So take this bit of advice: Make the most out of being in the infirmary. For the moment, it's not too dangerous; they don't seem to be carrying out big prisoner liquidations, just one or two from time to time. If you manage to get a bit better, you'll find a hell of a change when you get back to Ellrich. All the faces that you knew will be gone. It'll be a shock, so, for the moment, hold on, brother."

★   ★   ★

"You French really are idiots," said Jan the Dutchman. His five-foot-eleven frame was well fleshed, thanks to the extra soup offered by friendly officials. In his superior state of health, he dominated little Maurice.

The refectory had emptied after the barracks chief finished giving the Russian twenty-five savage strokes. He had cut the man to pieces. The Russian's back and buttocks were horribly lacerated and bloody; large hematomas swelled with blood were appearing. During the punishment, his screams were like the agonies of the damned, and now tortured sobs were racked from his throat as he lay stretched in front of the door. His buddies poured water on his back as gently as they could to cool and absorb the burns. A large piece of snot hung from his nose.

The Russian had been surprised by a Stubendienst while stealing sausage rations, and the barracks chief used the occasion for a "training" session to intimidate the other prisoners. He craved and loved such opportunities to inflict punishment.

"Yes, you French are stupid," repeated Jan, "because you don't understand. You see, this Russian stole those rations, perhaps yours or mine. That doesn't matter. He didn't deserve twenty-five lashes; what he deserved was to be killed. But it's us who should have taken care of that, not the barracks chief. It wasn't his survival that was in danger; it was ours. The damned barracks chief steals more himself, you know it. He doesn't hesitate to cut off a good bit of sausage when it arrives, and he puts it in his cupboard. He couldn't care less about us when he says the Russian is a bad friend. Well, during the punishment, I looked at the faces of the Russians. They looked like beasts ready to leap. They were watching the barracks chief with murder in their eyes; if they could have caught him, they would have torn him into fragments of bloody pulp. Yet their buddy had stolen food from all of us, meaning themselves as well. He would either have eaten it in some corner or sold it for tobacco. The Soviets would have been poached upon and would be enraged. However, the Russkis support each other and don't allow one of them to be touched by an outsider. Let someone else touch a Ukrainian or a Mongol and all Holy Russia stands up to defend him, no matter what he's done. They'll even let themselves be cut to bits because of some selfish bastard like this. Of course, it doesn't stop them from being just as unscrupulous amongst themselves. They'll execute one of their own in a minute—and savagely—if he has done something against the group, but they do it themselves, without letting others become involved in their business. They only accept the authority here because it is stronger, but they don't give in. They're waiting for their chance. Sooner or later, it will come. It may take weeks, months, or years, but the day when it comes, they'll jump on it.

"In fact," the Dutchman continued, "it has already happened. There have been Kapos who got the SS pissed off at them, lost their precious armlet, and suddenly found themselves back in the barracks with everyone else. They didn't last a day. Within twenty-four hours, they were dead from 'fatal accidents.' A legal doctor would have been surprised to find that a former Kapo officially cut in two by a piece of sheet metal also 'happened' to have a broken nose, his ears ripped off, and an eye hanging down his face."

Maurice didn't follow Jan's reasoning too well. "But tell me, Jan, what does all this have to do with the French? And how can you, being Dutch, know what the French are like?"

"I've known the French," said the Dutchman. "I was a student in France for a long time. You people are great talkers, you get angry with the government, the police, the bosses, and all the authorities, but when something goes wrong, you go right to the cops or file a lawsuit. France is a paradise for lawyers and wine-makers. I was there in 1936. I saw the workers demonstrate, revolutionaries out in the streets wearing flags as big as bedsheets—it was a hell of a show. Fascism and the owners were being beaten up, and now they were to be eaten up. The final fight, it was there. But when the Germans marched on Czechoslovakia, what a drastic change of direction. The cursed of the earth became fighters for peace at all costs! The Czech proletariat was quickly forgotten. Besides, Hitler didn't look too bad for a fellow with a tiny mustache. When war was declared, everyone went but with no intention of fighting. And when the great disaster arrived, all these former revolutionaries were marched off to the Stalags."

"So what are you getting at, Jan?"

"Well, what I'm saying is that you French are a big group in the concentration camps, perhaps proportionally more so than any other nationalities. You have the weight of numbers, but you don't defend your compatriots. Now take the Russki and the sausage. You say the

Russians are savages and thieves, but they have an excuse. On the other hand, if a Frenchman steals a sausage, he'll be thrown out of the community immediately, and you'll consider it normal for him to be punished. But who'll punish him? Not you. You people would rather let the barracks chief massacre the man. So, first, why do the Russians have excuses and not the French? Second, why not make your own policy? You're great talkers when it comes to demonstrating in the streets, but once everything is lost, you can't count on yourselves for your own survival. All of you here accept dying. Of course, you haven't any choice, but you don't organize anything to save your group. We Dutch aren't numerous in Dora, but we're well united, and we don't drop one of our guys as long as we can do something for him. It's the same thing with the Belgians, the Czechs, and Poles as with the Russians.

"Notice," the Dutchman continued, "these despised Russians who have no positions, no armlets, no stripes—these backward illiterates. Well, the Kapos now think twice before giving one of them a hiding. You know that if you find yourself alone surrounded by Russians, you're scared because they represent a fearful threat. And the Poles are a united group, but look at the French. The French could have dominated the camp with their elite. Instead, they're singled out by even the smallest Vorarbeiter because he knows he can attack without the slightest risk of reprisal. You'll call him a shit or trash, but no one will think of going after his scalp. You just saw the barracks chief dish out a hiding to that Russian. Well, you can be damned sure he's going to watch out for several days because with these savages, anything can happen. But if he'd done the same thing to a Frenchman, he'd be able to sleep like a baby. Just wait and see, Maurice, if we get out of this alive, the French will have any SS and Kapos they find brought up in front of tribunals—and the poor suckers who testify as witnesses will be shouted down by a bunch of damned pro-Nazi lawyers. But you just watch, Maurice. On the Russian side, rest assured, there won't be any so-called legal processes to block justice!"

Little Maurice had listened attentively. "It's true," he thought, "we are stupid cunts."

★   ★   ★

Simon sits in front of his arc welder. Since the machine is low, he has a stool, the height of comfort. He is at the far end of the hall, near the big exit gallery with its endless freezing draft. God! Well, you can't have everything, and it's better to catch pleurisy sitting down than standing. And also to the good, he is slightly hidden by the cabin of the arc welder, which screens him and affords a brief sense of peace.

Simon makes directional elevators, one of which will serve each of the fins of the V-2. An elevator itself is not a large unit. It is made up of a steel axis carrying a ball bearing and two perforated ribbings and trimmed with two formed pieces of sheet metal. Altogether, it resembles a small battalion flag: full around the staff and narrowing down along the two sides. It measures about twenty inches by sixteen.

A jig allows the first rib, which will be on the inside of the elevator, to be well situated on the axis, where it can be welded. The ridges of the two formed sheet metal pieces are then welded, and the axis is placed inside with its ribbing, which is welded all around. It only remains for the workman to spot-weld all along the leading edge and position the second ribbing, which acts as a cover, and spot-weld it at close intervals. With that, it is done. The elevator is then placed on a control instrument to both check for any faults and determine that the ridges are properly aligned.

The welder consists of two long copper electrodes that can easily be inserted within the elevator. It has a control ring that can vary the current according to the thickness of sheet metal to be welded. Use too much current, and a hole will be burned through the metal. With too little current, the metal will fail to melt on the selected point, with the result that the weld will break after a few seconds in service.

The art for which we aimed consisted of calculating the intensity of current so as to make a weld that would appear perfect to the eye and solid when not under strain but that would break apart under the brutal forces of acceleration, compounded by the vibrations and heavy stresses on the elevator during launch and flight. This "treated weld" is better known as "sabotage," and the SS had hideous punishments for even suspicion of such activity: the agonizing death of slow strangulation by hanging, among others.

Simon was almost subconsciously led into sabotage. Before his arrest, he had been a student who knew nothing about electric welders. When he found himself in the tunnel and, one day, they asked for welders, he was the first to leap forward. It was far better than shoveling tons of debris under constant clubbing by men with the SS armlets that allowed them to beat prisoners to death, if they chose, for no more reason than the perverted pleasure of committing a legal murder under the law according to Hitler.

But Simon was also keenly aware that a mechanic is someone who is respected; you must leave him in peace if his work is to be well done. After fumbling about, he soon understood the working of the machine and the uses he could make of it. He made some trial welds on bits of sheet metal of the same thickness as the elevator, then separated them with a screwdriver. Examining the bits enabled him to determine the exact amount he needed so as to make the apparently faultless welds.

Simon isn't really conscious of carrying on a campaign of sabotage—at least, not in the sense of agents being introduced into armaments factories with precise instructions. He simply thinks of himself as an anonymous part of a large group who, without scheming, happen to botch up their work.

The only problem with Simon's method is that a trained ear could detect when something is amiss. For when a weld is good, the machine gives out a rounded, reassuring purr, whereas an imperfect weld only produces a short little "bzzz" sound.

One night, Simon thought that his time had come, that his career was really over. He was at his machine, very carefully making defective spot welds, when he suddenly sensed a presence behind him. He turned around, and his heart leaped within his skeletal chest. *"Mon Dieu!"* It was Ironface.

Ironface, the most notorious and bloodthirsty of the SS sadists, was only two yards away, nervously hitting his left palm with his club as he watched Simon. The fragile man thought he was going to faint, and he could hear the little "bzzz, bzzz" sounds of the machine echoing through his thoughts. He leaped up at once, whipped off his beret, and stood at strict attention. His legs were trembling, and his vision blurred.

"Weitermachen!" (Continue!) And Ironface walked slowly away, still tapping his left palm with the gummi. It was several minutes before Simon's pulse rate returned to anything near what might have been considered normal.

Simon has noticed that when the prisoners speak of their work in the tunnel, which doesn't usually come up in conversations, they always mention bits and pieces of V-2 equipment that don't hold, are badly designed, are badly placed within the rocket, and will break away under the first stress of launch acceleration. True electricians and fitters say that if they had been asked for advice, they would have done things this way or that. But as the prisoners have done it, these bits and pieces will shatter into a thousand bits at some point after the rocket has roared skyward from the earth.

So there are, figuratively, a hundred ways of botching up the work, if not actually sabotaging it. Different parts of rocket machinery, fabricated in machines from many different areas, very often won't fit each other properly, meaning that touch-up work is necessary. Then, once a piece has been assembled, how could the inner faults and malfunctions be seen? No inspector could then detect pop-rivets that were badly set or had already broken between the sheet metal and the ribs, or screws that were defectively threaded and hammered into place, or control panels that remained in place only by some random miracle, for their threads had been so turned that the female thread was almost completely worn away, or electric circuits so fragile and delicate that they couldn't stand the slightest imperfection in flight.

The rockets, of course, are checked before being taken outside, but within the tunnel, they are handled as delicately as frightened young girls. The hidden vices and defects are numerous, but they won't become visible until the V-2 is into its flight. Many thousands of innocent folk in target areas will live out their lives after all when these monsters veer off course into the countryside, away from London and other cities.

Sabotage is a damned risky effort when prisoners are working on large pieces, especially when they are of different nationalities. The animosity between groups is so great that systematic sabotage is quite dangerous. Poles, especially, are to be avoided. You can well imagine them shouting loudly and accusing the French of shoddy workmanship. But in the right group, the mistakes and accidents that could be repaired with a little effort are silently passed along by tacit agreement. In fact, any change in the working pace in order to repair the fault would immediately attract the attention of the German Meister, who might cry out, "Sabotage!" So, mum's the word, and the group continues working as if nothing at all had happened.

In its final stage of construction, the V-2 is a beautiful machine, without equal in the world. However, it suffers from so many potential illnesses that it has every chance of ending its career by losing key bolts and coverings and, in any case, falling to earth far from its target. The beautiful rocket won't reach targets of strategic value or dense population. Instead, it will destroy itself in a market garden or, at worst, on or near some unfortunate, isolated human habitation, but, after all, that is war.

★   ★   ★

Toward the end of September, the inmates discover a convoy of strange prisoners on the roll call square. They had arrived during the night and had been standing for several hours along the side of the quad. They are dressed in the usual striped uniforms but wear funny little woolen caps instead of the usual Mützen. There are several hundred, all of whom seem in extremely exhausted condition and all of whom are unbelievably thin.

After inquiring, we find that it is a convoy of Hungarian Jews from Central Europe and that they had arrived by train, in open trucks, during the night.

There are several immediate reactions. The first, essentially, comes from the Poles. For them, to see this pile of human trash constitutes a most marvelous spectacle. "Look at those filthy Jews," we hear, "they really are disgusting. What a shame that we can't go and smash in their faces. At least, when the war is over, we won't see any more of these horrible guys who had all the good jobs, had all the business, and earned all the money. Even at school, they outnumbered us, and they had whole districts to themselves in the towns. They worked in beautiful offices and lovely shops, while we had to hustle like mad in the factories and sweated in the fields."

The general reaction, though, is less radical, and it has a more practical side. Having Jews in the camp is an excellent idea, for everything is aimed at them.

The SS, the Kapos, and the barracks chiefs must be rubbing their hands with glee. Now they'll be able to concentrate their talents without having to spread them throughout thirty-six nationalities. For the Nazis, the Jews are a blessing fallen from the sky. If they didn't exist, they would have to have been invented because it is such a pleasure, a duty, even an honor to fall upon them with might and main.

"Since they're so numerous," the SS are saying to each other, "there will be enough for everyone. We're going to enjoy ourselves for a while, and when we've finished with these, they'll have to send us some more. These vermin breed so quickly that we don't risk running short, so why go easy on them?"

Watching the new arrivals, the other prisoners are sure that the chiefs will sound the hunting horn but that they will be spared most of the blows as long as the supply of Jews lasts. The Russians, particularly, feel that they have climbed the social ladder. Though their traditional anti-Semitism isn't as virulent as that of the Poles, they notice with satisfaction that they now have a "race" that stands lower than themselves. It is always good to have someone who is more hated than yourself. The other prisoners almost go as far as to encourage the Jews to hold out as long as possible.

Once these widespread knee-jerk reactions have passed, however, we begin asking ourselves why the Jews have been sent to Dora. The Jews have a camp of their own, Auschwitz. So what are they doing here? There are no gas chambers, or do the SS have the quaint notion of carrying out trials? But that isn't too good. If the shower barracks were to be transformed into a gas chamber, anyone could be sent there, and each time you went in, you had a good chance of leaving feet first toward the crematorium.

Or perhaps they have an excess number of Jewish prisoners at Auschwitz and have decided to decentralize. Now the older prisoners begin looking worriedly at the sanitary barracks and the crematorium. We have become set in our views of dying in a well-known manner, and the changing of death into a possible production-line scale is far from something to cheer about.

The last and most elaborate reflection is the one that finally marks our minds. It is the first time that a group like this has arrived in the western camps. In Dora, we have prisoners who have known the main camps like Auschwitz, Mauthausen, Dachau, Flossenbürg, and others, and these were all ordinary transfers, but this arrival seems quite abnormal to everyone, entirely opposite to the norms.

It is thus that one central idea begins to germinate. Is this the beginning of the evacuation of the eastern camps now threatened by the advancing Russian armies?

The old hands look more closely at the convoy and note several things. These poor souls have traveled for at least several days, perhaps a week or even two. They have been without food or care. They must have passed through a camp earlier since they all wear striped prisoner garb. They are not escorted by Kapos and Vorarbeiter, which is usual in transfers from one camp to another. These men haven't a single personal belonging, even the most basic that all prisoners carry with them, not even a spoon or bag made out of some bit of rag. Their deteriorated state makes it obvious that they are going to die quickly.

So what will happen as the Allies approach? Will the SS evacuate Dora and go to the east? The Russian armies are still a long way off and, according to the latest news, haven't yet entered Poland. With an American offensive driving into Germany, perhaps in a few days or weeks, will the SS load the fifteen to eighteen thousand prisoners into railroad wagons and make them wander until no one remains alive? Or, lacking transport, will their captors force them to march until they fall dead from exhaustion? Now a new worry begins to circulate among the prisoners. The approach of liberating armies could be the signal for the SS to murder them en masse.

Toward midday, the Jews are still on the square. They have been made to advance to the middle of the concrete slab, and just this move of a few yards has knocked out a good number of them. The dead, who had been lined up at the start, now form several piles. Among the living, few are able to remain upright without moving. Most of them stagger about as if drunk. From time to time, one falls and moves slightly, just a few jerks, and moves no more. Huge gaps appear in their ranks, and their moaning becomes weaker.

By afternoon, there seem to be more dead than alive. The sun, which is still strong, strengthens the smell of rotting bodies. Not a single man is able to continue standing without help. Wavering and pitching about, the skeletal Jews shoulder together in twos and threes. From their position at the gate, the SS look on, chuckling with delight at this hilarious spectacle. The women within the nearby SS whorehouse have closed the shutters so as not to see the "show" that so entertains the masters of Dora. Prisoners avoid going near the square, and the kommandos detour as far from it as possible. Even the Polish Stubendienst have stopped their sarcastic remarks.

At the end of the afternoon, orders come from the gate. The survivors are pushed, along with the bodies, to the upper end of the camp. Several more of them die along the way.

★   ★   ★

Sylvestre felt his throat tighten up. "In the name of God!" he cried to Paul, with whom he shared his straw mattress, "they have stolen my shoes!"

"Stupid idiot," snapped Paul, dressing quickly.

The Stubendienst had just burst into the dormitory, so there wasn't a second to lose. Sylvestre and Paul quickly entered the Waschraum to splash water on their unshaven faces, then get to the refectory for their rations.

"And where did you put them?"

"The usual place, under the straw mattress beside yours."

"You couldn't have pushed them under far enough. Some rotten Russian was able to slip them out while you were sleeping. But hurry up. Don't hang around like that, or you'll get a beating."

Completely helpless, Sylvestre got dressed slowly, mechanically. He was suddenly out of tune with the turmoil in the barracks. "But what am I going to do now?" he worried. "What is going to become of me?" A man without shoes doesn't exist, especially a prisoner. In the extreme privation of camp inmates, their few possessions were vital, and not one could be taken away without endangering its owner's life. A beret, a shirt, underpants, a jacket, trousers, socks, shoes, and a spoon were essential to staying alive; they were indispensable.

The Polish Stubendienst who controlled the awakening of the prisoners looked toward Sylvestre and saw that something wasn't right. *"Was machst du, Franzous? Los! Los!"* (What are you doing, Frenchman? Quick! Quick!)

"Meine schuhe weg! Comme çi, comme ça!" (My shoes have disappeared! That's the way it goes!)

The Pole let out a huge laugh. To drown these French with vexations while at the same time giving himself the appearance of a moralist enthralled him. "These idiots," he thought, "don't know how to look after themselves. They only know how to say that something is unjust, that they're being picked on, *que çi, que ça.* They talk, they argue, and they all die without understanding where they are. They look for trouble, and they find it. If I woke up to find that my shoes were missing, it wouldn't have been long before I stole a pair to replace them, or a buddy would have done it for me. These French cry in their corner and wait for things to fall into their laps."

"Franzous kapitalist, kein Packete! Kein Schuhe! Alle fertig." (French capitalist, no parcels of food from your family? No shoes? All finished.)

"You fucking cunt," thought Sylvestre, "what have you got to snigger about? You'd better be doing something for me rather than giving me a shitty time. Try coming to France after the war, and you'll see how things are done."

But this didn't change a thing. Something had to be done because the situation could only get worse. Many weird things had been seen at Dora but not a barefoot prisoner. He decided to go and see the barracks chief before the Pole could give him a twisted version of the facts.

The German was at the door to his room. His mood could be good or bad. This could go either way. He was apparently in a neutral frame of mind, but that could suddenly flash one way or the other, from a dry laugh to a furious rage, and for no apparent reason. He watched as Sylvestre approached him warily. *"Was willst du, Mensch!"* (What do you want, slime?)

Sylvestre kept his distance, outside the reach of a straight jab, which could go off like a bomb. He repeated his explanation of what had happened. "Barracks chief, my shoes are gone. Stolen."

The barracks chief was flabbergasted. "To get up early in the morning here at Dora," he thought, "after eight years in various camps, each one as filthy as the others, and now see this Arschloch, this asshole, come and tell me that he's had his shoes stolen. It's impossible; I give up. And what number is this poor cunt wearing? A 43,000. That means he's been in the camps for nine months and, shrewd as he is, has managed to stay alive."

The barracks chief remembered the bloody fights for life that he had seen through the years. You killed or you were killed for a hundred times less than this. He looked at Sylvestre, something he never did. The new generations didn't interest him; besides, nothing interested him anymore. He had become a machine, a concentration camp robot who would continue along his trajectory for years if no trouble were to fall in his path. "This prisoner must be a peasant," he thought. "These mugs are unbelievable. They are ready to die for a cow but incapable

of saving their own skins. What saves them for a while is the fact that
they're thick-skinned and that they've learned only too well that life
is no laughing matter."

"*Franzose*, you're really stupid. You think you're still on your farm
where you can sleep behind closed shutters. Well, you're not on that
cozy little farm anymore, and there are no shutters to close. You're not
on a farm here or in a sanatorium, and if you aren't careful, you'll find
yourself bare-assed in shit up to your eyeballs. Come here."

Sylvestre didn't understand any of the chief's philosophical reflections in spoken German but followed the man into his room. Under
the wardrobe, there were some leather slippers, tap shoes, a sort of
babouches with wooden soles as worn by newcomers in Buchenwald,
and some shapeless things that had once been clogs. The German took
one pair and threw them at the Frenchman, who caught them in
midair. *"Danke viel mal!"* (Many thanks!)

Sylvestre put the old debris of shoes under his arm and quickly
made off toward the Waschraum.

"Poor idiot," thought the barracks chief, who went back into his
room and closed the door.

5

THE GATES CLOSE AGAIN

One October day, the sun disappeared after having ruled the skies over Dora for three months. A persistent, chilling rain came to soak the roll call square, the prisoners' barracks, and the camp routes. The summer was finished, that season of the wildest hopes and prodigious news of Allied victories that were not even denied by the Germans.

It was a fact that France was free at last! The Allies had crushed everything in the path of their advances. Even Italy had caved in. It was astonishing. The once formidable German army, stupefied, had lost every strongpoint in the west within a few weeks.

The days had been counted, one by one. Each bit of news was transmitted by anonymous reporters and translated into every language of the prisoners. We listened to topographical details given by men from regions crossed by the advancing Allied armies and heard commentaries from young prisoners who were former officers and had never accepted defeat and who had begun fighting with the underground Resistance as early as 1940.

For several weeks, Dora had experienced a continuing fever. The few Frenchmen who normally received parcels had eagerly marked crosses on the calendar because their families had been liberated and the nightmare would soon end. The camp had seen its worst and best hours; the glorious tunnel was finished, and the obscene misery of earlier months was now behind them. Even the food rations had been ever so slightly increased, the lump of bread for four prisoners having become *boule à trois*, for three. One hardly ever saw those hapless, frightening Moslems who, with a deathly grin on their lips, would unconsciously go and give their fleshless bodies to the final "lucky blow" and end their misery at Dora forever. But men still died in the secrecy of the infirmary.

Meanwhile, borders of flowers had grown around the barracks, and the roll calls, apart from some exceptions, were relatively short.

The hangings themselves had not changed, but now their frequency produced a strange and harmless added spectacle: The Gypsy orchestra often passed through the halls of the tunnel playing the inevitable "Yeux Noirs" and "Grande Berezina." In contrast with its earlier horror, Dora had become a quite proper place where living and dying were almost decent. A strange commission had even come to visit the camp, and they had most likely considered it to be a masterpiece of penitentiary architecture in which everything had been provided for the good of the prisoner.

The euphoric summer period ended abruptly in October with the first rain. Rain? In itself, it's nothing. It's needed for the earth, the plantations, the brooks, for the rivers and the frogs. But the rains of October 1944 awoke the prisoners with a shock.

The attitude of the SS is clear: You band of wretches, flesh for the crematorium, you think you'll escape just like that? You think the war is going to end and we'll all exchange addresses and go back home? What do you think?

And you, who for the most part are experienced prisoners, you should know that we, the SS, are always the masters. We need only a few seconds to transform any of you into a howling piece of wreckage fit only for the crematorium. Perhaps they're dancing to the accordion in France, where so many think the war is finished. But we have a firm grip on you. We'll never let you go; you hear that? Never! We'll always make you regret that you were ever born. When we took power, we intended to create an empire to last a thousand years. Well, if it won't last a thousand years but only twelve instead, they will be twelve years the world will not be able to forget. Starting with you!

So in the month of October, we feel the gates of hell closing again. We have good discussions about local fighting back in France. Baccara has just been taken, and everyone is horrified to realize that another winter isn't far away.

The Rhine, that ridiculous river only some tens of yards wide that never stopped the invasions of centuries past, across which a grandmother could swim with her grandchildren, won't be crossed this year after all. The young officers have told us if you want to advance, you must throw your opponents into continual disorder. You must never give them time to catch their breath, giving them the impression of being held at bay and that you'll never stop.

On the other hand, which, unfortunately, is the case, if you feel it necessary to pause, regroup, and rearm your forces before advancing again, then weeks or months may be needed before the attack can be renewed. An army has more to consider than its moments of epic bravery, such as the charge of the Light Brigade at Balaclava. War is a deadly business, and if it is better to pause, resupply, and concentrate forces before attacking, then we'll wait. So, guys, let's make do in between times, and we'll see each other next year.

Next year, indeed! How many of us will still be alive? The oldest prisoners have already begun their second year and have seen frightening gaps as their fellows died around them. The young ones of August and September 1943, the 20,000s and 21,000s who had swung the first picks and pickaxes into that Nazi tunnel and still live, now look like Egyptian mummies; and the great mass of the 38,000s to 45,000s can only be dimly remembered. The 77,000s, who thought they'd be here only a few days, discovered instead an alien universe that would crush them to powder. And there were the 14,000s, veterans of Peenemünde. All of these, gone, not to mention the countless Czechs, Poles, Balts, Russians, Belgians, and Dutch who saw the entrance of the crematorium beckoning, as if to say: "Come, my little ones. Soon you will moan from cold and misery. So let it all go. Hope is finished. What good is it to fight? Come and get roasted into smoke and ashes at once without wasting time. It's nothing at all, just a bad time passing."

Living conditions speed downhill with the readings on the thermometer. First the bread rations become smaller. Then Saturday's hungrily awaited bit of boiled beef disappears. The Sunday bowl of soup with a bit of pasta lingers a while on the so-called menu, but it becomes clearer and much less filling, if it could ever have been so defined. The barracks windows are closed against the cold. The barracks chiefs bring out their big clubs again. Had they, too, hoped for an end to the war? They show no impatience, for the moment, but instead more of a sleepy apathy.

The SS, for their part, look down upon the camp quite haughtily, contenting themselves with the extremely low food rations to the prisoners plus deplorable hygiene to maintain a death rate easily balanced by the arrival of new captives. Of course, the western well of human fodder is no longer available, but, *Gott sei dank!* (thank God!), there are plenty of others in Central Europe to fulfill the SS demands for more blood.

In the autumn of 1944, the SS left the slopes where they were lodged and came back down into the arena. Perhaps, in a moment of weakness, they thought they were going to lose their playthings. But the lesson had been learned and didn't need repetition. They brought their clubs out of the cupboards again and were seen among the kommandos, their very presence pushing the Kapos to renewed levels of brutality. Even the damnable fleas and lice, plus the multiform bacilli and streptococci, began proliferating again. The roll call square echoed with bad coughing spells that, in turn, brought on the rushes of the barracks chief, truncheons swinging mercilessly. The great endemic ills of the camp attacked the mass of prisoners without letup.

Once again, in the evening, you could see scabby, naked prisoners in front of the barracks, fighting in the rain over a tin of Mitigal with which they smeared themselves from head to toe. You could see again the inflamed and bloated faces and the pus-filled eyes of prisoners suffering from skin infections. There were countless men whose necks were deformed by monstrous swellings from the clubbings and others with foot injuries infected by the mud, which had hollowed out holes in their flesh. Crowds of sickly prisoners would surround the entrance to the infirmary, where the Polish guards would begin striking out with their clubs at their groaning victims.

The pitiful few ounces gained and kept during the recent "better" days vanished rapidly, as dysentery twisted men's guts once again. What had been healed or contained suddenly turned worse. The very slight color that had returned to prisoners' cheeks was soon erased, and their faces again became the deathly gray of the previous winter and spring.

Little by little, news of the fighting fronts became limited to reports of skirmishes, as in 1939. The prisoners became disinterested, and veterans, with death in their hearts, knew they must prepare for a new winter, like those already known. Instinct told them there would be huge losses, with most of them already in a pitiful state. They had long since lost their body fat, and even their muscles had disappeared. Their knees and elbows formed grotesque bulges amid fleshless limbs. The skin on men's buttocks hung so emptily that even sitting became painful.

Cold autumn rains soaked their uniforms and shoes, and the overall humidity in the tunnel kept anything from drying. The friction of ragged, wet clothing irritated their skin. Sores formed in the groin, the creases of the elbows and knees, and other sites of infection aggravated by the filthy clothing. Thus, men shivered for twelve straight hours before climbing again to the surface, where it was still raining.

But the rain was only the beginning, an hors d'oeuvre on your winter menu. Icy winds, snow, and cold weather would soon arrive: winds cutting into your face like a thousand razor blades, snow penetrating everywhere, and freezing cold turning your jacket and trousers into an armor plating of ice, not to mention hands tortured by chilblains and feet becoming no more than a bundle of sores. It was all about to start again. The unending roll calls, which could be endured in summer, would become murderous. The unprotected square would be swept by blizzards, as ears became martyred by the cold. Your feet would slip on concrete covered with frozen blood spittles. And those bastard dogs would howl all through the night.

So we weren't interested in hearing of skirmishes between patrols on distant battle lines or artillery duels in far-off sectors. Our thought was: Attack now or leave us alone. We need the little strength we have left just to survive. We are going to close up on ourselves and grit our teeth because this new winter in itself is too much. There are hundreds of men whose fate is already sealed; it shows on their faces, and it won't be difficult for the SS and Kapos to make them take the last plunge—they only have to be pushed a little. These poor devils were already deteriorating toward the crematorium when they still believed that the war was about to end, and the first cold spell will speed them on their way to a flaming departure.

You others, prisoners who think you are cunning and that nothing is impossible with a strong heart—you who promised wives or mothers to come back, hoping that such a promise would be like life insurance—you would do well to take a good look at yourselves and think again. If you seriously list your strengths and weaknesses, you'll be astonished at how slim your chances for survival are, and this without even considering the booby traps that the masters of your fates, the SS, the Kapos, and barracks chiefs, will set for you.

Spring is at least six months away, and during this half year, merciless winter and even less merciful men will do everything they can to bring you down. You can believe that these sadists will agree beforehand on the best methods to trap you, leaving you wide open to vicious blows. Seeing how much time they have left, they don't even have to rush themselves, but they want the pleasures of brutality to last. The savagery of the tunnel at Dora will be transferred to the Ellrich diggers, and these demented minds will come up with other ruses just as cunning—and you'll fall into their traps like newborn babes who have had no time to learn or understand what is happening. So hold on; six months lie ahead of you that you will never dare risk forgetting.

★   ★   ★

"*Pausa!*" The order is shouted in the tunnel. It is three in the morning. The machines stop for half an hour, while the exhausted prisoners stretch out and try to sleep. The handling kommandos lay down their loads and collapse wherever they are. The Meister light up cigarettes, exchange pleasantries with their colleagues, and seek out comfortable corners in which to catnap. The tunnel is cold and damp, and the only noise now to be heard is the sound of the extractors along the length of the two big galleries.

Vincent climbs the ramp leading to the gallery, which follows the V-2 rocket being assembled. Last night, he had noticed Hervé during the kommando's arrival and agreed to go and visit with him during this break. Hervé works almost at the far end of the tunnel, a trip of three to four hundred yards. In the stillness, his wooden soles echo noisily, and this worries Vincent, so he tries to move very carefully. The gallery is big and quite clear, and the halls off to the right are filled with bodies scattered about or grouped together in efforts to share a bit of body heat.

The gallery walls are lined with stocks of spare parts filling shallow metal shelves in all directions. The railroad follows its route with space to pass on both sides. Toward the end, however, available space becomes confined. The shelves become real cupboards, and a buffer marks the end of track. Free space in the gallery shrinks to a passage about three yards wide. So far, everything is fine; Vincent has been on his way for only a few minutes. He is nearly there, so he can visit with Hervé for a good quarter of an hour before galloping back to his hall. What a precious fifteen minutes, when you go over your childhood and all the good years. But he and Hervé won't speak of those memories; it's no good to revisit such things like a couple of old women. Instead, they will look at each other, then tell each other, without speaking, to hold on, and then drift away on a marvelous Makhorka cigarette rolled in a bit of cement-bag paper. Their conversation is harmless, but it is kept "between the lines." Vincent leaves, and they part, each one comforted yet anxious for the other; each one thinking, "If only he can hold on; if only he doesn't let himself slip!"

Vincent is about to enter the narrower section when a silhouette suddenly emerges from a hall and into the middle of the passage. He is gripped with fear. It is an SS man, a big, slender man with shiny boots and his cap down on his forehead. Vincent can see that he holds an object unlike a truncheon but more like a whip, almost a long cane. The SS man stands, legs akimbo and hands on his thighs, staring at the frightened prisoner. Terrified, Vincent is frozen in space for a fraction of a second. He'd like to turn about and run into the darkness for his life, but his legs don't answer the impulse. Then he continues, carried on by his scarcely interrupted momentum. Words come into his head. Above all, he thinks, be transparent, as if there was nothing unusual about his traveling during the break. He raises his Mütze, his beret, in the regulation manner, puts his two hands along the open seams of his trousers, and advances, his expression empty and eyes fixed straight ahead.

"Was machst du hier, Mensch?" (What are you doing here, slime?)

The SS man doesn't look in a mood to hit anyone; he has asked a question. In the sleepy atmosphere of the tunnel, Vincent realizes that his being out of place is somewhat out of line. Even the SS respect the rest break, the letup when everybody can stretch out, but he has broken the rule allowing all prisoners the leisure of sleeping on the concrete for thirty minutes.

"*Ich will mein Kamerad sehen, Halle zwei und zwanzig.*" (I want to see my friend, Hall 22.) In that rough German, Vincent stammers out the few words that come to his mind, which is already shaken by sudden worry.

"*Kommst du mit, Drecksack.*" (Come with me, shitbag.)

No need to draw Vincent a picture; he gets in step with the SS man. He crosses the hall without turning—what prisoner would try to dash off and save himself, only to get a bullet in the back?—and heads toward the tunnel entrance.

The underground world is still asleep, and they walk over the outstretched bodies. A few waking Kapos and Vorarbeiter take on a respectful attitude, looking at Vincent with quizzical expressions. Their eyes have the look of people seeing a hearse pass by, wondering whom it might contain.

At the guard post, the SS man turns and gestures for Vincent to enter. Inside, he sees a group of civilians. They look like highwaymen to Vincent. Long black leather raincoats and Tyrolean hats hang in a line across the wall. "In the name of God, it's the Gestapo!" Vincent recognizes them at once. The Gestapo is there and in strength. They have taken over the two tables in the place and are busily filling out forms and writing reports. The air is overheated, and Vincent feels bad. He is sure that he hasn't felt such heat for a century.

A Posten with a joint missing on his index finger is fiddling with the strap of his Mauser. His nose is bent slightly to the right, giving him the appearance of a faun. Along the wall, architectural blueprints show all the halls in detail, plus the exact location of each machine. A glass-covered board holds a list of names and various instructions. The air is rank with smells of cold tobacco and bitter sweat. Vincent moves further forward, where he notices a dozen prisoners, all facing the wall. Their hands are handcuffed behind their backs. He cannot see their faces but can tell that they are in a pitiful state. The men are having a tough time staying on their feet; they stagger from left to right, and he can see coagulated blotches of blood staining their jacket collars. The hapless wretches try to hold up their trousers because the string or electric wire formerly used as belts has been taken away from them. They try to push against the wall with their heads, but a civilian guard promptly kicks each one in the small of the back, and the agony straightens them for a while.

"This is it," thinks Vincent. "I'm booked for the hanging on Sunday." His mind goes blank, his face a mask of indifference. Then he thinks about the bunker; it frightens him. What happens there? No one knows. But how many times has he seen condemned prisoners gallop from the bunker toward the gallows like puppets who seemed to look toward the rope as an escape? In the beginning, he had seen men sobbing, rolling on the ground, and crying for mercy, only to be dragged by force onto the stool. But now, with a bit tied in their mouths, they make no sound and climb onto the bench on their own. They are probably already dead, he thinks, and their awful, slow strangulation is only a formality to make their condition official.

"But I'm well and truly alive!" The protest fairly screams in his mind. "I don't want to be strangled. I've done nothing. I just wanted to see a buddy, a childhood friend, a guy I played marbles and hide-and-seek with at school. You don't hang a man, even a Häftling, because he wanted to go and see his friend." Vincent's thoughts flash images to his brain of the bunker, of the gallows, of bashed-in faces and martyred bodies, but his own body doesn't move. Months under the savage SS discipline have turned him into a perfectly depersonalized robot. He stands at rigid regimental attention, his look impersonal and empty.

The SS man goes up to the table and addresses a civilian, the chief of the Gestapo detachment. In precise terms, he describes the circumstances under which he has found Vincent prowling about the hall during the break, in a place where he should not have been. His report, given in dry military terms, is perfect, neither too long nor too short. The prisoner's behavior was suspicious.

Vincent doesn't understand a word that is being said and is almost disinterested. He has gone through a new stage in his life as a prisoner. His fate is beyond his control; he can do nothing. No doubt, he will be on the square next Sunday after roll call. He'll emerge from the bunker, hands tied behind his back, the wooden bit tied into his mouth, and will gallop with the others to the gallows. He will have to be careful that his trousers don't fall down because it looks ridiculous. Neither would he like to piss or shit his pants in front of everyone. Vincent is ready for the great departure and everything that will precede the moment.

At the table, everything seems to have been settled. The quota of arrests has been filled, and Vincent makes one person too many. Orders are orders, and there is nothing to do with an extra prisoner. Send him back to his kommando.

"Du, Drecksack, raus!" (You, shitbag, out!) With a blow of his whip, the SS man pushes Vincent out, toward the tunnel. Toward a blessed reprieve!

★   ★   ★

The long line of night-shift kommandos makes its way toward the tunnel in rows of five, those in front carrying the banner with the number of their kommando. They go in cadence, the sound of their hollowed-out clogs echoing off the walls. A Kapo, bringing up the rear, shouts out the pace: *"Zwei, drei, vier, links, links."* The first ranks follow the cadence, but farther down the ranks, it deteriorates. The lame cannot hold the pace. Swearing, the Kapos rush at men who are out of step, aiming crushing blows of their truncheons at backs and heads. As if that were not enough, an already freezing rain soaks into the uniforms and turns bandages and Russian socks alike into sticky sponges.

What's this? We aren't going toward the usual tunnel entrance but to the exit. This corresponds to the second large gallery, from which the finished V-2 rockets emerge. This change is worrisome, for these sudden changes of habit are ominous at Dora. While we wait to proceed further, the prisoners exchange questions.

"And what is this brainstorm about? We've never come this way; this is the first time. The day-shift kommandos don't seem to be arriving, either. Perhaps they're going to seal us all up in the tunnel; us on the left, the other shift on the right."

"Don't talk crazy," comes a reply from a big fellow as he tries to adjust, under his jacket, the hooded chasuble he has fashioned from a cement bag. In the rain, however, it is turning to pulp.

Another man asks, "What would they do with two teams inside? The engineers are already screaming because the work isn't going as fast as they'd like. So the SS aren't going to mess around in the tunnel just for the pleasure of upsetting us. No, it's gotta be something else. Maybe a landslide."

"A landslide? Are you crazy?"

Roger is horrified by news of catastrophes. "Well, if there has been a landslide, you'll see how everyone reacts. The SS look cool. It's not a revolt, either, or they wouldn't have brought us down into the tunnel. They would have locked us up in the camp and kept us isolated."

A revolt! An uprising that could break out at any given moment, which would mean death for all the prisoners. Then new inmates would be shipped here, and that would be the end of that.

"Hey, look. There are the day-shift guys."

There is, in fact, a column coming, which presents itself at the control post. With their numbered banner in the lead, marching at attention, berets in hand, the kommando passes before the SS man, who counts them with his cane. The men are gray and worried-looking but no more so than usual. On seeing the rain, their expressions become, if anything, a bit gloomier. On the whole, however, they look just the same as yesterday's and earlier crews. It's nine in the evening, and they hurry to go and collect their rations and go to bed, hoping no one will devise some devilish fatigue duty to rob them of sleep.

A question comes from the arriving column: "Well, then, what's happening?"

"Well, guys, you're going to have the right to see a great show, something new."

Among the new arrivals, Roger asks, "But what sort of show?"

"You'll see in a little while. You don't need to get all worked up; you'll have a surprise."

From Sergei, a thin old bit of Russian debris, *"Chto ta Koi, Franzousky?"* (What is it, Frenchy?) He, too, wonders what is going on.

"Nitchevo, tovaritch of my ass. You'll know when I do. This idiot annoys me."

Now it is his kommando's turn to head for Hall 41. In cadence, with little fingers against their trouser seams, the men pass the SS man, and he counts them by tapping his whip against their shoulders.

The column passes in front of the final control hall, which is very deep and contains the V-2s set on their fins. Then the promised spectacle meets the gaze of the prisoners. Just beyond this point, a rolling bridge blocks the whole gallery. It is used to lift the rockets from their cradles and bring them inside the hall. For the moment, this rolling bridge is blocked halfway up, at about twelve feet above the ground. All along its length dangle an obscene bunch of hanged men, a dozen. Most of their bodies have lost both trousers and shoes, and puddles of urine cover the floor. Since the ropes are long, the bodies swing gently about five feet above the floor, and you have to push them aside as you advance. As you make your way through, you receive bumps from knees and tibias soaked in urine, and the corpses, pushed against each other, begin to spin around. Their trousers and shoes have long since disappeared, recovered by careful hands. Contrary to popular legend, the dead men don't have hard-ons. Here and there under the rolling bridge, truncheons in hand, the SS watch the changing of the shifts. They are laughing; it's a big joke to these bastards.

"Hey, Fernand, you better come and see. You shouldn't miss this!"

From Hall 41, Roger sees the rolling bridge with its dozen hanging dead. He awaits the reaction of the Meister and engineers who have entered the tunnel. They stop in sudden shock. They know only too well that these tattered fragments of humanity have been liquidated—

but up until now, these executions have been handled within the comparative secrecy of the surface camp. Most of these Meister and engineers have arrived after the cutting of the tunnel was completed; they haven't been here to witness the great murder waves of autumn and winter. Oh, they have been confronted with the sight of human beings worn down to their very bones . . . but they have never seen the results of the final act, the killing itself, and this shocks them. The puny human remains dangling from the ropes are filthy. The Meister and engineers make their entry between the wall and the last body, trying to avoid any contact with the awful things. Then they move along while exchanging jokes and light banter, but they are greenish in complexion and avoid looking at any of the living prisoners.

"There, then, Roger, I think it's worth the effort." The engineer's secretary, all blonde, pretty, and attractive in her little suit and white blouse, appears at the entrance. She has worn her high-heeled red shoes today. She has moved along her way without noticing a thing, her handbag tucked under her left elbow. She pauses briefly upon seeing the spectacle of the twelve dead men dangling from the rolling bridge, defacing their nakedness, one after another. Then, not wanting to modify her route for such a thing, she pushes onward, pushing aside with disgust a denuded leg of which only skin and bone remain and, head held quite high, enters Hall 41, making her heels click with feminine emphasis on the cement pavement.

"Look at that bitch," groans Roger. In spite of her pretty face and attractive looks, she's trash just like the rest of them. "On the day when we hang these SS bastards on the rolling bridge, we should think of her as well. We can't miss her because if one day she has kids, they'll be monsters just like her, and we'll never get out of this shit!"

★   ★   ★

Henri has managed to get into the visiting room of the infirmary. He has been eaten by a fever, suffering terrible pains on the right side of his chest. "Good God," he thinks, "it's starting again, like last year. Only now it's worse!"

In front of the infirmary, he has found the door obstructed by a wailing herd. The fleshless rags of men display their wounds before the Kapo, trying to soften his heart. But he, a well-fed Pole, drives them back with truncheon blows. Curiously, he lets Henri into the barracks, undoubtedly because he is in better condition than the others.

"Komme!"

Henri ends up in front of a French doctor, realizing the fact because of the way the other man pronounces the word *komme*. That's lucky; maybe the French doctor will have more consideration for him.

"Oh, you're French, too. So, what's wrong?"

"Well, sir, I have a terrible fever and pains in my chest. I find it hard to breathe."

"You know, you can drop the 'sir,' we're all in the same boat here. Take off your jacket and shirt."

Henri strips to the waist. He is ashamed of his poor thorax and of having arms like spiders' legs. He notices that his body smells malodorous, but what is worse, his breathing is difficult, like a flimsy fireplace bellows.

The doctor spots his stethoscope at the top of Henri's chest, then on his heart and over the last ribs. "Turn around." More soundings are made upon his back, particularly in the area of the right lung.

"Breathe deeply and regularly. Good; now, cough."

A painful cough shoots pain across Henri's chest.

"Well, my boy, I can tell you that you have pleurisy in the base of your right lung. I'm going to have you hospitalized."

"If it doesn't bother you, Doc, I'd rather not."

The doctor is astonished. "But you are mad! Listen, and then you'll see what I mean." The doctor shakes Henri's chest, and he can hear the sound of a wave within himself. "You're full of water. You're risking your life. You know, the infirmary isn't like it was last winter. They aren't transferring our patients, and we manage to cure people. Pleurisy can be treated if we have the patients here at hand; otherwise, there are no miracles. How long have you had this condition?"

"I had a pleurisy last winter."

"Were you treated, Henri?"

"No. I didn't want to go to the infirmary."

"Last year," said the doctor, "you were right. The infirmary was best avoided. But you were very lucky; you must have a very solid constitution. But now it's a different story: With a second pleurisy and that lung full of water, it's a 50–50 chance that you'll make it for more than three days."

"I couldn't care less. I don't want to go into the infirmary. I've never seen any of my buddies again once they've gone into that damned infirmary!"

"Well, do whatever you will, but I'll give you an order form. With that, you can come back tomorrow, and I'll give you a lumbar tapping. It'll relieve you greatly for a while. Afterwards, it'll be up to you to hold on. Here, take these aspirin for your fever, they'll help. I wish you good luck, my boy. And, deep down, I understand your feelings about this place."

Henri gets dressed. His eyes, raging with the fever, find it difficult to stay open. He thinks, "I only hope that the Americans arrive quickly. Otherwise, I'm done for."

⋆   ⋆   ⋆

Zawatsky, the company responsible for production of the big rockets, has, it seems, made a great fuss with the Nazi powers about its workers.

This does not, of course, cover the listings of prisoners who are ill, injured, or dead. For these, the SS has all the desirable official documents; they are part of the normal run of operations, and nothing more can be said about them.

The reports available consist, in fact, of lists of prisoners regularly signed on in the kommando workforces who, one day, don't appear anymore. Zawatsky has encountered delays in production and has discovered that the rockets delivered are of a very inferior quality.

The minister concerned must have commented adversely to other officials who, in their turn, complained to the SS of deliberate poor workmanship—or sabotage—and, as a direct result, the SS will increase the number of daily hangings.

For the disappearance of prisoners, they will now systematically seek out all the Zawatsky surface workers who have managed to become incorporated into other kommandos. Instructions relative to this order will be given to the Arbeitsstatistik.

In the small working class of the camp between the powerful and the lowest, this produces consternation. A good number of prisoners, especially those with a chance for some rest in the infirmary or those who, thanks to the help of a well-placed friend, have managed to be assigned to duties on the surface, share a sudden fear.

Some had been assigned to digging or construction kommandos, and though these might be murderous, they were much preferable to the tunnel, where death was almost a certainty. Afterwards, they made up the pool of workers from which the SS drew for their transfers to Ellrich and Harzungen. In fact, they had only been able to postpone worse duties as new tunnels came due for digging, and they would leave for these assignments in far worse physical condition than they had known on arrival at Dora.

Some men had managed to get along for a time in the same kommandos, but death caught up with them in the form of a clubbing, if not a terminal dysentery or proliferation of bacilli. Fate, in Dora, was inescapable.

A certain number, though, mostly Poles, have managed to escape the worst of it. They have jobs without responsibilities in the administrative services, the kitchen, the Effektenkammer, and the infirmary. These are extremely interesting from the point of view of living conditions. The men are Stubendienst or Schreiber in the barracks. This allows them to get soup and potatoes at will, have good clothes, and often have a bed of their own.

A few have even been allowed to let their hair grow, which is the ne plus ultra (ultimate privilege) of importance in Dora. Thanks to their jobs and the relationships that thereby develop, they get into a series of profitable little schemes that support a clientele of compatriots, which flatters their vanity. They are sure of themselves. For example, it would never cross the mind of a basic prisoner to enter the roll call square during the day. He will walk along pathways around the square because it seems to be a dangerous place and, for all he knows, forbidden. But the privileged prisoner walks across the concrete space with the calm and assurance given by his clean and well-ironed clothes, rested face, and well-fed silhouette.

Now everything is to be reexamined, following the directives from Zawatsky. It's a catastrophe. You can feel the tension of worry running throughout the "middle-class" prisoners. In the barracks, the Stubendienst speak in low voices. In the infirmary, dismayed minds feel the blade of the administrative guillotine threatening their existence. Within the kitchen and the Effektenkammer, which contain the most beautiful and easy jobs in the camp, all the men are worried and begin to look like desperate animals. It isn't possible; how can they play tricks with our fear? Something must be done, but what can we do?

We can start by trying to seduce the chief; perhaps he'll be able to do something for us. He only has to say that we're indispensable, that losing us would disorganize the operation, and that it would be difficult to restart such a well-tuned machine. Without boasting, we can say we're so good at our jobs that it will be impossible to find someone else as good as us.

But the chief, as a rule, scoffs at the sentiments of his subordinates. If the orders come through, they will be followed, and the little people will taste the joys of labor in the tunnel again. In the chief's view, all these workers are so fat, like real pigs, that the tunnel will do them some good. Shake any old tree and such types will fall by the hundreds. So the chiefs keep firm faces and make it known that it is useless to protest.

So we will approach officials in the Arbeitsstatistik, the Politische Abteilung, and the Arbeitseinsatz (manpower allocation office). They are important people who can't be approached as easily as a bank clerk.

So these people roam around their barracks in the evening. We let them know that we have come from so-and-so, who is a friend of so-and-so, who knows the official. If the official agrees to meet the unfortunate seeker of influence on the doorstep, he confirms that the rumors are correct but that the actual search has not yet started. As soon as the official orders are given, all the "gate-crashers" will be tracked down. To deal with a gate-crasher and try to get him "approved" seems the a priori goal. It's difficult, but if something can be done, we'll do it.

"You say that you're indispensable in the kitchen or infirmary? Perhaps you are, but it's not up to me to judge. If your Kapo feels that it's necessary to keep you, he will tell us, and your case will be presented to the SS for approval. That's all I can tell you for now since we don't know yet how things are going to be done."

The men holding little jobs begin to look more closely at the tramps around them, and their chests tighten with worry. The easy luxury of potatoes and soup, the tobacco they can buy without any problems, the decent clothing, sometimes tailored, will all disappear. And those with hair, will it be shaved off? It is out of the question for anyone to have a good head of hair when the Kapo himself still hasn't received permission to let his own hair grow!

And what of the danger, the beatings, and sudden death? All the terrors of the past that had been left to others less fortunate might now become their own fearsome daily reality. You don't easily return to a witches' cauldron once you have managed to escape its clutches. At the same time, the tramps also look at the minichiefs, those rulers of the selective soup ladle, the knights of the broom that caresses the jutting animal ribs and denuded skulls. These are the unapproachables who force the workers to wash and clean even their footwear before entering the holy of holies of the kitchen barracks.

The tramps begin speaking loudly, with expressive glances for emphasis, of handling kommandos that have become lovely messes, just like last winter. Once again, their prisoners fall and roll about in the sticky, freezing mud while the baton blows fall upon them as thick as rain. The losses are heavy, and it seems the SS are looking for new recruits. Some kommandos are actually growing bigger because the tunnel work is running at a good pace, and the Nazis are bringing in the manufacture of some of the items most difficult to transport: the liquid-oxygen tanks and the unique fiberglass material that turns men into bleeding hedgehogs. As if that were not enough, the Kapos of these kommandos are maniacs with their clubs. They have even been heard to remark that they can't stand even the sight of ex–surface prisoners, with their self-satisfied looks, nice clothing, and manicured fingernails.

As a result, some of these small bourgeois try to be reported ill and hospitalized. A few manage to do it, but they are only putting off the big day of the Kapo's vengeance. In any case, they find themselves facing nurses and orderlies who are in the same boat and who look resentfully upon allowing these men, so much more full of health, to take up beds and demand the diet soup, while they themselves may be living their own last days of plenty. It is a situation generating bitterness and powerful enmity. Most of the caretakers, however, prefer to remain at their posts, ready to follow the turn of events and, eventually, to act at just the right moment.

They realize all too well that they are trapped in a ferocious world, one without pity, a world where a man's life has no value whatsoever beyond the cost of his upkeep during several weeks or months of life and, finally, his incineration.

For a while, these privileged ones had been anesthetized by the fantastic riches of unlimited access to soup, to comfortable leather shoes, to the window through which, warmly dressed and comfortable themselves, they could see the less fortunate kommandos leave morning and night, to the bottle of alcohol and the cigarettes shared with their friends during quiet, cozy moments, and to that relaxed quarter of an hour allowed by the SS Blockführer that he shares with some Untermenschen but only with clean subordinates who smell of good French soap and wax.

Alas! It is all only temporary; it only exists because the SS want it that way. They have created their own world, well sealed off from the outside. The routing is one-way; you may enter, but you cannot leave.

This savage world, with big chiefs, midchiefs, and underchiefs, has been organized knowingly, thoroughly, almost lovingly by these strange, inhuman minds. It is an isolated world in vitro, which you penetrate by the air lock of "transport" and where you are supplied with the equipment deemed adequate for your job by the masters. As with all worlds of this kind, life is organized with its own unique rules, so long as the deadly acid is not spilled. But at any instant, the masters can pour in some new acid or simply adjust the balance of the organism and make it swing toward death.

The same causes always produce the same effects. When these kitchen and Effektenkammer prisoners receive stripes to put on their sleeves, they soon find that the sleeves aren't nice enough and look for better clothes. Losing all notion of where they are, suddenly nothing is good enough for them. Now they are out of the handling kommandos. Their uniforms are recut by fine tailors, and the striped shirts give way to civilian shirts, functional but of good value.

At the other extreme, when times become worrisome and uncertain, you must never show off such scandalous wealth. You need standard but solid clothes, warm and comfortable but not the least bit pretentious. You must not provoke some future Kapo by wearing an extravagant outfit that will make him feel envious of you; on the contrary, you must give him confidence and fill his head with the idea that you believe he can become an excellent Schreiber.

But this isn't the hour for dreaming. All those thoughts are unreal. Dora has to be looked at realistically, and it is enough to make your blood run cold. For Dora is now and has always been death. It is a death that can strike in many ways and that has nothing to do with pyramids of age, or diplomas, or strength, religion, diets, and all of the bric-a-brac that fills minds and bodies outside the barbed wire.

You only have to look around to see which men have survived in this potpourri of terror. First of all, there are the biggest bandits, the sadists or brutal killers who have bought their own lives for the price of thousands of others dead. Then there are the politicians, who judged it right to sacrifice whole groups of the uninitiated to a cause.

Even if you are a Schreiber, a Stubendienst, or an orderly in the infirmary, you have zero weight compared with the real aristocracy of Dora, which holds all the power and will be ruthless in keeping it.

But . . . on the day when that power falls, vengeance will be swift. The monsters will lose their armlets of authority, and within a few hours, at the hands of their former victims, they will be torn into shredded bits of bloody flesh. As for many of those nothings, those assholes, the wild horde will have its revenge for days and weeks during which it will be their turn to cry out in agony. The Russians whom they have kept at bay with their little stripes will then turn loose all the savagery and hate within them. What were once sneers will become deliberate violence. The Russians remember being surrounded by madmen who were after their skins. They survived, through circumstances unlikely ever to recur.

But the Westerners, verbal idiots unable to defend themselves against such mindless savagery, are almost all dead. Only the hardiest have survived, and these might remember all the bastardly things done to them that they would like to erase from human behavior. However, they are the only ones who, if things go wrong, can save us. They are so stupid that they won't be able to hold a grudge, and they will forget us after a few days of telling-off and a little ragging. *Mon Dieu*, how hard it is to be back in the real world of Dora, this unearthly shitpile that swallows men by the thousands.

Above us all, on the slopes, the crematorium has begun giving off smoke again, the crematorium no one has looked at for ages.

★   ★   ★

Marching along in a typically Russian mode, knees slightly bent, left foot in line with his march, and his right foot scraping the ground at a forty-five-degree angle, Sachka paces up and down the hall. With his beret pushed far forward just above the eyebrows, his stealthy glance takes in everything. His squat body is clad in a ripped-up, filthy uniform. The number on his jacket is almost illegible, and the one on his trousers has disappeared. His clogs are held together by an impossible net of wires. Sachka appears to be prowling haphazardly, as if he were looking for some random spoil, but, in fact, he knows exactly where he intends to go.

Like a hungry animal, he has noticed that during the rations handout, Victor swallows down his soup but keeps the bread, margarine, and sausage. He eats half of it during the break and the rest on returning to the barracks, which causes a lot of gastric acidity and desperate hunger in the men around him. But Victor doesn't care; it's his ration, and he can eat it in his own way. If the others want to gulp everything down at once and then go twenty-four hours without food, it's their business. Victor feels that even though it's hard to keep food when you are hungry, a certain discipline and restraint in that direction are necessary if you want to survive.

Victor is a storeman with Gilles in the store at the far end of the hall, near the passage that joins the large entrance gallery. Among these stores, there are piles of varying bundles of metal, long, short, and flat-ended, some as sharp as razors. He has used one of these sharp pieces to cut his bread and spread his margarine. At break time, he puts his tiny provisions on the little table near the entrance. Gilles, who has seen it before, no longer wants to watch the show, which twists his guts. He is going to lie down.

It is the moment Sachka has waited for. He has carefully spied out both the place and Victor's habits. He knows that the bread, margarine, and sausage are going to be on the table for a few seconds. All he needs to do is to slip his hands inside swiftly, snatch the provisions, then race off to the gallery, where he'll lie down in the midst of a handling kommando. Victor and Gilles won't have any idea as to who carried out the theft.

Sachka draws closer, straight on but a little to one side, so as not to give the impression that he is moving in. Through narrowed eyes he spots the table. It's OK, the bread is there. He corrects his approach, passes in front of the door, and, crack, seizes the bread with a quick hand. But Victor returns at the same moment. His reflexes are instantaneous; he wasn't born yesterday. He sees the hand stealing his bread, and in a flash, he grips the Russian sleeve and pulls hard. Thrown off balance by this unexpected reaction, Sachka falls inside the store, the bread still in his clutch. Victor calls Gilles for help, and the three men roll to the ground.

There isn't a single cry, it's a savage fight among beasts. There are silent blows, chops, punches, clawing, and biting. But Sachka has cat-

like strength and suppleness. Street fighting holds no secrets from
him, the knife-armed combat where everything is allowed, including
his opponent's death. With his wild kicking, strangleholds, and
thumbs gouging their eyes, he is about to get the better of Victor and
Gilles, who are not up to the job of defeating such a wild beast.

Suddenly, Victor feels his hand on the knife that has fallen from the
table. He takes it, stands, and throws a violent thrust toward Sachka's
face. But Sachka has seen the movement and quickly steps aside. The
knife opens up his cheek from jawbone to neck. With a desperate leap,
he escapes from the two Frenchmen and runs off toward the gallery.
He has dropped the bread.

The two friends have fallen on all fours, panting. Victor has also injured himself with the knife. His hand is bleeding.

Gilles is trembling, his nerves taut. "You see what happens with
your stupid ideas of wanting to save your bread? You'll get us murdered. You'd be better off doing like everyone else and eat the rations
when you get them. Besides, it upsets my stomach to see you stuffing
yourself all alone in your corner. It's inhuman."

"In any case, that bastard Sachka didn't get the bread," Victor pants.
"I left a souvenir on his face he won't forget, and he isn't going to
come prowling near us again."

With a bit of cement bag, Victor wipes off the blood running down
his hand. The cut isn't deep, but like all injuries in this filthy place, it
could become infected. He'd better put some cement on it. It will
make a horrible growth, but cement is a good disinfectant.

Gilles is not as complacent. He fought for something that didn't
concern him, and now he also risks suffering for the consequences of
his action.

"But, Victor, you poor idiot, do you think things will end there, that
it's all finished? I think it's just begun. This bastard Sachka is a real
hardnose. He belongs to a bunch of Russian gangsters who steal and
pillage all over the place. Now he'll stir up his friends, and one of
these nights, they'll have our skin. You know them as well as I do, and
you know it won't bother those bastards a bit. From now on, we could
have our guts ripped out at any moment."

"But what would you have me do, Gilles? I couldn't let him steal
my bread. No! Why not just give him my rations every day?"

"Don't be stupid, Victor. But since it's going to turn bad, we should
have killed him and thrown his body into a dark corner. Everybody
would have thought it was just an account being settled, and we'd be
out of the act."

"Well, it's easy to say that now. Anyway, it's too late. He's made his
getaway."

Gilles thinks for a moment. He knows exactly what is going to happen. After dispersion of the kommandos on the roll call square at about six in the evening—tomorrow night or in a month—a dozen Russians will quickly jump Victor and Gilles and batter them to death. And no one will dare help them; the execution will have been discreet.

"Listen, Victor, you know what we're going to do? We'll see Vassili. He's a good guy, and he has some clout with the kommando Russki. We'll tell him what's happened. We'll ask him to calm down the Russians and to arrange things. I think he can do it because Vassili doesn't like having his countrymen being viewed as a horde of murdering thieves. Of course, you'll also pass him your ration of bread."

"Pass him my bread?" Victor is shocked. "We nearly had our throats cut by a Russian for some bread, and you want me to hand over the same bread to another Russian? Are you out of your mind or what?"

Gilles begins to lose his cool. He'll blow up if this idealistic fool goes on.

"Victor, all of this was your own doing. Showing off your bread under the noses of starving men shouldn't be allowed. In itself, it's a provocation for murder. Over and above that, you've gotten me into the act. So it's quite simple. You can consider that your shit of a loaf now belongs to Vassili, and if you dare cut a single slice, I'll personally open your stomach."

Victor looks at his ration, now destined for the Soviet camp. From tomorrow on, if this business is settled, he promises that he will eat up his ration immediately!

★   ★   ★

Now a new rumor sweeps through the camp. The SS have arrested some Frenchmen. Exact numbers aren't known but likely five or six. There have always been arrests, but these are usually of prisoners recruited by the Gestapo to complete their inquiries, or of saboteurs, or in cases of planned rebellions. As a rule, this sort of thing doesn't create much of a fuss. The SS lead the men who have pissed on a machine or have taken a swing at a Vorarbeiter off to the bunker, and the whole business ends a few days later in agony at the end of a rope.

But this is more serious. This time, "personality" prisoners who have held key positions in the camp administration have been arrested. They aren't well known but have been well placed in different sectors. This has brought deep concern to the French colony. Have the SS come to think that the French have become too influential in the camp and decided to strike with an iron fist, perhaps with a pogrom affecting all Frenchmen down to the lowest level? Or do German prisoners want to recover command of all the machinery that was beginning to escape their control, and have they set us up with the idea of breaking up the French expansion within camp affairs? We just don't know.

The arrests could also be political, but most men don't see it that way. In the first place, palace revolutions have never been of especial interest to the small and obscure, but in the second place and perhaps more important, the elements at Dora aren't even assembled for such a conspiracy. In the concentration camps, the only real political force is the Communist party. And at Dora, Communists are few, at least among the non-German prisoners.

So it is thought that some Frenchmen in strategic posts, who knew of SS decisions, have formed a Resistance group within Dora.

When you have handled SS dossiers, when your ears are wide open, and when you regularly meet those who make decisions determining the prisoners' futures, you see things from a perspective that escapes most people. You put in a word here and there to save friends, and one day, a group is formed. Its purpose is certainly to save the greatest number by trying, obliquely, to oppose SS decisions. It's risky, however, because the slightest misstep could set off an SS witch-hunt, with incalculable results.

It has already happened among the Russians. A systematic search was made for all of the political members who might influence their groups, and those men were immediately hung.

Yet the French feel proud that their countrymen, even at the risk of great mortal danger and suffering, have continued a fight they could have avoided. Here are men more fortunate than most, with superior food rations, fairly decent clothing, and an enviable situation compared to the rest of us. It would be human to profit from their luck and let the rest go—but for one irrational fact. The Resistance workers are fools who have thrown themselves into the cause of helping and saving less fortunate fellow prisoners.

When France collapsed in 1940, a few men lifted their heads against the invaders. Like ants trying with their tiny legs to dig through concrete, they were caught in the act, but they were determined. They continued their resistance in the concentration camps, disregarding the risks and refusing to think of possible savage consequences to themselves.

By now, the French have regained some much-needed esteem from the other nationalities. Whatever absurdity there was in the reproaches against them, they overcame the sniggers concerning France's attitude of earlier years. The mistrust of the Czechs and the incredible animosity of the Poles had, for a time, generated tragic results against the possibility of the group's survival. The Belgians and

Dutch, who had nothing against the French, had somewhat reluc-
tantly stood up on their side. But the Russians, in particular, who so
easily forgot their government's unbelievable double-dealing in the
Nazi-Soviet pact and the division of Poland . . . these Russians had
only mistrust and contempt for the French, such bourgeois little chau-
vinists.

These earlier prejudices come under brisk reexamination with the
arrests. Until now, the French had the numbers but didn't make the
weight. The Normandy landings had raised their prestige, but with
the war seeming so long, the old stories had returned. They went as far
as discussing the reasons for their presence in these camps. Stories of
the black market and sharp affairs, not to mention the fantasies related to the legends of la minette, had tarnished our image. The ladder
had to be climbed again, and it's been done. These men arrested, who
had thrown themselves into the madness of Dora, sway opinion
throughout the concentration camp.

Life in the Nazi camps is Russian roulette in the flesh, a permanent
game of life and death. Old concentration camp inmates who had held
on for more than a few months need reasons for continuing the fight.
Here it is so easy to lie down and wait for the final blow. Within minutes, the affair is settled, and one is in paradise among the veterans of
Dora!

If you have nothing to back you up, what's the use of being a clay
pot going against one of iron? But if you can suddenly whisk trump
cards like these men just arrested—which no one of any nationality
has done—then everything changes. Even the Czechs, those cold witnesses, give us some consideration, and to be considered by the
Czechs at Dora is the best recommendation that can exist.

As for the Poles and Russians, their truce will last only until the day
they return to postwar life, if such a day can ever arrive. But here, the
inch-by-inch struggle for life will have to go on, an endless fight
within the trap, facing an existence that can turn to death in seconds.
But now, thanks to a handful of dedicated men, their fellow Frenchmen have become respected guys, real men! In the stock exchange for
shields of honor, the French have scored highly.

★   ★   ★

A strange and mysterious kommando exists in Dora, where no one
speaks to anyone else. It was formed in May: the crematorium kommando. Up above, on the edge of the hill, there is a group of prisoners
we seldom see but who are never approached. Only the Todträger, the
undertakers, go as far as their workplace. The undertakers carry the

dead from the infirmary and the work kommandos. The bodies are naked, identified only by the numbers marked on their stomachs in indelible ink. The crematorium Schreiber notes the numbers, and then the bodies are taken to the stockroom and piled atop each other like so many logs to a cord of timber. The furnace operators then come in to use up the stock of corpses as needed. They pull on heads or legs, and if all goes well, the bodies slide easily. But there are moments when bodies have become entwined or stuck together, and then the prisoners have to use hooks that penetrate the skin and unravel body parts and organs. The bodies are placed on a sort of giant shovel and thrust into the incinerator. The furnace door is closed, and that number of once living men leave Dora for good as wisps of smoke bound for the heavens.

All this is known by hearsay and guesswork, although no one wants—or has the right—to go and see how things really happen. No man wants to go near the crematorium. You see it all too clearly; it's there before your eyes, and its constantly smoking chimney gives witness to its endless work.

The Todträger who enter the building each day are never questioned, and they never speak about its operations. If there is a taboo subject at Dora, this is it; yet death is a part of the daily routine, touched upon with no particular recognition. You see men's dead bodies every day, and if you chance to look at one, death has become such a daily experience that the memory is lost in minutes.

If death is accepted as an inevitable, normal consequence of man's existence in a Nazi camp, then the final treatment of one's own body remains as a support to reality. The prisoners are used to seeing the piles of corpses stacked in front of the infirmary door; it bothers no one and doesn't really attract attention. However, if the same pile were seen at the crematorium, it would bring about shocks of horror and denial, a subconscious reaction from the depths of being.

Thus, all the prisoners are called upon to become martyrs of this insane planet, and they have accepted the supreme sacrifice as inevitable. They can't retreat; it is their destiny. A body, then, is no more than the envelope that temporarily houses each one of them. It is of only secondary significance, and the multiplication of these dead envelopes only serves to make them a commonplace thing.

At the same time, the way in which said envelopes are disposed of, the manner in which they are stacked and piled like deadwood—so far from the traditional cremation process used in many nations—is taken as a final gesture of mistrust among men who, in one way or another, have set themselves against the German state of Hitler. If the SS could have gotten rid of the bodies by dumping them into the toilets and flushing them away, they would surely have done so.

The recruitment of a crematorium kommando is done in a strange way. Ordinarily, when a kommando is to be made up, the Arbeitsstatistik has two solutions. If the team needs specialists, then professionals, electricians, plumbers, or mechanics are called for. If hands are needed for digging or handling, they are just chosen at random. All that is known and done openly. However, no one has ever heard of the method used in selecting a crematorium group. Nobody has apparently been able to say, "My friend so-and-so who was with me has been sent to the crematorium kommando." The questions remain: Who are these men, and where do they come from? The answers are obviously known within the Arbeitsstatistik, but no one would ever dare to go there and ask.

There is, in Dora, as in the other camps, a subclass of prisoners who can be convenient for such assignments. They are the NN, or the "Nacht und Nebel" (Night and Fog) group. Prisoners in this group can neither write to their families nor receive mail, for whatever reasons. They are kept under special surveillance in a secret area of the camp. Could they simply be ordinary prisoners transported here for such a purpose? Poles who came from Auschwitz say that anyone there can be assigned to a crematorium kommando. The prisoners therein receive better rations, but, from time to time, the SS liquidates the entire kommando. Therefore, it's an extremely high-risk assignment.

The prisoners we can see near the crematorium make us feel bad. If we happen to glance in their direction, we see them entering and leaving the building, talking among themselves, and occasionally laughing. They appear well clothed and wear leather shoes. They seem relaxed and don't appear to fear the beatings. When the Todtträger arrive at the door with their loads of bodies, the Kapo or Schreiber comes out and examines the delivery just like some butcher receiving cattle or mutton carcasses. The number of "pieces" is counted, the forms are signed, the job is discussed, they laugh a little, and the undertakers go off to pick up the next shipment.

These prisoners do the most terrifying work. Nobody would want to change places with them, even in exchange for as much soup and bread as he might desire. It is a cursed kommando that makes you shiver to think of it. We are ready to do anything, dig a new tunnel if need be, rather than do work like that. These poor guys must be drugged or have passed all limits of dehumanization to live with such horror day after day. Having to stick a grappling iron into the pile of bodies to pull them out, one after another, then to open the furnace and smell the redolence of a burned body, then to push the next corpse onto the big shovel and push it right into the oven—here is enough to kill any man of decent sensitivity. It even appears that this kommando has to open the mouths of the dead and search about inside with pliers to extract solid gold teeth that are already black with coagulated blood. These hapless men, living nightmares and beasts of hell, their dreams must be filled with empty orbits and mouths spitting out endless pints of rotten blood. Wherever you may be, stay where you are; you frighten us beyond reason!

6

THE WINTER SNOWS

"My God, it's already started, just like last year! What's all this muck?"

Marc slips in a puddle of mud already trampled a hundred times. Hands in front, he falls forward into the slimy soup. The entire front of his coat is covered up to his chin with the sticky, frozen mess. Ironface lets out a howl, and the Kapo rushes at Marc and clubs him. The Russians are pulling against each other on a machine that has slipped off its runners and is sloping dangerously. Everyone is shouting, and the Kapo is clubbing backs and necks indiscriminately. Searchlights at the tunnel entrance light the area like a sort of metal fairground, and the rain, which has fallen continuously for several days, has turned the workyard into a gigantic mire.

"*Franzous, lizopizdi, scheisse marschieren!*" (Frenchmen, pussy lickers, shitty marchers!)

"Shut up, you asshole Russki. Go and get fucked by hounds!"

The Vorarbeiter has returned with a steel bar to be used as a lever. Some men push against the bar, while others get a grip under the machine and lift it up. They pant and shout *"Dawai"* (Quick!) and *"Bystro!"* (Quick!) feverishly. They retrieve the roller, which had torn away, and put it back in its proper place. Rain and sweat alike run down the prisoners' backs, and each man's clothes seem to weigh a ton.

Marc is the only Frenchman left in the handling kommando. All the others have either died, have been sent to Ellrich, or have been transferred to the tunnel. Unhappily, Marc had been so sure that the war would end soon that he didn't try to improve his situation. Why change, he had thought, since he'd be back home in a month or so? Poor Marc, his tombstone might well carry the epitaph, "Died of pernicious optimism."

The handling kommandos, which had become less murderous during the summer, now have the highest death rate. First came rain and mud, followed shortly by snow and freezing cold, and then came the arrival of hundreds of machines of every sort from every part of the Reich. Whole trains have followed one another on the side line to Dora. Because of the Soviet advance, they must dismantle all factories that could be captured by Russian forces. The Germans are also forced to retrieve and ship out all usable equipment from enterprises flattened by enemy bombs. All these materials are loaded aboard railway cars and forwarded to Dora.

The tunnel entrance workyard is the same confused mélange as it was last year; a weird bric-a-brac of machine tools, lathes, and drills, bores, planes ad infinitum. They are scattered by the hundreds in the mud, and their outlines reflect in ponds that have formed. At night, under the rain and spotlights, you'd think it resembled the superstructure of a nightmare ship.

The crew is present, but it is made up of mad seamen, whose petty officers strike them with clubs again and again. Different teams are working against each other. Rollers dig out channels of unsuspected depth. Narrow-gauge trucks with steel wheels sink to their axles in the mire, and stout ropes are needed to pull them clear, then drag them to the next hole. It is bedlam.

Some of the machines are packed in crates covered with tar paper. The rain, however, has penetrated the paper, drowning the delicate parts. When you try to handle one of these crates, your fingers puncture the softened paper, and gallons of water spurt on your trousers and shoes. When this happens, prisoners jump back, swearing, and the crate slides into the mud. Then the men have to lean it to one side onto one roller and hold it straight while the other roller is put back in place. All this gives rise to a multitude of suction noises echoing those of the men's clogs.

The mud is everywhere, sovereign and icily triumphant. Thick layers soon build up on your chest and back. It reaches as far as your belt, then runs back down inside your trousers to the Russian socks, which roll up and bulge, tearing your skin open.

The mud gets into your eyes, nose, and eyelashes. It gets into your ears and into your mouth with a dirty taste of fuel oil. After being soaked for hours, the skin on your fingers becomes so softened that the mud cuts out horrible grooves, which become infected. Because of your uncoordinated body movements, the skin on your stomach gets the same treatment. Twelve hours in this rain and mud is an incredible nightmare. Afterward, you no longer even want to go back to the barracks. You'd prefer to lie down right where you are and wait for the end.

But the twelve hours aren't over; the night has only just begun. Now there are alerts. For some time, Allied bombers have flown over Dora in huge formations, the RAF Bomber Command by night and the U.S. Eighth Air Force by day. The cry goes up: *"Flieger-Alarm!"* and everything goes dark. Then there is a feeling of panic; you must drop everything and run for the tunnel.

The men slip and slide in the mudholes, many losing their clogs and hopping to the entrance. The Kapos and Vorarbeiter shout, curse, and kick the forms held in the mud.

In the tunnel itself, confusion rules. It's as black as pitch, and the last soaked souls, blocked by the mass of prisoners who preceded them, are jammed together. The SS arrive and begin clubbing heads to get this magma into motion. Once the prisoners are inside, it becomes silent, and you can only hear the sound of the rain. Somewhere off in the sky, very far away, so high that any rain is far below them, beings from another world, chewing their gum, are about to dish out fitting punishment to the Führer's Third Reich.

End of the alert. The lights come back on; the men are feverish and haggard. But prisoners aren't allowed to have feelings. The clubbings begin again, and you have to get out as fast as possible under the rain of blows and insults.

On the surface, everything is desolate. All these machines, which are useless here, continue to arrive from all directions and have to be taken into the tunnel; they'll be dragged, pushed, pulled inside, and left against the walls. We'll never manage it; there are just too damned many. The ground outside has turned into a massive soup with multicolored streaks, and the situation worsens from night to night. If this rain keeps up, we won't need rollers but a small fleet of boats, barges, and mud dredges. In some places, the mud is as deep as a man's legs, and new routes are needed to avoid these quagmires. Teams of laborers try to solidify them by dumping in loads of stones, a hellish job.

As if there were nothing more important, the SS, in their long green raincoats with black tabs, run here and there, hunting out unfortunates who have just gotten their breath back. These black angels of Hitler have found that it's less profitable to carry out daily executions of half a dozen or more themselves—a waste of time without any real effect on the general atmosphere. Instead, by transferring the terror into the hands of the all too willing Kapos and Vorarbeiter, the results are ten or twenty times better. Even Ironface, most brutal of the sadists, understands the benefits in this system.

Relentlessly, Ironface prowls the alleys, the streets and lanes, the cul-de-sacs and twisting ways within the stock area. The rain that makes his oilskins shine also makes him almost invisible in the midst of so much metalwork. He lurks in shadowy areas, camouflaged at the corner of alleys, sees the groups working and gesturing to one another, and seeks out a prey. He doesn't have long to wait this time; he marks his victim.

Marc is with his Russian teammates in the middle of an alley. They have to carry a big crate to the trolley. It is at the end of a muddy trench. With no way of going forward, it would soon disappear into the hole. With his philosophical mind and his pidgin German, Marc tries a bit of high strategy. "There's too much water here. It's impossible. This other way is better. No holes." The narrow eyes of the Russians—better called wolves—shine under their berets. They have stuck their hands in their pockets, the rain running down their jackets. One of them answers Marc.

"Du, Franzous, du bist verrückt. Wasser, kein Wasser, das ist ganz egal." (You, Frenchman, you're crazy. Water or no water, it's all the same.) "We couldn't care less; we're going to throw this fucking thing into the hole."

The Russians laugh. "Wolves, that's what they are," thinks Marc. "I had to come here to see that. If I'd been told, I wouldn't have believed it. These guys are crazy!"

One Russian walks away from the team. He goes and pisses against a crate.

At that instant, Ironface steps out, virtually on top of the team. The men are glued in place, standing to attention. "Kapo!" he howls.

The Kapo, who was a few yards away, rushes forward. He sees the prisoners standing at attention, their berets in their hands. The pisser also has his beret in his hand, but now he is pissing on his cloak. The Kapo sees the situation at a glance. With his club poised, he lands on the Russian and strikes with brutal force. The Russian gives a horrible cry and falls, his broken arm hanging at an unbelievable angle to his shoulder.

Ironface comes closer. His boots have just a few spots of mud along the sides. He looks down at the agonized Russian. The man's broken arm has no more strength, and its inert hand sticks into the mud. *"Prima!"* Ironface laughs and stands clear. His oilskin catches the glint of the searchlights. He walks along the crates and machines where the ground is still firm. "Bunch of shit! If you're looking for trouble, you're going to have some."

The Kapo is completely mad. His thick woolen cloak, soaked with rain, must weigh a ton.

"Throw that trash in a corner. We'll pick him up in the morning if he's still alive."

The team regroups, and the Kapo takes charge. They'll use planks to make a gangway over the mudholes. Marc takes two planks and places them as well as he can. If it isn't just right, the operation will be a catastrophe; the load will become stuck in the mud, and a lifting hoist will be needed to get it out. Faced with potential disaster, the Kapo makes a heroic decision. He puts down his club, bends down, and pushes along with the prisoners. The planks bend and groan, the team shouts, swears, and curses, and the crate is over. The job is done, the hole is crossed. There is a trolley a little way off, and one of the Russians runs to get it.

The Kapo is proud of himself. He laughs and flexes his biceps. He is still the man he was before the camps. The prisoners laugh with him. Kapo, the big chief! *"Danke viel mal, Kapo, du bist stark."* (Thanks a lot, Kapo, you're a strong man.) For next to nothing, this idiot Kapo would go half-naked to be admired.

It is still raining as the hours tick by. From time to time, the din of the work area is broken by cries of pain or distress. The night seems an eternity—the long night of winter. When crates and machines arrive at the normal track, they are loaded onto flatcars and pushed into the tunnel.

Although it doesn't rain in the tunnel, there is a glacial dampness invading body and mind. Although the physical effort is less, anguish nonetheless grips the prisoners. They don't feel the wild, uncontrolled, howling death of the surface workyard; it is something else. Voices are kept almost to a whisper. You are scared.

It is a strange world, frightening, inhuman. This unearthly place has held us in its grip since we arrived at Buchenwald, after three deadly days and nights in cattle cars, followed by the "grand reception" organized by the ever bloodthirsty SS. Your grandchildren, if you live to have any, will never believe this!

Suddenly, we met up with our first "extraterrestrials"—quiet men who looked like the living dead. The same living dead are also in the tunnel. They don't seem to have a rough time of it; they do their jobs, and things go on. Strange glimmers shine out of the workshops.

The flatbed trucks arrive at their destination, and the machines are unloaded. Lined up along the walls, they are covered with water, grease, and oil. The crates have lost their tar-paper wrappings. These bits of tar paper are now hidden, cut up into hooded chasubles under the prisoners' coats.

The machines look dirty; they are dripping all over and will soon begin to rust. There are good jobs ahead: Rub down all of this with sandpaper and a soft rag. It will be fun. Why, if we could manage to get signed up for that sort of thing, it could be stretched out for months. We could have our asses on stools, and we could talk with neighbors. Machines of this type are fragile, you know. You have to blow out all the little holes and talc their bottoms and bring up a good, gleaming shine. Kid stuff!

With the trucks unloaded, we have to go back outside into that freezing rain. For two or three days, the temperature has fallen steadily, and snow is expected. Now the men and women of the hills, those jolly mountain folk, can enjoy their skiing vacations. Seen from here, it is all very interesting. You vacationers will see the first snowfall of the season and whoop with joy! A Merry Christmas for Christ's sake!

At Dora itself, the spotlights shine over another planet!

★   ★   ★

Now, for a while, strange transfers begin to arrive at Dora. These aren't fresh troops or new members of the club coming in, bewildered as they wonder what is going on. Nor do they resemble the Hungarian Jews unloaded a few weeks ago and guaranteed a quick murder. No, these are veterans, authentic concentration camp alumni; you can't go wrong. A first, quick glance tells you—their clothes, striped uniforms or filthy cheap civilian garb, are worn in the style of old prisoners. Their uniforms are patched up following the mode of concentration camp dress and worn in a way that is at once both personal and anonymous.

The beret, whether pushed down to the eyes or pinched forward so as to form a small peak, is the mark of a veteran. As for those men still wearing old civilian clothes, most of them have pulled off the peaks from their old caps and arranged their trousers so as not to look like clowns. Even in the camps, you've got to be as respectable as possible.

The way they stand on roll call square shows which men are regulars. These are the men who stand at ease without being out of line. They are the men who have developed the art of pushing the dying toward the edge in order to fill in the emptied spaces themselves before the Kapos can rush in, bashing everyone with their clubs to reestablish lines of five. They have learned how to turn up their jacket collars surreptitiously to make them just a bit more windproof. These are the men whose reflexes have been acquired only after months of hard experience. They can remain standing on the square, speak among themselves without moving their mouths and without being heard by the Kapos. They have learned how to stand for hours in rain that transforms their clothing and clogs into a spongy mess.

Seen from the heights, the area might seem to be a market garden. The stalks stir, as if moving in the wind, but their feet don't move; they remain firmly planted. From time to time, the Todträger come, taking away the dead and dying. Then an SS in green oilskin raincoat and boots counts and re-counts the numbers. And the waiting goes on interminably.

New prisoners have appeared. On the walkways climbing the hills and around the barracks, the old-timers of Dora watch and wonder. Who are these new guys? Where are they from? It's a mystery until we learn that other transfers have arrived from camps in Germany, Austria, and Poland. These men represent a thinning-out in the numbers in overpopulated camps bursting at the seams with too many prisoners. But whatever the possibilities for piling up prisoners elsewhere, there are certain concentration camp norms that cannot be overlooked. For one thing, uncontrollable islands of prisoners must not be created, crowds impossible to index, file, and subdue.

The roll call square, where all prisoners should assemble, has a limited surface area. The SS have tried to do their roll calls in or in front of the barracks, but that takes far too long, even for them. In itself, that wasn't as important as the fact that the results of the count were very uncertain and left doubts as to the accuracy of the final figures.

To sum up, when a camp reaches its maximum number of prisoners, it must pass on its excess to other camps that still have room. At this point, the SS organize a great raid; a net is thrown among hundreds or thousands of these men, their numbers are noted, and they are all shipped off to a new destination. It is the epitome of Nazi methodology.

Dora has become one of these destinations. Regular transports now arrive from other Hitler "metropolises." From afar, the newcomers are measured for their capacity. They are, of course, at the end of the line. For days, they have been carted about, piled into open trucks without shelter from the rain and icy cold, without rations from their moment of departure. Their losses have been great, and the bodies are piled high in front of the crematorium, but at the moment, there are a lot of men still standing. These guys have a chance of getting through, unless or until they are sent to Ellrich or Harzungen for their terminal health cure. It doesn't look good for them because Dora is stuffed to the hilt. The population has grown astronomically. There are enough prisoners to sell off.

We'd like to be able to talk with these guys and ask questions. Where are you from? What happened there? Why are you here? How was your journey?

Are we getting panicky? Is liquidation coming or what? But we aren't allowed to go and talk with them or even go near the square. They don't even know where they are, but even if they did, it wouldn't help them. Dora? What is it? But the question blocking every throat is: Is it the evacuation?

Evacuation. The terrible word has turned in our minds for some time. For a long time, up until the Normandy landings, we had imagined the camps would be liberated when the winners arrived in Germany. The most optimistic envisioned GIs or Tommies knocking on the gate and telling the survivors, "There you are, you're free now." No one really thought things would turn out this way, but they didn't want to add the worry that liberation might be their moment of greatest danger. Worry was already a permanent feature of life, and one concern a day was enough.

Most of the prisoners, especially those who were less optimistic, added fuel to the rumor that the SS, when the Allies approached, will seal us all in the tunnel and then blast it. Thus, fifteen or twenty thousand men will be crushed by the mountain within split seconds, with no question of leaving a sole survivor. If the princes of Hitler's evil empire are to disappear, why should they allow their prisoners the privilege of surviving their masters?

The execution order will come from authorities at the highest levels, and there is no doubt that it will be given. Up until now, there haven't been any preparatory works and no buildup of explosives for the job, but it will take only a few hours or days at most to turn the tunnel into the most beautiful rattrap on this mad planet. Worried prisoners begin looking over all the works for arrangements that might seem suspicious. A few begin saying that if everyone is suddenly ordered into the tunnel, we should refuse, even though it will bring on a general massacre. In a case like this, there will at least be some with a slight chance for survival, whereas in the tunnel, death would be certain for all.

Before the landings, these hypotheses were only academic; the war could still last for months, if not years. In any case, death would be dealt out daily and generously by the SS and their minions.

After the invasion, the Allied advances quickly revived the question as to what our fate will be. Obviously, something will happen when the Allies come closer to Dora. No one imagines that the SS will be drawn up in meticulous Death's-head formation, magnificently uniformed, while the commandant exchanges salutes with the Allied commander and then hands over the keys to his kingdom, along with lists of inmates, to the conquerors. Even the simplest-minded prisoner couldn't believe such a story.

The one phrase, spoken or implied, that every prisoner knows by heart is the SS promise: "You will *never* leave here!" Then what? Will there be shootings in groups of one hundred, while the others, menaced by machine guns, look on helplessly? Will it be the tunnel as a trap for the Zawatsky kommandos and murder in various forms for the surface prisoners, with the help of the Kapos and barracks chiefs? These are the thoughts racing through every mind—on-the-spot liquidation, every last man dead, and no one left to tell the tale of the fate

Hitler and Himmler planned for all of humanity wherever the Nazi rule could spread.

The arrival of camp-to-camp transfers gives new direction to our wondering. It had been common knowledge but now comes back to our minds that the SS and their prisoners had an absolute, triple-A priority on all German rail lines. Our captors can form up trainloads of prisoners throughout the entire network, wherever and whenever they so desire. This arrival of prisoners merely proves it.

At a time when the shipping of supplies, troops, materials, and ammunition toward the west is vital to Germany's survival, the SS are organizing, at short notice, transfers of prisoners from one camp to another. Some had just arrived at Dora, and more must be arriving at other camps.

So we look upon the new prisoners with dismay. Is this what's waiting for us? These men are at their extreme limits; they're going to die in great numbers. A human being can draw fantastic, often unsuspected, energy from his body, and this is what they have done. He can march for days through rain, snow, and freezing winds, can be crushed into open trucks for days and nights on end, soaking and frozen, and this, too, is what they have done. Those who survive will now be sent to the Ellrich oven, and that will be their ultimate and very bitter end.

Yet the situation in Germany itself is still normal. The Führer is in firm command. There is no panic, not even a shadow of disorganization. The country is calm and working effectively. Apart from the Allied bombings, it is completely quiet. In such optimal conditions, a prisoner transfer can suffer enormous losses as dying men drop like flies. So if they do the same to us in midwinter, the real and pitiless winter, we will have no chance of surviving. The mortality won't merely be great, it will be total. No one will escape.

We think things over, talk to each other, and begin telling ourselves that if Dora should be evacuated one day, we should do all we can to delay the process, to stay put so that we do not have to leave. After all, twenty thousand prisoners, along with the camp annexes, can't just be moved in a day. It will take some time, and each day won will mean an extra chance for our getting out of here alive!

No, we must not leave. Dora is big. There are lots of places to hide, maybe even to set up a defense. Of course, the SS will go over the area with a fine-tooth comb and finish by rounding up virtually every prisoner, and they will be shipped away to God knows where. But the craftiest, the fleetest, and the most determined men will manage to gain a day, then two, then more until the Allies arrive. Only then can the world know what awaited them if the Nazi dictator had had his way!

All these men from unknown camps have begun to die on the roll call square. As their souls depart, their bodies drop like so much dirtied clay.

Things are stirring at the infirmary. The place is full, with no possibility of taking in these new dying men. Not only that, it would be pointless to accept them since they have no chance of surviving. What is the good of going through the formalities of admission, of the whole auscultation procedure, when these wraiths have only a few hours or minutes to live at best? They can end their careers in front of the gate, and that will avoid the need to give them numbers or even notate them in the registers. They'll simply be written off as "dead in transit," and that's all.

★   ★   ★

As December began, the first snow fell. The dull gray day broke with low clouds rolling in the skies. The rain began just as the kommandos arrived on the roll call square. It was a rain such as could be expected almost daily, not too heavy but one that quickly soaked uniforms and shoes, mashed up the toilet-paper bandages, and irritated foot wounds. The men bent their backs instinctively to try and keep their stomachs dry, home of the terrible, wracking dysentery.

The roll call of kommandos went quickly; in any case, they had to be in the tunnel at nine o'clock. The road leading to the tunnel was full of ruts and covered with puddles, despite daily efforts by laborers who poured in whole wheelbarrow loads of stones. Even the walkways were swampy, and the Posten had built up little islands of stepping-stones to keep their feet dry. The dogs growled menacingly as the column of prisoners passed, and Dora was once again wearing the sinister look of the bad old days. From the direction of Nordhausen, a light but cold and cutting wind began. It started as a common wintry breeze, then strengthened as the temperature dropped. In just minutes, an everyday autumnal cold snap gave way to winter's freezing cold.

Wind-borne rain slanted obliquely, cutting into chests and faces. As the coldness increased, the rain became snow, which quickly became heavy. Just in front of the tunnel, there were still a few drops of water here and there; then they vanished, and it was winter. Now the wind came strongly, almost horizontally, throwing swirling snow into the eyes, getting into jackets and coats, and turning the uniforms into metal-hard claddings.

The birds had long since disappeared, and there was no longer any sign of life on the plain. Puddles of water filled with snow, which became freezing slush. The wind no longer cut through the men's frozen clothing; soon they, too, would harden into immobility.

Around the tunnel entrance, the camouflage net collected a solid blanket of snow across its mesh until a heavy gust of wind knocked everything down at once. Liquid-fuel tanks that were piled up like so many glass bottles quickly welded themselves together. The tunnel entrance itself loomed through the blowing snow like a black hole, while the Totenkopf (Death's-head) SS on guard stamped their feet and blew into their hands.

Above on the hill, the fir trees had turned white, and the rustling of water here and there had stopped. A whole network of stalactites hung downward at an angle following the slant of the wind.

Thus, winter set in at Dora a few weeks ahead of the calendar. The German winter arrived with the same brutality and suddenness of everything that was German. It ended the period when the most optimistic among us still had hopes for a miracle, putting a final stop to those wild dreams. When General Winter speaks, human generals and field marshals keep quiet and give way before him. He has the last word. Armies stop and dig in.

Snow closed the gates of Dora. The prisoners heard the noise of the drawbridge lifting and the portcullis coming down. The noise penetrated every heart, causing many to skip a beat. A new winter was starting, one that would last a millennium, an impossible winter that no worldly beast could survive.

★   ★   ★

"All the Russians to the roll call square!" echo the loudspeakers throughout the camp. The barracks chiefs go to their doorsteps to see what is happening. It's ten o'clock in the morning, and the kommandos have just come up from the tunnel. The soup cans under the Stubendienst's control are ready to be served. The men are in the Waschraum, busy doing a quick cleanup, with shirts and coats firmly clutched between their knees to avoid having them stolen.

"There must be some pop-off who's made another major fuckup."

Michel laughs. He suffers from an incurable allergy to the Russian prisoners. He doesn't miss a chance to show his bad temper, fueled by months of fighting in different kommandos.

The Blockältester comes into the barracks shouting out the order. *"Alle Russki: Antreten!"* (All Russians: Assembly!) The Russians quickly get dressed, bawling and swearing, and form in columns in front of the barracks entrance. They weren't able to dry themselves first, and the outside cold begins freezing their wet clothes. A glacial wind is twisting through the area, sprinkled with snowflakes. A few wily dodgers try to mix in among the crowd of other prisoners, but these are soon spotted by the Stubendienst and led to the barracks chief, who greets them with a clubbing. A Russian stands out in the crowd, and the orderlies have trained eyes.

In front of the barracks, you can now see groups of Russians. There are thousands split into small groups beginning to descend from the heights to the roll call square. It's a fascinating spectacle to see such an anthill of prisoners emerging everywhere, making for a central point. But when the men are all Russians, the sight is even more gripping. They give out such a sense of force and savagery that they compel respect. Here is the horde of the accursed going forward on command. They have no idea what it's about, but they move out welded together into a single block that will accept anything but won't let itself be trampled under. The great Russia is marching to the roll call square.

Little by little, the square fills up, each barracks number distanced from the others. Behind the brothel's windows, the SS whores can be seen watching the proceedings. At the camp gate, only a few SS men, accompanied by officials, are talking among themselves. The senior officers are undoubtedly still enjoying the warmth within the offices.

The Russian prisoners are assembled. The Lagerschutz hem in the quadrangle on three sides. They are wearing their long green coats and boots. Their eyes don't stop roving over the compact mass, where at any moment, uncontrollable violence could be let loose. Guards in the lookout towers aim their guns toward the square. Even behind the protection of electrified fencing and machine guns, the SS are afraid of the Russians. That horde of madmen worries them. Individually, the Russians are only bundles of tattered rags, but in a group, they are terrifying. The SS hope God will save Germany from seeing Russian armies breaking into their territory, for that would be the apocalypse.

The cold intensifies as the wind howls through the groups, knifing between the men, getting into their coats, freezing their backs, stomachs, hands, and ears. The Russians from the tunnel have no coats, and the wind whips into their buttonless flies, freezing their balls. Their eyes weep, and their noses run. It is no longer snowing; the last flakes have danced about and disappeared toward the hilltops. The Blockführer now leave the command post. They make a roll call of the numbers present and sign the registers, and the barracks chiefs go back to their barracks. At last, we will find out what is happening.

It appears that two Russian prisoners were surprised while pissing on some machines in the tunnel. They are now in the bunker and will be hanged in the afternoon. In reprisal, all the Russians from the night shift are going to spend the day on the square and will go back to work without having slept or having received any rations.

As to the missed rations, the Stubendienst think about the money they can make with this fabulous excess. There is more than one mess tin that never left the Blockältester's room. The Blockältester appears, in fact, in the refectory and makes his usual little speech. "We are all friends, and the Russians who are suffering at this very moment on the roll call square are our friends. So we are going to keep their soup rations, and tomorrow they'll have the right to a supplement because they are good friends who are suffering for us all. To show that we are with them, there will be no supplement of soup this morning. *Kein Nachschlag.* (No extras.) Understand?" The Blockältester belches and swings his truncheon. "Your Russian friends are going to suffer all day long, and you're going to sleep now, you bunch of swine. So I don't want any noise, filthy as you are; your chief needs peace and quiet to look after you and these Russian cunts who are our friends. Now, everyone in bed."

"What a shit!" groans Michel. With the extra tins of soup, he would have been able to buy a few gallons of schnapps and be dead drunk for days. But this Russian thing will start the ball rolling for the chiefs instead. "They'll stuff themselves, buy good clothes, and think themselves masters of the world. But for us poor bastards," he thinks, "it means that nobody will have a supplement, and what's more, we'll have to tighten our belts. No supplement! Shit, these chances are so rare, and when I see all these tins filled with soup and with potatoes at the bottom, it gives me one hell of a stomachache. All these NCOs and politicians, the criminal prisoners and damned queers and you name it, I never want to see any of them again. They're a lot of trash, and if I get through this, you'd better never mention them again. All these bastards think about is their homosexuality and their political group. The poor guys like you and me, all the assholes who are here because these radical, social, thingummy sweet cunts didn't do their jobs, everybody forgets us. Here in Hitler City, you have to be a criminal, a queer, or a revolutionary, and if you don't fall into one of these categories, you just shut up and hope that your soup won't be too damned watery. *Ponimaich!*"

So it's everyone to bed. The soup is eaten, and the bowls are put back in the cupboard. You must sleep as much as possible if you hope to survive the next night. Through the windows, you can hear the freezing winds howling through the camp. The men have to sleep in twos and squeeze against each other to get even a tiny bit of body warmth.

Toward midday, everyone is awakened. What the hell is happening this time? It seems that, following the SS roll call, some Russians are missing from the square. The barracks chief personally checks all our numbers and badges and compares them with his own list. Everything is OK; there isn't a single Russian in the barracks. We can go back to bed.

Outside on the freezing square, the Russians are still standing, forming stationary masses through which the wind howls. From time to time, officials or the SS emerge from the guard post, go toward one group or another, count and re-count the prisoners, and then check their registers.

Just before six, the sleeping prisoners are awakened. It's time to get ready so that we will be at the tunnel by nine. A glance through the frosted window shows that the Russian prisoners are still in place, standing immobile against the rising wind. At the end of each group, we can see forms laid out cold and straight, those who could no longer resist the terrible ordeal. We go to the Waschraum quickly, then sit down at the tables to get our tiny ration of bread, margarine, and sausage.

Then, as we pass the Blockältester's room, we glance inside. It fairly bulges with soup and bread. The packets of margarine and whole sausages are piled on the table!

Now the night-shift teams go down toward the square and the formation points for their kommandos. An order blares from the loudspeaker: All Russians must join their kommandos.

Their joints are so stiffened from the arctic cold that the Russkis find it very hard to walk. They are neither gray nor white, they haven't any color. The men can no longer speak and can make only the feeblest mild gestures. Just a tiny push with a finger would make most of them fall over. Some lean against others and walk as if they had artificial legs. Others have not moved; they lack sufficient energy or strength to take a single step. Each of these stands like a statue that has lost all of its life.

"Go and get your friends." One after another, the Kapos give the same order. Can it be that there is a bit of humanity somewhere among them? It's difficult to say, but in any case, the square has to be cleared of these freezing people, and the kommandos must be completed before leaving. Frozen workers may not work very well, but dead men don't work at all. So much for the mercy of our captors. So we're going to get the Russians, supporting them on both sides and keeping them in the middle of groups where they are the least exposed to the wind. We help them as much as we can, but at the camp exit and the tunnel entrance, they must find the strength to walk alone, in cadence, with heads bared and hands on the seams of their trousers. And if they manage to survive the night, they can eat in the morning.

★   ★   ★

A concentration camp is a strange invention. Usually, it's a sort of area situated between somewhere and nowhere—not too welcoming but not necessarily too forbidding, at least from the outside.

On its grounds, barracks become living accommodations for its prisoners, along with some basic buildings. There will be an infirmary, a kitchen, an Effektenkammer, some workshops, and a bunker. And of course, no self-respecting Nazi concentration camp could hold up its head in the Third Reich without its very own crematorium.

The entrance is surrounded by anonymous, unpretentious administrative buildings. Only the gate can make claim to some small architectural research. The lot is surrounded by a system of electrified fencing about twelve feet high, with lookout points that have interlocking fields of machine-gun fire, which make any attempt to escape over the wire suicidal.

None of this is very impressive, and in any case, it is far from the sort of image that could be born of a romantic mind. It is, in fact, commonplace. There are no high, turreted walls, no worrisome rampart walks, no barred windows or firing ports. On the whole, it's banal. The gate itself is only a little bit higher and more barbed than a simple prairie barrier gate.

And yet that gate, rudimentary though it is, separates two entirely different planets. On the outside, there is the Planet Earth, with men who are born, live, marry, work, sleep, eat, drink, and finish by disappearing as men have always done.

Inside Dora is the Planet KL, the Konzentrationslager. Here everything is different; nothing is as it is on Earth. A simple network of electrified barbed wire is all that is needed to send this little world into another galaxy. However, the prisoners can look out and see the other world with ease. No one stops them from looking to the Earth that lies just beyond the deadly wire. They can see the houses just a little way off, with men and women going in and coming out; they can see towns and villages, cars, carts, and a peaceful daily activity. Yet prisoners never say that beyond the barbed wire life is free and that you only have to pass beyond this apparently fragile threshold to be on the other side where everything is marvelous.

They never speak or think of that freedom because their minds are already blank, because they are now without hope. Even the sight of this freedom doesn't penetrate to their hearts, already too brutalized to dream of better things. Even the electrified fencing doesn't have any of the magical attraction you'd expect it to have. After all, what ecstasy it would be to get up speed and run toward it. At the last moment, with your last step, you cry, "I am free!" There would be a crackling for several seconds, and you would, indeed, be free from all this endless misery.

You rejoin the concentration camp paradise. All that remains stuck to the barbed wire are the miserable—or grandiose—remains of someone who has already suffered that ending. So you don't take this great leap toward a final, marvelous freedom.

You're a prisoner, and as such, you'll do your job to the end. It isn't a case of saying, "A minute more, Mister Hangman,"—it's wanting to push death back, day after day, minute after minute.

As days go by, you become detached from all that has made you a man to begin with. You avoid all the traps, detect the slightest danger; you become craftier than the devil. The losses are huge, but a few manage to become mutants and thereby live a bit longer. The first beings on Earth took millions of years to emerge from the sea and swamps, to reach the surface and become acclimatized, but as a prisoner of the Nazi Reich, you don't have millions of years. You have to become accustomed to the ways here very quickly—or else perish. The great final leap into the barbed wire isn't a solution, at least not yours. The world that lies just beyond that electrified network doesn't exist for you, so you don't look at it, or if you are looking in that direction, you fail to see it. Your real life is here inside the perimeter, and it's here that you must fight; here where you must win or lose. There are also, of course, engineers, civilians, work gang foremen, and secretaries. These humans land on this planet for so many hours a day but have nothing in common with you. You don't even envy them; no real contact brings you together. They are people from the Planet Earth, that's all, and only visitors to the Planet KL. If some civilian occasionally is humane toward you, it seems suspect. Between these strangers and the prisoners, there is no possibility of understanding or coming together. Each must live his own life, and the concentration camp inmates live theirs as helpless prisoners. Here there mustn't be a missionary allowed to blow on the dice and alter the results. Welfare ladies, worker-priests, and other comics don't have a place in this strange world. You can't throw a gangway between these two planets.

The prisoners' universe has been created with representatives of the whole social body. All the hierarchies and religions, civil and military powers are there, but they have collapsed, leaving the prisoner population with nothing but themselves to counter the insane rule of the Death's-head SS. A weird anarchy is the result, a pitiless society forged in misery, anguish, and death.

Behind the barbed wire, the prisoner is alone. There are no charitable groups or sympathetic tribunals to treat their wounds and rehabilitate them. There is only either a pure ferocity or a friendship that may extend as far as the supreme sacrifice. For here, the bishops have lost their crosses and miters; the judges have lost their wigs and power; the unionists have lost their ability to unite; and the military have lost their sabers. There are only naked men left, stripped of humanity, men who can become saints if they are up to it.

The prisoners' ages vary. Using official standards, the average is about thirty, with the youngest (very rare) about eighteen and the oldest thirty-five to forty. However, they all look extremely old, "without age," as it is said for Armagnac bottles. They have no more illusions, and when they behold newcomers, their diagnoses would astonish university professors. They never look beyond the barbed wire except to see whether the weather may be changing. They know that, like a wine, the more they age, the more they will improve. The prisoners make their own carapaces, hard outer shells, to help defy the slings and arrows of outrageous physical, moral, and meteorological inclemency.

The captives look at the SS, who also seem very old. Then they scrutinize their fellow prisoners, sizing them up. The run of their thoughts is probably along similar lines: "Obviously, one of the two will let go first, and doubtless, it'll be me, but that's no reason for giving up without a fight. I'm watching you, you bastard, and you won't get my skin for a dime. You'll have to pay a damned good price for my skin. A few months ago, it wasn't worth much, but I've made some progress since then, and if you want my skin, it'll be damned hard to get! And don't count on me to do anything stupid and allow you a checkmate without any difficulty. I have only one skin, and I'm not about to give it up just like that!"

News of the invasion and reports of Allied progress are far off now. Because of them, we had dropped our own fighting guard, so they must be forgotten, at least for now. Reality is not on the other side, it's here. What happens out there on Earth is of no consequence inside the barbed wire. If liberation ever comes, it will be immediate. The prisoner will change from a concentration camp inmate to a free man. But there will be no preparation nor lengthy evolution, nor even a quiet passage. It's one or the other; so what good is it to strip off your armor for a dream? He who does it is only condemning himself to death. In giving up the only arms he possesses, he becomes a virtual suicide.

Winter will be hard, and numerous unknown perils will multiply. Tremors have begun to nudge the Planet Dora. So far, they are only slight, but they are omens of fantastic jolts that risk crushing everything, down to the last prisoner. Yes, the months to come will be hard.

★   ★   ★

Gilbert gasps, loses his breath for an instant. His eyes open wide in amazement, and he lets out a huge, involuntary laugh. "Look! Will you look at that? Am I dreaming? Or what? What the hell *is* this?"

The kommandos are just coming back from the tunnel and have crossed the gate when they notice it. In the upper area of the roll call square, there is a huge Christmas tree. Not a tiny tree bought in the village market, no. It is a magnificent tree of the best quality. The effect on the men is so gripping that they stand stupefied in wonder. At last, a laugh breaks out along the column.

"Putting up a Christmas tree in Dora," says Gilbert, stunned. "That took some great thinking! I'll bet they put up candles and presents for each other on Christmas Eve!"

There, Gilbert is a bit optimistic, but the very idea of the Death's-head SS taking the joke so far as to celebrate the Christ child's birthday in this murder hole is deliriously droll. On this planet, all religious practices, even any recollection of such, are verboten—strictly forbidden!

Priests arriving in Dora are the object of special worry. On arrival in the camp, when they are asked their profession, they have quite innocently stated that they are priests, bishops, etc. The officials of the Arbeitsstatistik and the Politische Abteilung candidly suggest that they list any profession but this. You simply don't let it become known that you represent God when you are a prisoner in the Devil's own house. However, these priests, unswerving, insist on being inscribed as such. When a man has traveled a good way along the road of supreme sacrifice, he doesn't tell a ridiculously little lie just so as to blend into the safe anonymity of the masses.

"As you wish," answer the officials, and they notate "priest" or "bishop" without even lifting their heads to see what one of these might look like when naked. The officials couldn't care less. They have already seen the fanatic Bibelforscher, the Jehovah's Witnesses, and marked their religious convictions with violet triangles. Soon thereafter, the SS responsible for such matters would examine the files of the newcomers, and they would see to it that those listed as priests, bishops, or whatever—if they lived past the three-week quarantine—would be sent out on the most murderous kommandos.

Whatever the reason for the Christmas tree's appearance, its very presence represents the SS's supreme derision of everything sacred to normal, decent Christian life. It was not put there to generate a ray of sunshine or goodness in the prisoners' hearts but rather to destroy their morale. It's well known that the holidays, especially Christmas, are a torture for the poor, for the lonely, and for the underprivileged of the world.

At Dora, everyone knows that Christmas 1944 will be a hard time to live through. We fight it day after day; we put blinkers on our minds. Our memories are forgotten or at least deeply buried, when, without warning, Christmas is suddenly thrown at us. The reaction is instantaneous and inescapable.

All at once, we remember our families around the fireplace and think of Christmas Eve, with tasty fresh oysters and other snacks, of roast turkey, and of Yule logs covered in rich cream. And we think of parents, wives, and young children opening their gifts Christmas morning with enraptured eyes. We remember when bottles of wine were uncorked amid the sweet smell of candles burning, when the radio, in its beautiful metal cabinet, announced the joy for every man, woman, and child on Earth. And we think of the midnight services; what marvelous moments! We all attend together. The candles smell so fragrant, and everyone is happy. The whole world is happy, full of joy and passion, for Christ's sake!

Gilbert, like many others, feels that he is going to give in, but he must refuse to let it get him. He is there in his striped uniform, filthy and covered with grease and mud. He has no buttons left on his fly, and his clogs are broken. His body looks like a cadaver in anatomy class, and his ankles are badly swollen. His hands, cut up by the cold, are large red, raw things, and a swelling has begun to grow on his left ear, reminiscent of Hieronymus Bosch's classic artworks. Torn up though he is, Gilbert refuses to be drawn into the SS trap. Since they want to have him quietly, destroy him a little more by shameful means, he, trying to hold onto his life with both hands, means to give out a big shout.

"Why the hell are they screwing around with this Christmas tree? Have you seen it? I wouldn't have a thing like that at my place. It looks like a shit of a tree. I can't even look at it; it makes me sick. Anyhow, it's all a joke. Do you guys remember when we arrived at Compiègne, how they handed out prayer books, even to the Arabs? By the way, I don't know whatever became of them because I haven't seen them since. And as to the guys who handed out these prayer books, I don't know where they got them or who paid for them, but it was money wasted because they burned our asses with them in the trucks that took us to Buchenwald. So let's talk about the little Jesus, the stable, and the Christmas tree after the war, when I'm back home. For now, they can stick their goddamned tree wherever they want it; it's all the same to me. I've seen it once, and that's enough. If the SS want it, they only have to put it up at their place because it blocks my view where it is. I can't enjoy the scenery as it ought to be."

"Listen, Gilbert," says another man. "You shouldn't talk like that. There are some people it could upset, and they wouldn't like it."

"Well, then," responds the irate Gilbert, "maybe you'd like me to mention bygone Christmases, when everyone was kneeling around the manger? Are you dreaming or what? Where do you think you are, buddy? This is Christmas Eve; do you want to come and cry on my shoulder about your mother-in-law who is so kind and of your kids who are growing up and waiting for Daddy to come home? If you try and tell me such things, I'll give you a faceful of fist; I don't want to hear about it. Tomorrow, there's work to do, and that's serious. We're workers, not merrymakers. If you wanted to celebrate Christmas, you should never have come to Dora. You should have stayed quietly on your farm, avoided the Resistance, and milked your cows. However, we would have missed you . . . but we could have made up a reason."

Gilbert's declamation has its positive effect. The prisoners perk up a little, and those who were about to soften up forget about Christmas and take a fresh look at where they are. However, there are still a few days before the fateful date, and the awful anguish can return at any time. To plant a Christmas tree on the roll call square is to plant a dagger within every heart in Dora!

★   ★   ★

The Blockältester turns over in his bed. Despite all his efforts, he cannot sleep. Just a while ago, he thought he was going to fall asleep; he felt tired and wanted a nap. After handing out their rations to the night shift, he warned everyone. "Listen, you load of shit, *Schweinerei*, your barracks chief needs a rest. So you are going to bed, and you won't make any noise. Understand? *Compris? Ponimaich?*" The prisoners tiptoe about, and even the snorers hold back their snoring.

But now, the quiet upsets the barracks chief and worries him. What sort of concentration camp is this where the prisoners sleep quietly like little bourgeois? So what, the SS no longer do their job; they don't care about a thing. The Blockältester recalls the terrible years when prisoners were awakened several times a night for the so-called keep fit exercises in the snow. The death rate was terrible, but the hardiest survived, hardy like him. In the name of God, what a rough time we had! So to see this unworldly garbage sleeping quietly gives him fits of fury. "We veterans," he thinks, "have suffered a thousand deaths, and our stripes have been won over a mound of dead bodies. The armlets were given to us who survived the first great killings. Even the SS have a sort of respect for us. Well, not really respect, more like consideration. Only they don't bother with anything anymore, and everything falls on us."

He gets up. He can't stand the quiet; it isn't like a concentration camp. Dora is noise and fury, cries, beatings, and desperately running men. Fear must be maintained. If prisoners feel at home, they'll quietly await the end of the war. If they're left alone, they'll begin questioning orders and turn the barracks into a pigsty. Already, some have stopped washing their shoes before coming in, and they go to bed fully clothed. They have to be shown that Dora isn't a sanitarium. The Blockältester takes his club in hand. It's a fine piece: three twisted copper cables clad in rubber. It's both hard and flexible enough for effective beating along its whole length.

In the refectory, two Polish Stubendienst sit opposite each other with a bowl of soup between them. It is thick, almost wholly potatoes. They take turns at filling their spoons with the rich mixture. The sight of the Blockältester, club in hand, paralyzes them, spoons motionless in midair. As if confronted by a large cobra, they resume their movements in very slow motion so as not to create a complete break in their activity. They realize that all hell is about to break loose and don't want it to come in their direction. The barracks chief looks at them, hesitates, and then makes off toward the prisoners' sleeping area. He slowly opens the door and looks inside, but everyone is sleeping; there is only the sound of men breathing. Frustrated, he shuts the door again and goes toward the second sleeping area in the other wing of the barracks. Passing the Waschraum, he hears water running and pushes the door slowly open. It is well oiled and doesn't make a sound. Inside, he sees a horribly thin man whose back is to him. The feeble prisoner is stripped down as he washes his shirt and underpants in the basin. He has the runs, and brown streaks run down his fleshless thighs.

The barracks chief enters noiselessly, stands behind him, and taps him on the shoulder with his club. The prisoner turns, sees him, and shows the white of his eyes in terror. His knees give way, and he totters backward like a drunkard.

"*Blockältester, Scheisserei!*" (I have the shits!) His voice begs for mercy, moaning, already racked with sobs.

With a kick, the barracks chief shuts the door again. He slowly walks around the basin without really approaching the prisoner. He feels the fury building within himself.

"You trash! You garbage! You stink, and you shit everywhere!"

The prisoner can't understand his words. His eyes roll; he has no strength left and stands still. He can only repeat, "*Scheisserei, Blockältester, Scheisserei!*"

The barracks chief stares at him. "What a filthy rag," he thinks, "the most disgusting thing there is!"

Suddenly, he shoots out the club like a rocket and hits the man's shoulder at the base of his neck. The prisoner howls and falls on all fours. He is lost. The German hurls himself upon his victim, and he hammers the club all over the man's body. The great force of his terrible blows quickly reduces a once living being to a bloody, disarticulated mess. It is finished.

The German is out of breath; his hands are trembling. He inhales deeply to catch his breath. With the tip of his foot, he turns the body over.

He calls to the Stubendienst, who are hovering behind the door, quiet, attentive, and obedient. "Throw this rotten meat outside. And if I see anyone else with the shits in this Waschraum, he'll answer to me. It's not a pigsty in here."

In the barracks, all is as quiet as a cemetery. All the prisoners could hear the execution, but no one moved. You could hear a fly in the air.

★　　　★　　　★

"It doesn't take much ambition to be the Kapo of a shithouse. If such a man had told that to his wife, she couldn't be boasting to the neighbors."

Everyone laughs, at least the French; it's above the heads of the others. Charles rushes to the only free toilet and quickly undoes his trousers. The runs don't wait, and it's prudent to shorten the ceremony.

"You'd think we were still children at school here," he tells himself, "when I think that we must ask the Kapo for a token just to go to the shithouse. Sometimes I wonder just where the hell we are. If I could keep one of these coins, after the war I'd go and play it at Deauville's casino, just to see the look on the croupier's face!"

In the narrow, well-lit passage, magnificent toilets are lined up along the length of each wall, ten on each side. The tunnel latrines are at once the last room where men can exchange facts or rumors and also the place where men with the severe runs can feel their lives ending. Men who aren't too far gone are allowed in, but the others, at the end of their days, are thrown back out with awful clubbings by the Kapo, a colossal brute who jealously looks after his toilets. He has a sharp eye, and gate-crashers have no chance at all for a long stay.

At regular intervals, he rushes into the shithouse to rain truncheon blows, chasing out the prisoners, who flee holding their trousers in their hands. Outside, other prisoners are anxiously waiting, some moaning, "If only I can get in before it's too late." The needy groan and try to soften up the guardian, *"Kapo, Scheisserei,"* but he only looks with disgust at these tattered bodies with their legs crossed in desperation. He feels all-powerful and so much above these miserable shitbags. Twelve hours of listening to the moaning and begging of these bastards makes him ill tempered and quick to strike out with his truncheon.

Inside, well seated, the prisoners try to prolong their stay as long as possible. It's the moment of blessed relaxation for men whose intestines aren't knotted up, but for the rest, it is a brief respite. Aching stomachs give them rictus, but the Kapo soon chases them out, still with horrible colics and nowhere to go.

Charles has saved a bit of grudgingly handed-out paper and rolls a cigarette. It's verboten for prisoners to smoke, but then, what isn't forbidden in Dora? Anyhow, in the rank atmosphere of the latrines, maybe the tobacco smell won't be noticed. He has made himself an ingenious tinder lighter, lights his Makhorka cigarette, swallows a long draw, and holds it in his lungs as long as possible. The strength of the tobacco staggers him, and his eyes roll a bit. "Lucky I'm sitting down," he thinks. "Otherwise I'd fall on my face." He blows the smoke back toward the toilet to break up the incriminating cloud. Two-thirds of the way through the cigarette, he takes the fag end and inhales two or three quick puffs on a single draw. The smoke burns as it invades his lungs. How marvelous! He carefully saves the little bit of paper that's left. If there's no more tobacco, at least the paper is impregnated with it and keeps its smell. He can always chew the paper later.

At the door, other prisoners are fidgeting about in protest. It can't be normal to leave people inside so long. What are they up to? If the Kapo was doing his job, he'd have sent them out a long time ago. They're not the only ones; we have the shits, too. If this keeps up, we'll do it in our clothes, we can't hold on. Men with extreme dysentery hold their stomachs to try and ease the spasms. They are greenish and know they won't be able to contain themselves much longer.

Towering over the crowd, the Kapo looks them over. He'd like to rush into this infected lot and bash their necks and heads, but he thinks of the dodgers who have been inside too long. They don't care about him, of course, and he doesn't like that. He frames himself in the doorway and, with a wave of his truncheon, indicates that everyone must leave. A few quiet protests are made. The ill men are afraid of leaving and shitting in their trousers, so the Kapo flings himself into the room, striking left and right with his club. At once, the prisoners, backs rounded to protect their necks, retrieve their coins and rush out of the exit.

★ ★ ★

The tunnel is strangely quiet this night, with only the noise of the machines to be heard, nothing but the machines. The SS, whose regular rounds serve to animate the prisoners at their work, have disappeared; not a single one has been seen all night. The Kapos, who usually chat with their colleagues on the hall steps as if they were department heads of big stores, stay locked up in their offices instead. The Meister whisper among themselves in small groups that come together, break up, and then form new groupings. There are no cries of pain, no desperately galloping men, no howlings. A padded atmosphere takes over the tunnel. Of course, you can hear the panting of the electric welders, and in his corner behind the sheet metal of his office, the arc-welder throws brilliant rays of light against the roof. Further on, in the gallery entrance, handling kommandos echo the banging of their clogs, while on the other side in the exit gallery, the rockets advance slowly in their cradles. But all in all, the impression is different from other days. It is December 24th, Christmas Eve.

"*Pausa!*"

The shouts and whistles reverberate. It is the blessed hour for the break, wherein, for thirty minutes, you can stretch out and drift into unconsciousness. It is three o'clock in the morning.

Each night when the call goes out, Jacques puts a stool in front of the workbench with its articulated lamp and falls asleep, his head between his hands. Tonight, though, he does nothing, his eyes blank of any expression. Henri comes to him, sensing that something isn't right.

"What's wrong, Jacques?" Henri sits down at the bench and looks at his friend.

"But yes, everything is very good," replies Jacques, "and what do you mean? Everything is perfect. I'm in great shape."

"Don't be stupid, my friend," says Henri. "You're off daydreaming about Christmas. But why? Christmas is a day like all the other days. I think you've been taken in by that stupid SS tree. Maybe you thought they were going to allow you an exit pass so you could share the festivities with your family? You're such a kid, letting it tear at your heart whenever you're reminded of something Christian. The minute I saw that those SS bastards had planted that cursed tree, I knew that caring people like you would have a hell of a bad time."

Jacques begins to cough. He's very cold and turns up the collar of his jacket. His skin, shrunken over his face, is gray and marbled with slabs of beard. "Listen, Henri," he says, "if you've come over to tell me off, you can just go right back to your corner. I'm like you; Christmas doesn't worry me, and if I heard there was a midnight mass in the tunnel, I wouldn't move a muscle. Christmas doesn't interest me, but it's my family who must be thinking of it. This will be the second time that they have been tormented, wondering what has become of me."

"Here we are," thinks Henri, "another delirious idiot. He couldn't be in a worse state, but instead of thinking of himself and a doubtful future, here he is, worrying about his family, who must be quite warm, worried but really warm."

"Last year," continues Jacques, "I was in prison at Christmas. There was, doubtless, a guy in the chapel playing the organ. The prison was star-shaped, with buildings going out from the center, and some were still occupied by the French administration. It was from there, I'm sure, that the concert was coming. I was all alone in my cell, and that music annoyed me. When you're in trouble and you know no one will come and save you, carols and hymns sound ridiculous. If I could have, I'd have told that organist to knock it off because it was doing more harm than good. It's no time to soften people up when they need all their strength to survive the shock of being imprisoned by these damned Germans."

"Go on," thinks Henri, "it'll do you good to get it all said. Otherwise, you'll keep turning it over in your mind and end up by losing your grip completely."

"Christmas in prison didn't break my morale," continues Jacques. "I was as solid as a rock and told myself that, if the Germans didn't shoot me, I'd hold on, no matter what happened. But when my parents sent their first card in February, they thought they had done the right thing in saying Christmas had been sad without me. So, you can see, I imagined them huddled together and crying. Because they aren't fools, you know. They understood fully that being imprisoned by the Gestapo and SS would be no bundle of laughs. And now that they've been liberated, they must have some idea of what a concentration camp is like. Yet here we are; it's all starting again, and it eats me alive to think of them."

"Ah, but Jacques," says Henri, "everybody here is like you. Do you think the rest are all crying like babies? OK, your parents must be having a hard time of it, but even if they're wondering, they can't imagine what Dora is really like. So forget the worries. You'll see your family again, Christmas or no Christmas."

What a mess these "festivities" can be!

7

THE PENULTIMATE HOUR

Coming back up from the tunnel on the road to the camp, the kommandos saw piles of scattered debris, especially berets and clogs. The road itself was covered with a thick coat of frozen snow, and it was terribly cold. The Kapos kicked the debris away to avoid any fights. The prisoners understood what had happened. A transfer of evacuated prisoners from some other camp had arrived during the night.

After passing the camp gate, they saw the new group. On the square, two or three hundred men were staggering weakly. It looked as if most of them wouldn't last through the day. They were at the extreme limits of endurance, and many lay dead at the ends of their ranks. Some hadn't even the strength to pull up trousers that had fallen to their ankles. A long, low groaning came from the group. They must have traveled for days in open trucks. A few escort Kapos prowled around the groups, but they had given up trying to be understood. No orders even reached the frozen minds of these ghosts, men who fell into line only through well-conditioned reflexes. The officials, at a loss, walked around them, not knowing what to decide. At the gate, a few SS men watched the spectacle while they laughed and talked among themselves.

"Hey, guys, look over on the right!" The men turned toward the side of the hill, between the crematorium and the camp facade. There, halfway between the kitchen and the electrified perimeter, a large wall about 300 feet long and 5 feet high had been built up. The men who built it must have worked all night long, but the result was well finished. It was a wall made of dead bodies.

"My God, there are thousands!"

There they were, layer upon layer of corpses piled up head to tail. Seen from a distance, the wall appeared solid, showing no protuberances or gaps, everything seemingly in perfect alignment.

Except for the pitiful few survivors we had just seen, the entire transport had perished. These Auschwitz prisoners had left that camp alive and arrived dead at Dora. They had begun the transfer as living men, still able to walk. After a roll call, the SS had picked a number of prisoners, carefully noted their serial numbers, and then formed them into groups of fifty or a hundred.

Undoubtedly, they had been issued a ration of bread, margarine, and sausage for the day. The Nazi administration is very strict on that point: A prisoner must receive his daily rations, at least if there hasn't been a collective punishment.

After getting their rations, all the prisoners were crammed into open wagons. Then it was, "Coachman, crack your whip; we're off to Dora." Along the way, however, the prisoners spent at least several days, if not a week or two, exposed to frosty 15-degree air, helpless against the wind and blowing snow and without food, drink, or even the ability to move. It was certain death. Those men who had looked at the crematorium chimney at Auschwitz, thinking it would be their final route to eternity, had been somewhat misled. Their chimney was to be the one at Dora, in the province of Thuringia.

The placement of this wall of corpses posed a genuine challenge for the jolly folk at the crematorium. The place could never cope with such an overwhelming number of bodies; there were too many. It would take days on end just to convert this wall of the dead into wisps of smoke leaving the chimney, yet the daily death rate at Dora already kept the crematorium working full-time. Not only that, all the cripples near death on the square would soon arrive to enlarge and heighten the wall.

The transport from the station to the camp must have fallen to the "kommando of the punished," the Strafkommando, which got all the dirtiest jobs. They must have needed trolleys or some sort of vehicles, maybe just a few Central European types with two large wheels at the rear and two smaller, steerable wheels at the front. The undertakers would have loaded these to the maximum, losing some bodies along the way, which they then had to pick up and throw back on top of the macabre pile. They would have pulled and pushed the vehicles as far as the slope.

At the entrance to Dora, the SS at the guard post let the convoy pass without bothering to count the load. Dead lumps, the hell with them. Let the crematorium crew do the counting if they ever got to that point on the job. Without a doubt, the convoy chief had a list of his load, but what good was it now?

The cold intensified horribly, swiftly deteriorating the situation on the square. Glacial winds whipped the little group of survivors, as more and more empty spaces appeared among them. Without a word or a cry, men fell, stirred slightly, and curled up into fetal positions, the ones we share at birth and death. The Kapos dragged their bodies into line with the others.

An SS official came up from the gate and spoke to the convoying officers, who stood at rigid attention with hats off. The ranks were reformed, the SS man counted the survivors, signed a register, and gave curt orders to a subordinate official. This man now had to lead the survivors to the disinfection area. The dying men moved off, their legs stiff, their joints no longer functioning. They had a fixed, empty look, heads stiffly back. Slowly, supporting themselves, they formed a pathetic column that crossed the square to arrive at the bottom of the slope leading up to the sanitary building. A few made an effort and managed, but most had to be led, climbing the slight upward slope with stiff little steps. They couldn't help their continuous groaning, each one leaning against the other. At last, they arrived in front of the doors, and the indifferent Stubendienst pushed them inside.

These poor bastards were going to plunge into the bath, pushed forward by impatient, merry Kapos who love the fun of it. Then the prisoners would go under the showers. But the hot water would kill them.

★   ★   ★

The arrival of this horrible transport from Auschwitz revives the deep worries that have gnawed at Dora's prisoners.

One thing is certain. Within a more or less brief space of time, the coming weeks or months will see all the Konzentrationslager threatened with the greatest of risks.

The immediate risk is, of course, hunger and famine. Germany has now been pushed back to roughly within its boundaries of 1939. The Third Reich can no longer steal food from its neighbors. Now, besides its own population, it holds millions of foreigners to feed: the prisoners of war, the civilian workers, and, of course, the prisoners within all its concentration camps.

Like all armies, the Wehrmacht wastes its food rations, but that will have to stop. The arrival of the Russians at the German threshold will involve the breakup of civilian populations, as was the case in France in 1940. The collapse of the Eastern Front means disorganization throughout all that territory and the onset of strict rationing in Germany.

Even during the times of plenty when Germany ruled over Europe and ate up food and wealth prodigiously, concentration camp prisoners were allowed rations that not only did not assure survival but also meant certain death. If a slice of bread or bit of sausage were taken from daily rations, the death rate would skyrocket. Now it is happening at Dora, where the cutting of bread rations goes beyond the survival limits of men already reduced to living skeletons. This peril threatens every hour of our continued existence.

The second peril to revive our fears is the certainty that the SS won't let us go. Why should they disappear one fine morning, leaving the camp and its prisoners to exult in a sudden discovery of precious life and freedom? It isn't their way at all. For a time, when we envisaged a longer war, we feared that they would shut us all up in the tunnel and blow the mountain itself down upon us. That extremity now seems improbable.

Until recently, Dora was held firm by a solid system of hierarchies, but now it is overpopulated, filled with an unstable population difficult to control. Hundreds of prisoners are barely even numbered, let alone assigned to work details. They are useless in the job market, but their presence constitutes an anarchy that is breaking up camp discipline. The tunnel kommandos are as firmly structured as ever, but chaos is taking over on the surface.

So long as the whole prisoner population of Dora was actively employed, the SS could always find a pretext to get everyone into the tunnel and thereby organize their eventual total liquidation. But to lead these shattered human remains from the latest transfers into the subterranean world would be flagrant proof of SS intentions, and it might complicate their plans. Members of Dora's master race have never made a mystery of the end to be achieved and its necessary means, but they have also left it up in the air as to the day, the hour, and the proper Nazi procedure.

So the prisoners conclude that there will almost certainly be an evacuation. Judging from the evidence, it will turn into a general massacre. From day to day, the men have weakened under inhuman nutrition and man-killing weather conditions. Soon, they won't have enough strength to drag themselves along the roads or to resist the effects of cold and hunger on the truck platforms.

The only hope among Dora's prisoners lies in the inertia of the Nazi administration. The tunnel makes vital weapons; therefore, it must operate, come rain or shine, until the very last day. That these weapons are no longer decisive and that the V-2 can no longer wipe out the enemy is not the question. An armaments factory doesn't stop in wartime. If no one takes the responsibility to turn off the machines, we have a very slight chance of surviving until the end. This will be the case especially if Hitler, in a final act of megalomaniacal suicide, decides to destroy everything that gave Germany its strength. In that case, not a single one of us will survive!

*　　　*　　　*

Christian takes his bit of bread and cuts it carefully into two equal parts. Now he has two little pieces, neither one larger than a small boy's fist. He puts one piece inside his shirt, then cuts the other down the middle, containing the heel, thick bread that feels so good in his stomach. He spreads the margarine and starts to chew the gray and slightly shiny paste. But his gums are rotten, and they hurt him.

"You're not still going to sell your bread for some tobacco!" His friend Raymond is enraged. "We have almost nothing to eat, and with the lungs this tunnel has given you, tobacco isn't especially good for your health!"

Christian, about to swallow a good mouthful, stops with his arm held high, as if he'd suffered a body blow. A bit of redness appears on his cheeks, and he retorts, "Not good for my health? Are you kidding? What the hell is good for anyone's health in this shithouse? If you're so worried about your health, what the hell are you doing here? You should have stayed at home sipping chamomile.

"And you think this so-called bread is good for your health? It gives us the runs, just like the rutabaga soup and margarine, guaranteed fat free. So if you allow me, I'm going to buy some tobacco. It cleans out the lungs and adds a bit of color."

Raymond and Christian, with their shaved heads, ravaged faces, and hollow eyes, look like two shrunken little old-timers from the poorhouse. Raymond wonders what good it does to talk sensibly with Christian. The man is a maniac who would rather give up essentials for the tobacco that is his vice. Raymond drops the subject.

Christian finishes his bread, gets up, and leaves the barracks. Outside, the cold is terrible; he begins to slip but feels a frozen hand grab him across the stomach, steadying him. His ears, which have been slightly warmed during the discussion inside, now burn him. The frozen snow is dangerously slippery, and he must be careful with his footing. In his dilapidated state of health, a fall would mean a certain fracture.

Arriving at the flea market, he notices that it is almost deserted. It isn't surprising; with the weather so cold, the small dealers prefer to carry out their negotiations in the comparative warmth of the barracks. "Good God," he thinks, "I've known some tobacconists at Dora! I don't know what's wrong with them; they're dropping like flies. These old Russians just can't stand the pace."

Now one of them emerges from the shadows where he has been sheltering. With his long cloak and thin silhouette, one would guess he was somewhere between thirty and seventy. From thirty onward, the Russians are called *"Stare"*—"old guy." Christian approaches him warily.

"Hey, Stare, Makhorka!"

The Russian lets out a moan and from his coat takes out a pair of leather shoes. He shows them off with the cagey look of a toothless old whore. *"Franzouski, Schuhe. Gut, gut."*

"I don't give a shit about your shoes, you poor cunt. All I want is some tobacco. *Makhorka, ponimaich, Makhorka?"*

Christian is angry for a moment, then realizes that this fleshless Russian carcass is at the end of his tether. In forty-eight hours at most, his body will have become part of the wall of the dead. By shaking him up a little, Christian knows he could steal his shoes and the tobacco. Anything the Russian has on him, he has already stolen from the dead or from guys too weak to defend themselves. Then too, there are worrisome shadows prowling the area, and it could degenerate into a massacre. Christian knows he is so weak that he wouldn't stand a chance of getting out alive. So he smiles at the Russian and continues. *"Ich habe Kleb. Du hast Makhorka?"* (I have bread. You have tobacco?)

Looking like a conspirator, Stare reaches under his coat and brings out a sack tied with a string, like those seen in prewar Westerns. He opens the bag and takes out a pinch of tobacco, enough for two small cigarettes. *"Ein portion Brot."*

Christian gulps. Are we that far gone? Two lousy cigarettes for a portion of bread? Then everyone in Dora is finished. There's nothing left.

"Go fuck yourself, you old fool, old bastard of a Russian shit!"

Scandalized by this galloping inflation, Christian breaks his negotiation and draws off, remembering to look behind him. The horrors prowling in the shadows now know he has some bread and can attack him to steal it. For at Dora, you kill for a lump of bread, for a coat, or for earmuffs. In fact, you kill for anything. Now you can survive only by another's death; there is no longer enough to enable everyone to live. So the weakest are stripped of life to allow the rest to survive a few more days, and when you become one of the weakest, those a bit less weak will attack you.

Christian has spotted a bush with leaves that look dry enough to give a good smoke. After all, tobacco or not, it's the smoke that he wants. It helps him to forget the hunger he has known for so many months, hunger calmed only by the smoke that arrives in his lungs. What's the name of this bush? Something *vulgaris*? Well, I'm going to enjoy the bread since I haven't sold it, and then I'll make a cigarette out of so-and-so *vulgaris*.

Christian gathers the leaves; they're frozen but dry and crackling. Just right. He wolfs down the bread and begins stuffing the leaves into a piece of cement bag. Drunk already with all this manna from heaven, he shouts silently to himself, "Go stuff it, you miserable bastards! But I'm holding on till the end! I'll never let go. NEVER!"

★   ★   ★

"How many ways are they splitting a loaf today?" The kommando is arriving for morning relief, and the night shift is worried about the rations. The men are exhausted, their faces worn to desperation. There is an obvious proliferation of TB and edemas, the most impressive of which are those of the eye, which give each ill man the protruding appearance of a lemur. Their stomachs are all shouting famine!

Inside the access gallery, the clogs are clacking on the floor in an unusual manner. The men's faces are joyful.

"They're splitting two loaves for every three men!"

Two loaves for three men? Are they kidding? That's double the best ration ever given here! It can't be. Someone must have been drugged to start such insane stories. Yesterday, the word was that there was no bread, and here are some nuts telling us we'll get the handout of the century!

The men of the relief kommando come down into the halls, all overexcited. They produce bread from everywhere, from their pockets, from shirts, from bags. They can't swallow it all; their shrunken stomachs refuse to accept such volume. So at break time, we'll have a snack such as hasn't been known for centuries!

"You know," says one man, "when we saw all this coming, we were like fools. The Stubendienst had to make two trips to get all the bread, and they were angry as hell. They told the guys to sit in groups of three, and at each group, wham! Two loaves of bread. We almost fell on our asses. It couldn't be true. There's been a mistake, an administrative screwup, and in a few minutes, they'll jump on us to get it all back. Anyhow, we split the bread in a hurry. Each loaf was cut three ways and handed out fast. Believe it or not, the guys who had two portions were making faces. For them, it wasn't the thing to do; they were greedily eyeballing the big loaves still uncut. Face it, when you have an undivided ration, it looks mad, as if it could last you all year!"

Lord Jesus, a double ration of bread! The night-shift men have tears in their eyes, uncontrollable tears, a Pavlovian reaction. Why, two loaves between three men is more than they have dared to dream of. It's the jackpot! Two loaves between three men means you can stuff yourself till you can't eat another bite and still save some for later when you're just a little bit hungry. Two loaves split three ways is like dinner at Maxim's, the Tour d'Argent! You'd sell your soul for less than that; Dora is great.

How did such a feast happen? Curiously, nobody gives a damn; we couldn't care less—we're going to eat!

However, this unusual handout of bread is clear evidence that the SS stewardship is running off the rails. If these bastards have decided to let us have a feast, it can only be because they've received more than they could stockpile. So now the question is: What will there be tomorrow? The factory that makes the bread may have emptied its reserves before closing its doors. Perhaps beyond the barbed wire, everything is beginning to go to pieces. Is this the beginning of the end? The SS must have sent their usual order and then been given everything left on the shelves.

Anyhow, if the day-shift kommando has come down, that means they haven't been given their traveling rations. Tough luck, but for the moment we don't move. We'll go right on making V-2s that could never make it over a suburban housetop and that often explode on engine ignition. Our sabotage is very effective, and it's good this way. And for the time being, there are extra rations waiting for us in the barracks.

★   ★   ★

Since the middle of March, the situation has really gone to hell in Dora. First of all, we were overjoyed by the extraordinary handout of two loaves of bread between three men, but there was nothing at all the next day. Ever since, the ration has fluctuated from absolutely nothing one day to a whole loaf per person the next. We don't know where we're going any longer. The Planet Dora has gone mad.

We hear that the Allies have begun their great offensive in the west, while somewhere to the east are the Russians. The idea of advancing troops doesn't enter our minds. We only know that a race is under way, and the survival of the last of us here depends upon its outcome.

This is our real world. Troop movements and air raids, all the rest of it is a bit abstract. All that matters is the fight against death, so we can only think about what's here and now.

The most important tangible item is food. The irregular deliveries of bread only add up to constant shocks to the stomach and intestines. One day, we're diving like animals into an enormous, system-destroying ration. The next, our stomachs are tortured by cravings for food that doesn't come. As for the so-called soup, it's a slop mixed with scrapings from the granary. The margarine and sausage often disappear. Tobacco, that opium of the people and the camps, is only a memory, and leaves from any available bush become its substitutes.

But the routine continues. The men, used to little or almost no food, continue their lives as prisoners. They muster for roll call, make up the work parties, work twelve-hour days or nights, and plod for miles every day. When men have reached their physical limits and know they can't hold on any longer, they climb to the infirmary at night. It is the prisoners' Way of the Cross, and for them, it's finished.

Although the tunnel workforces remain full, the surface komman-dos shrink drastically. Significant little transfers elsewhere lower their numbers of men. Assembled on the surface one morning, they take the route to the disinfection barracks. Then they receive their rations and march through the camp gate in columns of five. They're being sent to reinforce the dwindling manpower at Ellrich and Harzungen, where most of them will soon die.

The tunnel kommandos make their daily descent into the under-ground caverns. They feel almost like minor lords, the untouchables, for they think that V-2 rocket production will continue until the ar-rival of the first Allied soldier. But can they be sure the SS won't seal them all in the tunnel and blast the mountain down upon them?

For the moment, the German civilians remain faithful to their work, and the factory turns out its production with some degree of normality.

But if the worst happens, what can we do? You can be damned sure that we'll fight tooth and nail, shouting our defiance against such an end. Obviously, the result will be the same, but that isn't the question.

The point is that we'll never go meekly to the slaughterhouse of the damned SS. The fight may only be symbolic, but it'll happen.

For now, we refuse to give in to fate or any so-called destiny deter-mined by these master-race bastards. We want to know where, when, and how the last act will take place, and we seek out every possible clue. The German civilians begin to put on strange faces, so things can't be going at all as they'd like, which recalls certain days in 1940 to the French. We now see them as worried, tormented people who have listened to the news and slept badly afterward. They seem to sense the catastrophe of the Third Reich without having admitted it. They go about their jobs like well-trained robots, but you can feel that their hearts are no longer here. Their world is breaking up. It will soon be crushed, and they know it. Even the few glorious survivors of the Eastern Front behold the terrible face of war that is driving onward, following them into the heart of Germany. This time, however, they have lost their arms and mighty firepower. There is nothing left for de-fense, and their own wives and children are now the ones who will be blown apart by incoming shells.

Since the arrest of the Frenchmen who had, indeed, formed a Resis-tance group within Dora, news from Allied radios has been shut off from the prisoners, and no one really knows what's happening out there. It seems that the Anglo-Americans have crossed the Rhine, quickly penetrated the Siegfried line, and begun to invade all of west-ern Germany. That's what we think, but how much time will they need, if all goes well, to get here? It's out of the question, naturally, to pin up little flags on maps, and any discussions, besides, would be in vain. The progress of those armies alone will decide our life or death.

Those unknown, unseen soldiers alone, through the force of their spirit and will to win, even to sacrifice, will make the difference between liberating the camps . . . and simply finding areas like this and remarking that there are only dead bodies left to mark the spot. The dice haven't been thrown; the game goes on, with its high and low points. With a lucky throw, we find ourselves alive on the winning side. With a bad throw, there is nothing on the horizon for us all but an unworldly bone factory.

*   *   *

It is Easter. Sunday, April 1st. For the first time in its short history, the tunnel isn't working and has closed its doors for the day. The night shift has come out but hasn't been relieved by the day shift. The kommandos normally scheduled to go down below to work have been kept in camp.

This schedule change poses a slight logistical problem, for the day shift must give way to the night people. They have the right to the Waschraum, the refectory, and the dormitories. So now, the men are set loose on the pavement without reason or work assignments, and this, in Dora, is filled with risks of all kinds.

Apparently, it has been announced that the camp chief and tunnel enterprises, in the great gentility of their Christian caring, have allowed the prisoners a day of rest in which to celebrate the glory of Christ's resurrection.

Since we have nothing to do and since the surroundings around the barracks are quite dangerous, we go to visit friends with whom we can meet on neutral grounds, which is to say, in the streets.

We take advantage of this respite to pluck the last leaves from every available bush—maybe for our last smoke. What's really happening? It isn't at all like either the SS or Zawatsky Company to hold up V-2 production for anything. Therefore, the situation for the Third Reich must be very serious.

Can this be the end of Dora? But it seems impossible to end the existence of this alien planet in one fell swoop. We aren't hearing any artillery barrages, the countryside appears quite peaceful, and nothing a priori is likely to close up one of the factories making Hitler's "vengeance weapons," regarded by the Nazis as so essential to the final victory of the Reich.

Prisoners gather in small groups to discuss their thoughts and fears, then disperse and join groups farther away. Hunger, illness, the endless terror and miseries are far from our thoughts as we try to discern whatever will happen to each one of us. One says the tunnel will be open for business tomorrow as usual. Another answers, saying, "My foot! First of all, how will we manage to get everyone sleeping in the barracks when there are already normally two of us to a bed? We can't put in four; there isn't even enough space on the floor." Another picks up the thought: "So, it's certain; the last day shift will go down in the tunnel tonight. And if they do, it means that everything is just as it was before . . . that there isn't any danger in the area and the Allies are still a long way off."

Or, still more seriously, could the SS have some projects for all the prisoners? At the same time, however, it must be remembered that the SS aren't the only ones to decide our fate at this point. The tunnel enterprises (Zawatsky) now have a word in the matter as well.

Could there have been a conflict between the civilian and military authorities, leading to a decision as to which group will take over? It's obvious that if the Zawatsky civilians have had orders to close the tunnel, they won't give a damn about the fate of the prisoners when they are gone. Then the SS will have a free and savage hand with us, with no one to interfere, care, or even notice. However, if Zawatsky is ordered to maintain production until the last moment, then the tunnel civilians will have the advantage in opposing a liquidation that would strip them of their workers.

So for the moment, prisoners walk about and profit in this rest day, a day unique in all the history of Dora. Soup is even served at midday, and it's of fairly good quality, with potatoes and pasta!

Still, there's something odd and unnatural about the rhythm of the camp today, and worry eats away at the minds of most prisoners. All of us feel as if our fate is being decided at this moment. The wheel of our fortune can spin for another few days, but it can also click to a stop at any moment.

All too easily, the order can come—"All prisoners to the roll call square!"—and destiny will swing harshly in one direction or another. The machine guns of the lookouts can fire into the crowd and follow the stampeding groups. Then the SS, heavily armed with their Schmeisser automatics, grenades, and flamethrowers, can methodically wipe out each corner of life left in the camp, one by one.

Just as easily, it could mean an evacuation or at least its start. The SS would take a few thousand prisoners, then load them on highways or open railroad cars to march or ride for days or weeks without food or water, dying like flies along the way.

More hopefully, if the civilians have been ordered to continue production, then the night-shift kommandos will go down into the tunnel tonight.

The lowest-level officials among the prisoners, the only ones with any chance of having information, are invisible. The few who appear in public are immediately surrounded and questioned, to which they simply respond, "We don't know a thing. Nothing's happening; every-thing's OK, don't worry." Sure it is. And the moon is made of green cheese. The veterans have developed a sixth sense that lets them know when something is about to go awry. Their problems have been so considerable that they can almost smell it when trouble is in the offing. These diplodoci (dinosaurs), twenty or thirty years old, sur-vivors of a reptilian Nazi world without pity, must always be alert just to remain alive.

But on this Easter Sunday of 1945, we have no way in which to per-ceive the situation rightly. There are too many pieces in the puzzle, too many unknowns. An equation can only be solved if you have a basic minimum of the right inputs with which to find the solution. But in the equation of Dora, we have no inputs, only unknowns.

In the midst of all the suppositions, what can we do? The answer is: nothing. We're helpless. Even those who owe their survival to an in-credible ability to adapt and react feel unarmed, condemned to follow a fate they are powerless to oppose. Tomorrow or the next day—in a week or a minute—something will happen. Only at that moment will they be able to act to try and save whatever is left of themselves.

As always, the dice will have been loaded by their German captors, but they're used to that duplicity and will make do as best they can.

For the time being, then, what good is it to continue these discus-sions with anyone? Nobody knows a thing, so for now, let's make the best of this unexpected rest day. The Easter Sunday weather—for once—is perfect at Dora. The sun is shining on the camp; it's a real spring day. So let's roll a cigarette, somehow, out of something, and smoke it as slowly as we can.

8

THE END OF THE ROAD

Monday morning. It's eight o'clock. The kommandos are on their way down to roll call square. Everything seems normal, and most of the anxieties of the previous evening are forgotten. Already, the formations are lined up as usual. The roll call won't be long, and then we'll move down quickly into the tunnel.

But what's happening now? Instead of going off to the area assigned to their kommandos, the prisoners of Barracks 10 have been halted on the top side of the square, along with others who preceded them. Charles and Michel look at each other: This is it, the departure.

In this tiny corner of an alien world, Europe and Asia are side by side. There are the French, the Belgians, the Dutch, the Czechs, the Yugoslavs, the Poles, the Hungarians, and all the peoples from the immensity of Russia—every single one held in a trap of steel bayonets and machine-gun muzzles only too ready to open fire.

The setup has been so sudden and well prepared that no one had been suspicious. A section of Dora has been cut out and is about to be sent out on the road. The Lagerschutz begin to encircle the helpless prisoners. It's the end, there's nothing we can do. But yes, we can do something. A revolt, a jump into the electrified wire, a dash for safety. Michel screams at Charles: "Let's get out!"

Even as he shouts the words, the movement explodes through the thousands of separated men, and a stampede radiates in every direction. The Lagerschutz charge, clubbing right and left with their truncheons, but it's too late. They can't do a thing against the horde of demons scattering this way and that, rushing toward the heights, and searching for hiding places between the barracks. A few prisoners fight and are knocked out, but most of the thousands have disappeared. So a manhunt is organized. The SS stir up the barracks chiefs; the escapees are to be tracked down.

Charles and Michel have hidden with about a hundred others in a small yard behind one of the barracks, sort of a cul-de-sac. All of them

200

have run, and their faces are deathly pale from the effort, their breath coming in wheezing gasps. The Russians, very excited, have grouped together in a corner.

"The bastards had us in the bag, all right. That was a good trick, going down into the tunnel, but we were up to it."

Michel yells, but it's the cry of an empty carcass, a dying man getting excited.

Suddenly, noises break out in the barracks. A group of Lagerschutz led by the Blockältester appears in the yard. The prisoners are trapped like rats. With truncheons threatening, the Germans signal everyone to come out. It's the end; obey or die under those clubs. One after another, they emerge and go back down the hill to the roll call square. Slowly, the quadrangle fills again, with many men driven forward by steady beatings.

This time, the net is well secured; no one can escape. The fearsome Lagerschutz are everywhere, watching every movement or attempt to move. At the slightest gesture, they'll rush into the assembled prisoners, clubbing mercilessly. These are Nazi robots, more clubbing machines than human. As the minutes pass, everything falls slowly back into order. Kommando 34 has returned to its place. Michel, without seeming to, counts those who are present.

"Claude has managed to slip away," he breathes.

Claude, the small guy from Lyons, isn't in the group. He must have managed to find a safe place where the Lagerschutz didn't find him.

The Russians are everywhere, the immense majority as always forming the bulk of the prisoner troop. But where are we to go? Is this an evacuation? Are we leaving for another camp? Or is this to be the liquidation? The moment of stupor passes, and Michel regains his aggressiveness.

"You see, we're idiots," he rasps. "We were trapped like so many flies. Getting all piled into a yard like that is the stupidest screwup we could have made. For God's sake, even a newcomer wouldn't have screwed up like that. Now we'll all be liquidated like a bunch of idiots."

Charles is getting fed up with Michel's tempers, having been teamed up with him for months. "Shut your mouth, you piece of shit! We're trapped, all sewed up. If you want to be knocked off by the Lagerschutz, keep it up. They're just waiting for a chance."

After an hour, the group is taken to the disinfection barracks, and everyone strips down. It's been more than a month since they have been naked together, and the spectacle is impressive. The once flesh-less creatures have become skeletal wraiths, bones covered by little more than skin. Their buttocks hang empty above storklike legs. The cresol in the disinfectant hums in their mucous membranes, while the body lice fall away in death. The warm shower relaxes their tortured, stiffened muscles.

Officials arrive to note their numbers and take them off of the camp list.

"Don't worry," says one, "you're going to Harzungen. It's not too bad there, and you're all veterans."

"But why are we going there?" asks a prisoner. "We're from the tunnel. Is it the evacuation? Or what?"

"Don't worry, everything will be OK."

Anxiety grips the prisoners. Everything OK? What a lot of crap! Memories of the evacuees arriving from the east fill their minds. Those transfers, 95 percent of them dead bodies by the time they arrived and the remainder who disappeared within the next few days, are all too real. Those lost souls must have heard the same words when they started: "Don't worry, everything will be OK."

The infamous job is under way. They're going to take us out into an open field and kill us all. The Russians in their corner begin singing a wild song of the steppes and tundras. When the Russians start to sing, it's because they can smell death.

Now our clothes have been steamed. As always, they come back to us wet, with the bodies of dead lice making little red spots in the creases. We dress, line up in columns of five, and head for the heights of the camp, which has become the quarantine zone. From that perspective, Dora looks deceptively calm and fantastic: a magnificent camp, perfectly organized.

Under every barracks, however, and under each lump of concrete lie the endless terror and countless hundreds of bodies. Dora, you filthy whore, you hellish mess, you made us die a thousand deaths. But Dora, I don't want to leave you; I'm too scared of what's going to happen to us.

"Everyone go to bed! *Alle schlafen!*" It's the barracks chief, truncheon in his fist. Then he remembers that he's dealing with veterans and lowers his voice a bit. He, too, is beginning to worry about his future. It's the end, but only the devil knows how the curtain will drop. The disappearance, the death of Dora is no more than a question of hours.

★   ★   ★

The first real departure takes place on Tuesday, April 3rd, to Harzungen. It isn't far away. The prisoners only have to leave the camp and travel about ten miles around the hill, and they are in front of an electrified barrier, simpler than those at Dora. The weather is still fair, but clouds are building up, indicating a return of cold weather. The column of at least two thousand men stops. The guards here don't seem to be SS. They may be Hungarians or Romanians. Then, in groups of one hundred in columns of five, the prisoners move into the camp.

"I say, it looks quite rustic here. You'd think we were going to spread dung in the fields!" calls out one man.

In fact, Harzungen does look like a badly kept farm. Loose straw, scattered bits of wood, and all sorts of rubble are strewn everywhere. The area looks neglected.

"Hold on, guys, here comes the farmer!" calls another. He has spotted the red triangle with an *F* on the jacket of a prisoner who is approaching. The man is pushing a wheelbarrow and looks like a real idiot.

"I say, Toto, how are things here?"

The dung-spreader stops his barrow, then scratches his head under his striped cap. He thinks for a moment, but it's clear that his thoughts are struggling to leave his badly disorganized brain.

"How are things here? Oh, I don't know . . . and where are you from?"

"We're from Dora."

"From Dora? . . . Well, then." The hulk goes on with his wheelbarrow. He must have had some tough clubbings on the head to get that way.

The transfer party is regrouped on the roll call square. Perfect alignment shows that the prisoners are veteran concentration camp inmates. The square is surrounded by military men in German uniforms, but they are not SS. These men are from all over Central Europe, dressed in black and khaki uniforms.

"Attention!"

The camp commandant arrives and asks for interpreters.

"You have come from Dora, and you are now at Harzungen. Here, discipline is very strict, and I see to it personally. Today, you will move in, and tomorrow, we will form works kommandos. You are veteran prisoners, and I know you will respect the discipline. So tomorrow, we form the kommandos, and you will work."

Announcement over, the commandant leaves.

Shit, what the hell is this? Here we've been shipped in from Dora—the guys who have built the first giant rocket in human history—and they send us to make an extra hole in the ground when the situation is catastrophic!

We thought we were headed for the final liquidation. Instead, here we are with this clown who doesn't read the newspapers and wants us to go and push wheelbarrows in this shit of a hole.

For the guys from Dora, Harzungen is a real peasants' pit. This poor idiot of a commandant doesn't realize that it's the end of the road for everybody, for him as well as the prisoners. In a few days, maybe a few hours, the heavens will cave in on us all. Well, at least we don't work today, to our great surprise. At Dora, they didn't wait until the next day to shove a pick into your hands.

It is just after midday. The camp looks almost deserted. Only a few laborers are seen, spreading stones in the hollowed-out tracks under the tired eyes of a Vorarbeiter. The rest must be working in the mine.

The newcomers are led to the barracks, and the dilapidated look of these buildings confirms the sensation we have about the place. There is grass and rubbish everywhere. Inside, the barracks is dusty and completely empty. No crude bunks, no straw mattresses, nothing.

The windows are very dirty. The men go in and glance around, and almost all come out again. With no luggage, they don't need to mark out their places or look after their possessions. Outside, they can feel the temperature dropping. The spring of Easter is far away, and this place gives off an aura of great sadness. Groups begin to form, and conversations are the same in every tongue.

"Why did they yank us out of Dora and the tunnel to put us in this rotten camp, then tell us we don't start work until tomorrow? If we've evacuated Dora, it can't be to keep this place working."

"Well, maybe Dora is too big a chunk to evacuate all at once. Twenty thousand guys are a lot to handle. So the SS have a policy of dealing in separate packages. They'll send groups to all the small nearby camps. That way, when the whistle blows, they won't have just one enormous mass to roust out onto the highway."

For the moment, however, there's no question of leaving on the roads because tomorrow we'll start digging again. But if Dora's tunnel closes, what the hell are they going to want with this new hole? Nothing is clear at all here.

"Is there anything normal about this place?"

Suddenly, whistles are blowing everywhere. The Lagerschutz howl, "Everyone in the barracks!"

There is a rush for the barracks. And then we can hear the sound of airplanes, large numbers of them, it seems. They are coming overhead with the sound of hundreds of roaring engines. Then come the first explosions, which become a steady crackling thunder. The ground vibrates a little.

"That's it, the Americans are bombing Dora. But no, that's not Dora, or we'd get some, too. It's more likely to be Nordhausen getting hit!"

The bombing seems to be extremely violent from the mass of aircraft, and now we can again hear the planes flying farther away. From Harzungen, we can't see the town itself, but columns of smoke are visible in that direction, climbing into the sky.

The men are deeply moved. For the first time, they see that the war is getting close. Outside on the square, the armed SS are running in all directions. Haphazardly, the Kapos and Lagerschutz blow their whistles. The situation outside is getting panicky. Prudently, the prisoners draw back away from the windows.

★   ★   ★

"*Aufstehen!*" (Wake up!) The barracks chief, dressed in his cloak and high boots, blows his whistle. The men stand up on the board floor, fully clothed but pressed against each other to get a little warmth. They need a moment to remember where they are, then look out the windows. "But, good God, it's daytime! What time can it be?"

The prisoners knew they should have been awakened a lot earlier to form kommandos and go down to work. So why this unexpected late call?

"*Los! Antreten!*" Assembly. We're late, but apparently, we're going to work without rations or coffee.

The new arrivals from Dora get out of the barracks and line up on the square with well-polished discipline. Yesterday, they saw a dirty, empty camp. This morning, it's just as messy, but now there are people. The whole workforce seems to be present, signifying that the kommandos haven't started their workday. The Kapos and chiefs are prowling around the formations, speaking quietly among themselves. It all points to some major event, to big decisions.

"*Stillgestanden! Mützen ab!*" The whole camp executes the order amid an enormous sound of clacking clogs. Up here, the weather has rapidly deteriorated into a damp coldness. The few clouds from the night before have taken over the sky, while on the ground, the wind is scattering odd bits of paper and various scraps. Harzungen seems to have a lousy standard of cleanliness and tidiness.

Now the commandant appears, followed by his assistant. He is a small man, inclined to obesity. He has put on his regimental uniform and shining boots. He doesn't seem to be a high-ranking officer, perhaps a lieutenant or captain. He walks forward to the empty center of the square and calls the interpreters forward.

"I have been advised that the American army has arrived in this region and is progressing in the direction of this camp. I am telling you that I will myself put the camp and its prisoners in the hands of the American officer commanding the unit that will be presenting itself at the gate. There will be no evacuation."

The interpreters translate his words immediately into French, Polish, and Russian. In the ranks, the prisoners can't believe it. It's impossible. The war isn't going to end in a stupid whisper like this. Is he telling us that, in a few hours, everything can be finished and that, by this evening, the Americans will be giving us chocolates and cigarettes? That we are going home?

The commandant gives some orders and leaves the square. Without breaking ranks, the prisoners return to their barracks. Once inside, everything becomes merry madness. Joy bursts out in every language.

"That's it, guys! It's finished! *We have won!*"

Suddenly, everyone is joyfully embracing. The Russians, Poles, and French are miraculously reconciled. The barracks chief warns that the rations are going to be handed out and that we must be in groups of four to share a loaf of bread, margarine, and sausage. For the first time in the history of the camps, we're ready to team up with other nationalities, even the Russians. Nobody is about to try to cheat or steal. What do we care since the Americans will be here tonight? It's the Grande Entente Internationale.

"Did you see?" says one. "It's the commandant who's going to hand us over to the Americans. It's fantastic! And for him to say that today and not tomorrow means the American army will be here before tonight. He wouldn't risk announcing it several days in advance."

"I watched the commandant closely," adds another. "I didn't see him too well because he was too far from us, but I have the impression he wasn't SS. And then, can you imagine an SS man telling us such a thing? Why, he only just stopped short of calling us his dear little children!"

A third man is more thoughtful. "Well, if you think about it, he may be SS nevertheless, and he's taken off his uniform and badge. From now on, it's going to be hard to find an SS man."

Another adds grimly, "And what about the Kapos and barracks chiefs? Their truncheons have disappeared into thin air. All those deadly beatings never existed except in our imaginations. The concentration camp is about to be presented to the Yanks as a kindly sanatorium!"

It is an hour of total euphoria. All the thousands of men here, all of us are going to know that marvelous joy, the unique moment of Liberation! Even those at the end of their tether, condemned by fate and about to die, even they will taste the supreme joy of being freed. They will see the Americans, those superb young gods opening the gates of hell and saying, "As of now, you have become *free men!*" Then the doomed will lie down, and their souls will fly from their tortured carcasses, crying *"Merci! Merci bien!"*

In the midst of this rapture, the Russians suddenly seem distressed. They're happy, of course, and show their elation in sharp cries of delight. But something isn't quite right. The liberation is too sudden; it goes against all the dreams of hatred and vengeance they've developed through months of suffering, privation, torture, and death. Their dreams of punishment and revenge, so lovingly cherished, are being overthrown by this quick change of events. Vengeance is a thing distilled and savored, and it must be executed at just the right moment in the painful agony of the drama. But now, suddenly, the theatrical rule has become unbalanced. The Germans aren't playing the game.

In the afternoon, the Blockältester makes a new appearance, followed by the Stubendienst who have remained at the door with bread, margarine, and sausages. There is no coffee, but who worries about that at a time like this?

"Listen, everyone. You are going to come up in groups of four, and you will be given your rations. You'll cut them up, share them, and then go to the roll call."

Everyone laughs. It's the last roll call, the last one before liberation. We'll go gladly. What a shame that there isn't a camera handy. It would be something extraordinary to capture the last image of detention on film.

The men go by in groups of four and take their loaves of bread, bits of margarine, and sausage. They share the portions and go out to get in line. Everyone starts eating right away. We couldn't care less; tonight, we'll have caviar.

Outside, the square fills quickly with groups thinking less about a straight line than their rations. They just eat, not bothering to look to the left or right. Then, one by one, their eyes begin looking up, and in the ingrained habit of prisoner reflexes, they scrutinize their surroundings. But what's this? What the hell is happening? The truncheons are back in sight; they're everywhere. Kapos, barracks chiefs, Lagerschutz—they all have clubs in hand again! In the lookout towers, guards have their machine guns trained on the prisoners on the square. Soldiers surround the place. And the camp gate, that barrier separating two worlds, is wide open.

My God! It's the evacuation!

★   ★   ★

The long column of prisoners has now passed the gate of Harzungen, stretching out along the road. There are a lot of people but still not all those in the camp. No doubt, the others will leave later in one or several groups. The Kapos and barracks chiefs are loaded with boxes, sacks, and even suitcases. Walking in tight lines, they threaten the prisoners with their truncheons. The German guards are numerous. They walk along beside the column, rifles and machine guns in hand and ready to fire. Rain begins to fall, and it is cold.

Soon the road from the camp joins a real public road, and the prisoners can see that chaos has arrived, at least among German civilians. Carts, automobiles, bicycles, and pedestrians block the pavement. The vehicles are crammed full with suitcases, bags, and piles of clothing, with mattresses loaded upon their roofs. The bicycles they push are so loaded that their wheels are barely visible.

Cursing, the guards push the civilians onto the sidewalks. The roadway is a priority for moving the prisoners. Already, some of the weakest men begin to drag their feet. The ranks begin to break up, but the Kapos club them from behind. To the rear, there are shouts. The SS use their rifle butts to make those who are dragging break into a staggering run.

We haven't gone far from Harzungen, only a few miles, but the men are already tiring. After being conditioned to exhausting work, for months the prisoners have worked their daily journeys on foot; the routines have become conditioned reflexes. But now, when the route and length of march are so drastically changed, their cheeks become hollow, they lose their breath, and their legs weaken.

The column arrives at a station with a train already at the platform. It is quite long, about thirty open wagons and a few enclosed railroad cars. The men breathe sighs of relief—at least we won't have to make this journey on foot. Even the most exhausted regain their hope; perhaps now they have a chance of pulling through. However, the open trucks are small in size. If they load us at a hundred per truck, there won't be enough space for everyone.

Now the SS men push the column forward along the length of the train, breaking the prisoners up into groups of fifty. That may be OK. With fifty, maybe we can all manage to sit down somehow. The prisoners climb aboard and start to mark their places, but they haven't counted the German SS guard, who boards last. He uses the butt of his rifle to push everyone out of the corner he has selected. Then he fixes his bayonet to the rifle's muzzle for all to see and sits in his corner. The dislocated prisoners begin to shout and curse each other, but the SS man lets out a growl. Everything calms down.

Soon after this, the SS officers and women of the German army arrive; the women, known as "gray mice," are wearing heavy makeup. They are loaded with spoils, cases, bags, and cans of food; the officers have the same plus machine guns and ammunition. Shouting and laughing, they board the enclosed cars.

The waiting seems interminable, and the prisoners begin to feel cramps coming on. After all, fifty men to a small open railcar doesn't leave enough room after the SS guard has taken a quarter of the space for himself. We can already see that before long, the weakest will be crushed underneath the mass of the others. A steady, quiet rain is falling now, soaking the light uniforms of the men. There is no protection. On the deserted station platform, large puddles are forming, with not a single civilian traveler to be seen. From time to time, a uniformed railroad employee passes our open railcars, seeing nothing.

From within the covered railroad cars, we can hear a hubbub amid women's voices. Now two soldiers come up with a small lunchwagon and hand out food to the SS guards; bread, canned food, and coffee. For the prisoners, there is nothing. We will have the privilege of watching the guard put down his rifle, spread his legs, and open the can with his knife. The can is filled with potted pork, spread in thick layers. The very sight is torture. The German takes a large mouthful, chews slowly and conscientiously, and swallows his food with a grunt of satisfaction. He repeats the procedure, while our stomachs scream, until his rations are finished. Then he rolls a cigarette slowly and lights up with obvious pleasure.

The weather continues to deteriorate. In our hopelessness, we wonder how long we'll be kept like this. Will this train ever move?

Finally, a whistle sounds from up front. A very old type of engine has arrived, puffing out jets of steam as it backs to make a connection. Civilian employees emerge from the station and go toward the engine. In view of the circumstances, they seem to be hurrying to hook up the train and get it moving as quickly as possible. Some SS officers, doubtless the ones responsible for this convoy, go up to the station chief. They arrive together at the engine. There are discussions, and with much heel-clicking and "Heil Hitler" salutes, the SS officers return to their enclosed railroad cars.

There is a long, shrill whistle from the locomotive, and with great puffs of steam, the convoy is moving.

★   ★   ★

The day after departure is April 5th, and the train from Harzungen is rolling through the countryside. The prisoners have slept like less-than-animal creatures, crushed down on top of each other. It's a dirty day, sad, cold, and still raining. All night long, the German guard, cursing, has booted, bayoneted, and driven back the exhausted bodies. He is in a very foul mood; he'd like to sleep.

Shouts are heard from all the open rail wagons. We awaken to find that there are dead bodies everywhere. They take up room, and we'd like to throw them over the side, but the guards refuse to allow it. They have no orders about this, so we living prisoners must sit on top of the dead. That way, there will be more room, and the number of prisoners will remain correct.

The train comes to a stop in the middle of the countryside. Again, the SS guards receive their rations, this time bread, cold meat, and coffee. Nothing for the prisoners, of course. The train starts forward again. It seems as if they don't know where they're going because from time to time, they come to a stop near a station but far away from its platforms. Then they reverse and leave on still another line, only to stop again after an hour or two. At another station, there is a hurried conference between the station chief and the SS leaders, who elect still another direction. A fine, glacial rain continues to fall.

By talking with prisoners who understand German and have been listening to conversations between the guards, we learn that at least one train direct from Dora and perhaps a second from Harzungen are on the same line. The evacuation of the Harz Mountains seems to be general, but the convoys are apparently paralyzed either because of the bombings or because of military priorities. And no one knows our final destination.

The trucks are filled with prisoners who are frozen, soaked, starving, and covered with shit. The night guards have been replaced by others who had slept in the covered railway cars. Disgusted at having to spend hours among such an unearthly trash of stinking prisoners, they show their resentment with shouts, smashing rifle butts, and stabbing bayonets.

Slowly, desperately, the day wears on. Some prisoners who want to talk with men in the next wagon stand up, but they are immediately knocked out by the guard's rifle butt. The numbers of the dead increase. A stripped carcass, pushed from one prisoner to the next, ends up on the knees of a neighbor without a sound. These were living men, and suddenly, they are dead. They are under our feet, under our buttocks, already a softer cushion than the railcar's flooring.

The guards are changed regularly. It seems that, in addition to their food, they also have the right to a share of tenderness. The women with the convoy aren't typists at all but real whores. Each time the train stops, they put on provocative displays. The guards who have finished their shifts climb aboard the closed cars with them when the train starts again. It's a real pleasure for the guards.

Each time the train stops, the starving prisoners hope they'll get some food, but their hopes vanish. Nothing has been allowed for them. What good is it to feed them since their fate is already sealed? They'll never be left alive. So if some reach their destination, there will be time to think about it. For the moment, though, it would be a waste of good food.

★   ★   ★

Friday, April 6th, is the third day of travel for the Harzungen evacuees. Dawn has risen, cold and damp. All night long, the guard has smoked and used his rifle to push back the bodies piling up. New corpses are found, and they are laid out across the floorboards. A good bedding of insulation now covers the rude base of the car.

The prisoners are beset with worrisome shivering. Even though they press closely together, they cannot evaporate the penetrating rain. Their terribly hollowed faces are beginning to become greenish in hue. They regroup according to nationality, which causes brutal confrontations along the group boundaries. There are heated words about the space to be taken by each group. The SS guard shouts and begins clubbing heads. Then, seated and wrapped in his tenting, he kicks the nearest prisoners furiously. He is cold, too, and would like to sleep.

Surprisingly, then, the sky clears completely. The sun begins to warm aching bodies. The heat enters the pile of human debris, and a slight steam rises from their ragged uniforms. A marvelous sense of well-being permeates the bodies of those still alive.

The train stops at the edge of a wooded area, and the guards are relieved. Those replacing them demand more space, sit down in place, and take out their rations. They have bread, canned food, sausage, and mugs of hot coffee. The prisoners, piled in their corners, are hypnotized by the food. Sobs break out from some. From among the Russians, we hear muttering and bitter cursing, all in low voices. Their stares are hard and murderous. We pick up comments going from man to man when the thickly spread bread enters the German's mouth. Little would be needed, only the slightest impulse, and the famished horde would dive onto their torturer.

For several hours, the train hasn't moved. The SS leave their cars regularly to relieve themselves in the woods and stretch their legs. Then they inspect their convoy. With single jumps, they hoist themselves up the side of the open cars and glance inside. *"Sehr gut!"* Everything is all right. They go off again to talk with fellow officers. The women also appear from time to time to visit with nature behind the trees. One of them, an amazonlike female with an impressive chest, regularly jumps from the enclosed car ahead, giving out gales of loud laughter. In the distance, at the same time, we can hear the sounds of bombing.

From the changing azimuths of the sun, it's obvious that our convoy is running in circles, going in one direction, stopping, then branching off in a new direction. It has never crossed any large town or station or used a single main line. Nor have we encountered another single convoy.

Does the SS mean to have us roam Germany in endless circles until we're all dead? Judging from the capricious itinerary of a train that goes nowhere and meets nobody, it's very possible. The convoy goes forward, then back, in a continuum detached from the rest of the earth, leading its own solitary life.

But where is the war? Where are the soldiers? From time to time, we hear noises and explosions, but these are always far away. When the train does come into some unknown local station, the platforms are empty. Only the stationmaster appears to meet with the SS, wearing his almost military uniform. The stationmaster doesn't even glance at the dying prisoners. Good German that he is, he ignores the very fact of their existence.

Toward midafternoon, the convoy moves on very slowly. The sky is beautifully still, and the sunlight is almost warm. The prisoners begin to doze, their sleeping bodies tossed against each other with the rolling motions of the railcars. There is only the sound of the engine's puffing and the wheels clattering as they roll over the rails. The wooded countryside leads to a series of valleys. Now the train twists between rounded hills, alternating between zones of light and shadow. Lulled by the steady noises, the SS guards are heavy-eyed. They have set aside their canvas tenting and smoked their Zigaretten, and, with rifles cradled across their thighs, they dream of sweethearts or hum favorite songs.

The train moves between two wooded hills, and we can hear birds singing. A hundred yards ahead, a highway overpass straddles the rail line. There are several children who look to be about ten years old on the overpass, no doubt from a neighboring village. Having seen the train approach, they collect some stones and laughingly throw them at the prisoners.

At that exact moment, two of the prisoners jump from their railcar and begin to climb the embankment. It's well timed, with the guards only half-conscious. But the children cry out, and "action stations" sounds for the guards. The train halts, and SS officers jump from their cars with weapons in hand. The would-be escapees are trying desperately to climb the embankment, but they have no more strength. Like wounded insects, they frantically grasp at tufts of grass and roots, then slip backward down the slope. The SS officers go up to them, calmly and deliberately. They place the muzzles of their weapons against each prisoner's head and fire. That's all.

The officers give orders. Guards come, retrieve the bodies, and throw them into the open railcar. The children on the overpass applaud the brave SS officers.

★   ★   ★

On Saturday, the train enters a large station. It seems enormous to the prisoners, whose weakness has deprived them of all sense of proportion, but it is certainly very big. Rows of platforms and rail lines are laden with a vast collection of military equipment. There are trainloads of troops, material supplies, and ammunition. There are tanks mounted on flatbeds, their cannon pointing downward, and machine guns grouped in pairs. There are mortars precisely lined up on flatbed trucks. Behind the sliding doors of covered railcars, you can see great piles of munition cases.

The troop trains are filled with armed German soldiers looking tired and nervous. And everywhere, you can see ack-ack guns and rapid-fire cannons aimed toward the sky. On the railroad platforms, overexcited officers are bawling out endless orders. The sun bathes the scene overall, and it is amazingly hot for this time of year.

The Harzungen train pulls alongside a platform slightly away from the others. Farther on, between the prisoners and the rows of overloaded platforms, there is a rail convoy bristling with machine guns pointed skyward. The operators look at the prisoners, only about twenty yards away, with astonishment. Charles finds he is just opposite a gunner who is about his own age; one is a lord, and the other accursed. Tired by the hubbub of the station, the young German looks with interest at these strange, shrunken creatures. He may or may not have seen some prisoners, but he has certainly never met men in such a state.

The hubbub is drowned out when the sirens begin to howl, and there is pandemonium in the station; a panic in an anthill. Germans are running in all directions. They are caught in a trap!

"Everyone! Under the train!"

SS and prisoners are immediately piled together under the railcar. It wouldn't be fitting for the captives to be killed by the Americans. No, it isn't in the Nazi rules of the game. The prisoners belong to the SS, and they alone are allowed to decide whether the men will live or die.

Under the railcar, Charles notices the German. He has fixed his helmet and pointed his weapon, a double-barreled machine gun.

Suddenly, the planes are overhead everywhere, and the explosions begin. The ground quivers and trembles. Whistlings and groans fill the air. It's the end of the world.

Charles looks out at the soldier, the only one he can see. The man fires upward like a fool. He doesn't know what to shoot at. Suddenly, he straightens up, surrounded by flames and explosions. His uniform is torn and peels away from him like burnt paper. His face is covered with blotches and begins to melt. He falls with his weapon, its barrels aimed upward toward the sky.

"Everyone back aboard the train!"

The prisoners climb over the metal sides and take their places again. Only the dead haven't moved. The planes have passed overhead, but the station echoes with explosions, and fires are breaking out everywhere. Of the trains that were nearby a few minutes ago, nothing remains but masses of twisted metal.

Somehow, the convoy of prisoners has been spared. God is with the SS. Even the line allowing the train to exit is intact. The captives' journey begins again.

★   ★   ★

Charles feels a shooting pain in his stomach. He awakens or, better, comes back to life. In front of him is a wide-open face, gaping as if its jawbone had been broken off. "Good God," he says to himself, "I'm among the stiffs!" Around him, he can see only the inert forms of the dead. Above, he can see clogs moving about. He must have lost consciousness and been thrown in among the corpses. With great effort, he climbs back to the surface of the pile. The survivors nearby moan. "Why is this dead body coming to bother us?" He wonders whether it is morning or afternoon. It looks more like a morning. But what morning? Charles would like to think, but his head feels almost empty, as if his brain were full of cotton. Ah! It must be Sunday, the morning of the fifth day aboard the helltrain. Around him, he sees skeletal heads, with deeply hollowed cheeks almost thin enough to show the teeth inside. The sun is relatively warm, yet everyone is shaking. Even the guard on duty seems exhausted. He is shaven and spotless, but his features, too, are hollowing out. He groans while pushing away some feet. The slightest irritation will have him firing into the crowd, but nobody even looks at him. We no longer look; we no longer have the strength.

From time to time, cries break out and blows are exchanged between nationalities, but they are the sputterings of old men in an asylum. Not one prisoner is in any condition either to fight or to defend himself.

"Let's see," thinks Charles, "how many days is it? Five? Yes, that's it, I think, it's been five days that we've been going in circles. And have we eaten anything in those five days?" Beyond that, he doesn't remember anything. He tries to think, stirring the wet muddle within his brain, and thinks that, one day, they were given food, but he isn't sure, and, anyhow, he wouldn't know what or when.

Perhaps he hasn't had any food since leaving Harzungen—and what the fuck? First, he isn't hungry anymore, and if they gave him a bowl of really good, thick, warm soup, doubtless he wouldn't have the strength to swallow a spoonful. Careful, my old Charles, you're about to slip off the tracks for good. Remember the Moslems at Dora? They were like you, with those fixed grins. A push of the finger and they fell into nothingness; they turned into dust.

Charles notices Michel. He still has that stubborn look and clenches his teeth, but the full, rosy cheeks have now disappeared. Under the prominent cheekbones, there are deep hollows. Michel turns around and sees Charles.

"Oh, there you are! You disappeared. I didn't know where you were."

"Well, I'm back from the dead," says Charles. "I was among the stiffs where I had a little snooze. I think I was unconscious for quite a while."

The conversation stops. Speaking is too tiring. You must save your strength. So as not to become dazed but because it worries him a little, Charles asks, "Michel, do you remember if we have eaten since leaving Harzungen?"

Michel turns around, with a venomous expression and murder gleaming in his eyes. "Shut up! I hate it when people speak about disagreeable things."

It's Michel all over. Pigheaded and angry to the end. Charles recalls a night in the tunnel. They had decided that one of them would sleep in front of his machine while the other kept watch. Every two hours, the roles were to be reversed. But when Charles awakened Michel, the latter was in a deadly mood and snarled, "You make me sick with your turn of snoozing. I've slept badly, and I had nightmares. And beyond that, the cold froze me stiff!"

"But, Michel, we said each one would have his turn. Now I feel like sleeping. It's my turn, as we agreed."

"I couldn't care less what you want to do. I'm sore all over, and it was lousy. If you want to sleep, then sleep, but don't bother me."

Charles took Michel's reaction at face value. Perhaps Michel was right, after all, that sleeping in that freezing den wasn't a good system, that it was better to keep moving because of the cold and dampness. It was the way he said it that hurt Charles. And yet, they were two inseparable partners who couldn't live or survive without each other. Charles thinks, "Shit, this irascible cunt will be telling the world to go fuck itself right to the very end."

The corpses of our late fellow prisoners are piled everywhere in the open cars of this helltrain. Do you want some? Here you are. Serve yourself, it's all free. Of course, the dead are as thin as broomsticks, and they do stiffen quickly. Even as cushions, they aren't worth much. Well, so they're worthless. They could very well be tossed overboard to lighten ship, and we'd arrive in port sooner. But which port? And is there even a port? But you mustn't dream; for the prisoners, no port exists. After five days in the postal service, an ordinary parcel, even at slow speed, might reach Paris, Rome, or even Timbuktu. But five days in this ghost express equals zero travel. At the end of five days, the shipwrecked captives aboard this train are exactly midway between Nothing and Nowhere. The sails are run up, the main jib hauled, and we arrive in view of nonexistent waters in a port that doesn't exist.

Inevitably, our spirits weaken, and we drift into an apathy closely resembling a coma. We're delirious, as a group, and couldn't care less; yet, in the depths of our shipwrecked minds, a tiny glimmer remains, bent upon survival. For God's sake, we must hold on!

But another voice, false and insinuating, comes to say, "Why be stubborn, you shabby bunch of trash. Can't you see, even now, that all the gods of all the religions ever known have abandoned you? You're nothing but smelly shit. The SS are right; you're vile, and even your wives on the outside would ignore you if they could see you now. So what use is all this resistance? Let it go!"

Then another voice, still deeper and more resolute, responds, "Never! As long as I've got an ounce of life, I'll keep it and take it where nobody has ever been. Hitler and Himmler, you rotten bastards, I'll give Nazi Germany a royal salute, and we'll see which of the two of us will have the last word!"

The train to Hades continues on its way. It stops and then starts again. In the cold corners of the open railcars, strange ghostly figures move about. Their stiff limbs barely react to any stimulus; we no longer know who is still alive and who is already dead.

If you are looking upon me, I swear one thing: I will hold on!

★   ★   ★

During the night of Sunday through Monday morning, the train arrives at a mass of intersections. The rail lines now split up, with dozens crisscrossing and interchanging. Huge pylons that once carried searchlights now stand like so many dead trees. Water towers with their canvas sleeves and signalmen's huts are spread all over a lifeless railyard space. Here and there, a random switched-on light gives a surrealistic image of the surroundings. The convoy slips from point to point, then seems to hesitate between the lines. It stops a few minutes in front of one signal, then starts again and arrives alongside a remote, deserted platform and stops. A neighboring building, badly lit, still carries in big letters the inscription "Hamburg."

As far as the eye can see, there are hundreds of trucks and miles of platforms, but everything is as deserted as if it were abandoned by mankind. The city itself, which can't be far away, is invisible. Perhaps it doesn't really exist and all of these impressions are nothing but the imagined creations of hallucinating minds.

The convoy chiefs jump to the platform and briefly do some loosening-up exercises. Then soldiers and station officials appear, all in uni-

form. There is the usual flurry of Heil Hitler salutes and much clicking of heels. Then they all board one of the covered railcars. What the
hell does this mean? Have we reached our final destination? Are we
about to be off-loaded? Is this the end of the journey? If it is, a quiet
exit will have to be found because our appearance, dead or alive, isn't
the kind of thing that can be shown to everyone.

Now the summit conference is over, with another flurry of Hitler
salutes and heel-clicking. The welcoming committee goes on its way
to other matters. Time passes, but nothing happens. The prisoners go
back to sleep, and all apparent life stops on the platform.

Finally, the engine throws out jets of steam, and the train slowly begins to move. It follows the rail lines and crosses some intersections.
Little by little, the buildings become farther apart, and the number of
interconnecting rail lines becomes smaller. Our speed increases
steadily. Then there are no more lights or buildings, and the countryside reappears. The helltrain resumes its mad journey to nowhere.

In the open cars, the prisoners think for a moment that they are
going to arrive—no matter where—but arrive! Still, there are no excla-
mations, no movements or gestures. They have expected that someone would like to dispose of them, do anything with their carcasses
and whatever other life still holds on. But nobody wanted them in
Hamburg, and now it seems that they're not wanted anywhere else, either. Like lepers and the plague-stricken, they are being pushed farther
and farther away. Thus, what good is it to look outside the car since
nothing is happening there. The helltrain rolls onward, onward forever, and the prisoners once more drift into unconsciousness.

★　　　★　　　★

On the morning of Monday, April 9th, the ghost train arrives at
Lüneburg Station and comes to a stop alongside the platform. In the
distance, military convoys are moving amid great turmoil. The
weather is fine, and the sun beats down upon the bundles of rags that
the prisoners have become. But the men don't lift their heads. They
are too weak, and their bodies are mere masses of pain; their stiffened
limbs no longer respond. The guards no longer have to defend their
space; nobody moves. The prisoners' eyes, deep in their sockets, are
lifeless, and only some among the Russians still hold a gleam of murder. We're no longer fighting between nationalities, we merely clear a
crushed arm or push a leg away. For the first time since we all became
prisoners, coexistence has become a peaceful thing. Quarrels between
clans are no longer settled by battles or murder; we only show our
teeth. It's the peace of the Grand Necropolis.

A strange silence has settled over the convoy, this mixture of sleeping cars and private club cars. The silence is almost perfect, and one

respects his fellow club members' rest. The guards, tired by the journey and affected by the somnolent atmosphere, tend to doze off while
looking over their flocks. Their slogan could be, "I shut my eyes, but
keep one open." They have sore buttocks and believe that they've had
a rough time like no one on earth. Meanwhile, they're glad for the
calm that has taken over the whole train.

What is this place called Lüneburg? And why make a stop? They
won't want us, either. Lüneburg must be a town with a mayor, a town
council, important people, and mothers. They would all collapse if we
were off-loaded at the station square at school-closing time, tons of
stinking and groaning rotten meat. "Get rid of all this and quickly,"
they would shriek. "We don't want any of that near us. And all these
dried-up mummies flattened on the bottom of the railcars, you can't
throw those things in the town dump; it isn't sound. So move along,
we don't want to see you here. The war news is already bad enough. If
the Americans found a boneyard inside the town limits, they'd blame
us. So take our advice, and leave the station as fast as you can. *Raus!*"
We begin to move forward.

The load of castoffs and ghosts leaves Lüneburg behind. The
weather is lovely, and we can even smell the splendor of spring. There
is a sense of joy in the air, of rejuvenation. Buds are bursting open, animals are mating, and the first flowers have shyly begun to appear.
The countryside is flat and sharp, but it can't escape the sweet madness that is now returning to the Northern Hemisphere. Winter is finished and forgotten; long live spring! Sap is rising in roots, trunks, and
branches. Here and there, on the farms, girls begin to feel a warm sort
of languidness, and the great annual excitement is back again.

This trainload of the destitute and ragged coasts along, crossing
these scenes of beauty, but it isn't involved. It passes on earth only by
error. It has come to pollute this earthly space only because circumstances beyond control have brought it here.

Therefore, we can only think, "Excuse us, good ladies and gentlemen, we didn't want to come and bother you like this. It isn't our
fault, we swear. We were quite happy there in our camp, not bothering
anyone at all. And now those awful Jewish, Masonic, bourgeois,
Anglo-American, French gangster plutocrats have come and upset the
Fatherland. They have caused us to be thrown onto the highways and
railroads like this. We understand quite well that you don't want us,
and we agree, but tell us where to go. Otherwise, we'll be going in circles for centuries. We can't help it if some of us are still alive; it's because we were treated too well. When we think of our three-day journey from Compiègne, that was a million years ago. Another
twenty-four hours and almost everyone was dead. Now, after months

and years of camp and a terrible five-day journey, there are still a few survivors. It just proves that the SS have spoiled us too much. So if our presence bothers you, go and see the SS. We can't do a thing. We'd like to pop off out of this life straightaway, just to spare you our presence, but unfortunately, we have small, awkward flames within that do not want to go out. If that bothers you, too, then it's your problem, not ours. Our business is to hold on just a bit more, to go further than any humans have done since the beginning of mankind. So go and get stuffed, you rotten, uncaring bastards!"

The train starts off again.

★   ★   ★

During the afternoon of Monday, April 9th, our train draws into a medium-sized station and stops by the platform. The place is almost but not quite deserted. Alongside the opposite platform, there is a freight train with covered cattle cars.

Our convoy stops with a creaking of brakes, and the prisoners can hear shouting, groaning, and rattling from the other train. It holds women prisoners. Under a hot sun that is burning through the coverings, they are piled up, as if in communal coffins. They're going to die from lack of air. We wonder whether they're coming or going. But what difference does it make? They're making the same journey as we.

"*Alle raus!*" Everybody out!

The convoy chief has jumped onto the platform to shout out his orders. But the words have some difficulty in penetrating our benumbed brains. What's happening? Have we arrived? Are they going to feed us or what?

The guards become alert and begin to shout while kicking into the prisoners' bodies. Now they have to get out of the train—but how? For five days and five nights, they have been packed and piled up in their corner. The men have no more strength, no reactions or reflexes. Their joints have become so stiff that they no longer know how to walk. Yet somehow, a few prisoners manage to pull upright, move forward like robots, and get down from the railcars. Others, like paralytics, grip their way along the sides, slide along as far as the door, and then fall onto the platform. The guards force the slower men with kicks and blows from their rifle butts. They push forward against their backs, their hands, their faces. Finally, there is nothing left aboard the railcars but the flatness of dead, mummified things, piles of rags.

"*Zu fünf!*" Form columns of five. The prisoners begin to find their universe again. They are given orders and execute them. A long, grayish line snakes along the platform. Lord Jesus, what an army of shadows! It's a mob of the dying, an army of zombies!

The prisoners' heads are frightening. They aren't heads anymore but rather grinning balls with two big holes for their eyes, paired hollows for their cheeks, and a hole for each mouth, from which long yellow teeth protrude. Yet a large number of these scarecrows remain upright. They have suffered so much during their lives as prisoners that nothing more can affect them. They'll begin marching in step, then drop brutally, falling in an instant from life into death.

One group of ex-worthies tries to get to the front of the column. All the prisoners know it's the best place because there they get the least punishment. These ex-worthies are mostly Kapos, barracks chiefs, and Vorarbeiter. A few still have their armlets, symbols of power. Others, for safety's sake, have taken off their armlets and now regret it. The gates of hell are going to close again, and it's better to be among the elite than among the plebeians. These minions of the SS are still loaded with cases and boxes, material proof of their importance, but they, too, have suffered on the journey. Their faces are worn and tired. On the opposite rail line, the sound of women crying and groaning is like the sound of approaching death.

The guards are lined up, rifles at the ready. Some are carrying Schmeisser machine guns. Behind them, another group also carries automatic weapons. The convoy chief and his lieutenant walk the length of the column. Their freshly waxed boots shine as they stride the platform. After months of delegating power, they finally find direct contact with the prisoners extremely satisfying. These rotten lumps of stinking prisoners are more unearthly than ever, and this gratifies them enormously.

"Im Gleichschritt, marschieren!" (In step, march!)

The column leaves the station and heads toward the countryside. It is now very warm. After a few yards, the marching cadence comes back to the men. Marching in columns has become second nature to the prisoners. No need to shout cadence; we march quite well on our own.

After a few miles, death, which has quietly followed the group, begins to show its face. It slips insidiously into bodies, chests, and legs, eating away at their energy and breath. Mocking life, it awaits its prey. But don't think that it only attacks the unfortunate; it also has an eye on the "wealthy," the trustees. It even warns those in front that they, too, are only crematorium meat. It attacks their calves, thighs, and shoulders. The trustees, softened by the years of plenty, begin dropping their cases, which snap open and disgorge treasures of lingerie and sausages.

The most interesting, though, are the poor wretches who get tangled in the shirtsleeves or slip on the margarine packs. They march on mechanically, step after step, holding on for dear life to their remaining strength. They have left the train and marched, as always, at a measured pace. But they are soon finished, and the measured pace is lost.

Within minutes, the ranks break up, their form unraveling. Then, at the rear of the column, the first shots ring out—sometimes a single round, sometimes a burst of fire. The stragglers find a new store of energy and try to catch up with the column but not for long. The most exhausted drop to the rear of the column, fall, lie there, and receive a bullet in the head.

On the sidelines, it's the same. Prisoners walk normally but in an irregular way, without speaking. Suddenly, a man's head leans to one side, he staggers drunkenly and falls into the ditch. The SS man with a Schmeisser goes up to him and triggers a burst of fire into his head. The blood splashes onto his boots, but the column doesn't miss a step. It continues along its way and will keep going as long as there is the smell of life ahead. They're all holding on to their very souls, these poor bastards! After months and years of treatment no animal could survive, they keep marching, and some are even still in step. It isn't normal, but they are demons.

The miles go on, and the shootings increase. The Germans kill prisoners by the dozen, and there are still hundreds left, marching on to the very end. Several times, the men have walked over the coats of fallen Kapos—those marvelous coats so desired during endless freezing days and nights, that fabulous protection against the cold, the wet, and the snow. The men now walk over them so as not to risk tripping, falling down, and getting the ultimate peppering of lead.

For now, the Kapos have ended up by stripping themselves of everything that was their strength and reputation. These half-gods, with their insane anger plus the right to kill, are they getting short of breath? And we, who have suffered a million deaths day after day, we, the wretched, keep on marching. We who travel without luggage have only our carcasses to offer the SS killers, and we think, "Well, you bunch of bastards who subscribed to help the Nazis and betray us all, it upsets you to give up your seniority points and fine clothes, doesn't it? You're hustling at the front of the column because you have reserves of muscle and fat, and you hope to get through this. Unfortunately, though, there's a little hitch. You haven't foreseen that this little trot may be your last; you'll never know. And perhaps there's a bullet with your name on it loaded inside a nearby machine gun. All of it keeps running through your still functional mind, eh? Well, we no longer have brains; we just count the steps, one after another. Where to?"

After miles on the march, the column has thinned out. The liquidation of men who have fallen from the column or into the ditch, mostly to the rear of the group, has greatly reduced the number of prisoners still alive. The group begins to pass through a familiar countryside; first, control towers, then electrified fencing, and beyond this, men wearing striped clothes. Finally, we're in the type of surroundings we all have grown to know so well.

"What's the name of this place?"

Ah, Bergen-Belsen, very well. It'll be no worse here than anywhere else. But the column skirts the camp, doesn't stop, and continues onward. In the name of God, there are concentration camps everywhere in Germany! You just have to pass one and you find another. They don't seem to want us here, so on we go. We only have the problem of choice—to march or to die.

With SS machine guns for background music, the column rounds the camp and continues on its way. A little later, we arrive in front of a group of buildings, a sort of well-built barracks. They're not surrounded by electric fencing.

The prisoners arrive on a clean, tidy, and spotless square. The arrival is split up, and it's the first roll call in another part of Bergen-Belsen. My God, how many of us were there at the beginning in order to have so many still alive on arrival here? There must certainly have been several trains that followed each other within a few minutes, for there are plenty of people around. The buildings are two stories high, but we'll have to fight, more and more, just to find some room in this place.

Now the ex-worthies get busy. The armlets reappear, and their wearers are eager to take over the running of things. "Of course, *Messieurs les SS*, you can always count on us. And if you want to organize some work kommandos, we'll be there tomorrow morning at daybreak."

In Bergen-Belsen, life is organized according to a fixed system of barracks. But these are two-story barracks, with three levels split by a central staircase. The barracks are made up of a wing on each floor, with a barracks chief and the inevitable Schreiber and Stubendienst. The healthy little hiking trip in the open countryside is over, and we are now back amongst our own.

The first job is to note the number of each prisoner, but it's already a complicated business. The first big convoy from Dora via Harzungen has gone through disinfection, and they have abandoned their clothes to get newer ones. A later convoy has been given the abandoned clothes without the numbers having been removed, so in many cases, two prisoners have the same number. This provokes the fury of our captors, even while it confirms the fact that some evacuation trains left directly from Dora without going to Harzungen.

The barracks are completely empty; there are neither beds nor straw mattresses. The exhausted men collapse wherever they can find a place. How far have they walked from that station to here? From the number of bodies, it must have been a long way. A great many of the slaves have groaned their way up this route. Now, having arrived at the new camp, they lie down and never get up again. For them, it's finished. Their neighbors take them by the arms and legs and carry the bodies out onto the landings.

The barracks chiefs and their aides are outraged. What sort of camp is this, where prisoners drop like flies? Not only have the armlet-wearers lost all their treasures along the way, they are also reduced to noting the damages and registering the numbers on the bodies. And then there's another problem. Before, everything was simple. The dead went to the crematorium, and it ended there. But this part of Bergen-Belsen has no crematorium, so that won't do. Now the bodies of the dead will have to be thrown into an empty room. When it's full, they'll be piled up somewhere else, and so on.

It's really not like the good old days. From the first day onward, large numbers of prisoners slip from life into death simply because they have no strength left. Among them are veteran prisoners of nearly two years in the camps who finally arrived at the end of the trail, but there are also young lads far from having completed even their first year.

Although the quarters were built to very rigorous health standards—if anything Nazi could be termed healthy—nothing works anymore. These facilities weren't designed for so many people. So two enormous latrines are quickly dug, six feet deep and twelve feet long, surrounded by planks upon which we sit. But what can you still shit when you haven't eaten for centuries? Those with the runs, they know and arrive running to let out long jets of the last wastewater in their bodies. But they have no strength left; they are but empty bags, and they fall into the hole below. And so the next prisoners arrive and curl up on the planks, and they, too, empty everything out of their bodies. At the bottom of the hole, men die in a sea of shit.

★   ★   ★

In the meantime, the SS have set up an improvised cordon around this new camp of Bergen-Belsen. There's no possibility of installing an electrified fence; neither the time nor means exists. So posted around the camp, there are Hungarian SS dressed in black uniforms. These are rough, stubborn beings who have been given certain instructions and apply them. If the prisoners even approach the demarcation line, they are to shoot, and they do shoot.

The prisoners don't have the slightest desire to escape. They no longer have the strength; besides, where would they go in this hostile, horrible Germany?

There is one thing, however. Behind a line of Magyar guards there is a field loaded with carrots, beetroot, and all sorts of marvelous edibles we've only dreamed about. We saw them during the day, and we have decided to slip out during the night to get at them. Hunger is a hideous torture.

When everyone is asleep, we creep down in a group, make it out of the barracks, and then ease off into the dark. There isn't a living soul between the buildings, although there are a few stealthy groups all sneaking in the same direction. There are no Lagerschutz doing night rounds. From here on, it's a struggle for life—double or nothing. If we want to survive, we must eat—yet food and death are ultimately entwined together. We can eat without dying, or we can die without eating. It's like flipping a coin.

The prisoners creep along between the latrines, wherein bodies are already rotting. They approach the fateful line. The Hungarian sentries are there, like frozen black silhouettes. We can't tell whether they're sleeping or dreaming of the plains back home. But beyond them are the delicious plants into which we'll dig our teeth, those life-giving plants that will give us one, two, or even three days more of survival. We move on, crawling as carefully as possible. The food awaits, almost at arm's length. It has leaves, all juicy and just waiting for us to devour and digest it, until we have a rounded belly.

But suddenly, a groaning resounds in the darkness. The Hungarians get up and commence firing. They fire upon the shaggy silhouettes crawling in their direction. The bodies of the prisoners go prostrate, pierced by bullets that weigh almost as much as they. Their heads lift up for the last time and then lie flat. At last, there is only a pile of rags to be seen, only a bit higher than the ground itself.

Behind the line of Hungarian sentinels, the fields still lie there, untouched.

★   ★   ★

"There are some guys attacking the kitchens. There's some tough fighting."

Lucien thinks this is an interesting bit of news. He decides to go and see for himself. If he can get there in time for the sharing of the loot, maybe he can scrape up something, some potatoes, bread, or meat for himself.

The kitchens are on the ground floor in the middle of the barracks complex. A large entrance leads to a double door to the pressure-cooker room. Lucien arrives to find the entrance full of shouting, swearing people. Sticks and truncheons wave above the surging crowd, something like the storming of the Bastille or the boarding of a

Spanish galleon. The fighting is hot. On the side of the building, there is an open window. Lucien pulls himself up and over the ledge, then goes into the kitchen.

The spectacle inside is frightening. Lined up in the middle of the room, the pressure cookers are open and giving off wonderful-smelling steam. Most of them are full of soup, but one is filled to the brim with boiled potatoes. The food is within reach while the cooks fight at the front of the room. Some are trying to force the double doors closed while others, clubbing with pokers and iron bars, crush the heads, arms, and shoulders pushing into the entrance. The leading attackers collapse, broken in pieces. Some fall dead, their heads crushed and red with blood. Others with broken shoulders howl in pain. Behind them, other prisoners push and swear, even as the irons and pokers slash above their heads. They have gone mad en masse; it's murder on a large scale. Heavy stools thrown by the attackers crash against the fat cooks, who roar like injured beasts. On the few small yards of battlefield, broken bodies pile up. It's a fight to the death without pity. One must win, the other perish, until the last man alive becomes the victor.

But already, the fight is taking shape. On their side, the cooks have their physical strength, layered with fat like knights in armor, but the horde of attacking prisoners has nothing to lose. They rush on the kitchen defenders like buffaloes stampeding toward a cliff. Perhaps they'll die, but there will be nothing left in their wake. The doors crack, and soon the two halves will be forced back against the walls, flattening, knocking out, or killing those who try to hold them.

Lucien is alone for the moment in the large room. The cooks are still holding on, but sooner or later, the mass of hysterical skeletons will break through, climb over the pile of bleeding flesh, and dive headfirst into the pressure cookers. They'll kill him on the way and probably each other, too. He knows he mustn't stay here. It's a question of seconds rather than minutes.

He runs to the pot of potatoes, tears off his jacket, and throws it on the floor. He plunges his hands into the hot mass and throws potatoes onto his jacket. He doesn't dare look toward the door. God, don't look! Quickly, quickly, get potatoes! Within seconds, he has collected more than he has seen in all his months as a prisoner. Quickly, a few more! Then he folds over the flaps of his jacket, ties the arms together, and races to the window. Behind him, Lucien hears the loud cracking of the door giving way. He throws the bag out of the window.

Just as he's climbing over the window ledge, he sees a bundle of dirty clothes topped with a head rushing to steal his treasure. But the package is too heavy, and the man opens it to take as much as he can carry. Lucien jumps into space and lands, feet first, on the other prisoner's back. He hears a loud "squeak" and then silence. The Russian's neck is broken. Swiftly, Lucien reties the package, gets it over his shoulder, and starts to run. The potatoes burn his shoulder blades.

★   ★   ★

"I say, guys, there are the Gypsies from Dora with their musical instruments. I spotted them in the next barracks. They've got their violins and accordions. If we could pinch a few instruments, I could play you some music, music from home."

The man starts to recite the list of big hits he knows. First, there is the unbeatable "Je Suis Seule Ce Soir" ("I'm Lonely Tonight"), the smash of the forties. It's an air that makes the gals sob and cry beside their lamps while awaiting the return of their heroes imprisoned in the Stalags. Then there are the more lively songs that have brought their composers glory. Immortal, catchy songs that will be remembered for centuries. He mixes in a few notes and moving comments, warming up the guys in his barracks with some lovely phrases from home. In France, it's well known that every meeting always ends up with a song, so we're not going to let ourselves be done out of it. If we're going to die, let it be with music, and that will be that. That's France.

The prisoners go up to him. It's a distraction. The troubadour feels that he has the audience in his hands, young skeletons still in their twenties, a good age to be alive.

"Listen, guys, I've cased the place. The Gypsies from Dora are in the next block, and the instruments are there, a whole orchestra full. They've got violins, accordions, bandoneons—everything. So we could organize a little trip to pinch a few items, especially a violin. When we have some instruments, we Frenchmen could play some of our own music," and he hummed a few lines. "There's no reason why we should always have to hear the same old stuff from them."

The prisoners exchange glances. They don't see each other as they are, or they'd immediately go and hide in some corner. No, they know too well that their lives will be very short, that their life expectancy may not extend beyond forty-eight hours. So why not do something daft before giving up the ghost? When you're twenty years old, what the hell do you care? So they listen to him.

The writer-composer-singer looks at his audience. They are already doomed. He doesn't ask for volunteers, for a suicide mission can easily be set up here. The word isn't used; instead, he asks who wants to be a member of the glorious French team. He quickly finds five guys who agree to carry out the raid without even knowing whether its chief will be part of the team. Anyway, he doesn't suggest it. Besides, if he isn't there, who'll play the music?

The final details for the expedition are put together. First of all, weapons are needed. Some large, three-legged stools have been found. Two will be enough. The legs are unscrewed; they'll make good truncheons and can easily be hidden under their coats.

Now, the attack itself. The Gypsies' room is on the first floor of their barracks, just to the left of the stairs, which will help the retreat. We'll leave together but not too closely, so as not to appear grouped and therefore suspicious. We'll regroup in front of their door and go in swiftly. The Gypsies will be surprised and won't dare move for a moment. Three men will each quickly get hold of an instrument, especially a violin, and get the hell out of there. The two others with their clubs will stay behind, forming a rear-guard defense. But there's nothing to fear. In this barracks, there are Polacks, Russians, and a bit of everything, and nobody bothers about his neighbor. Besides, there are raids all the time, and no one pays any attention anymore. Once we're back in the courtyard, we'll quietly make off behind our own building, and we'll get back in by the small door at the far end.

It all seemed well planned, to the last detail. All that remained was to put the plan into action. The violinist looks like a field marshal in his HQ, set on not going out.

"See you soon, guys."

Gerard sticks his club into his belt; he's part of the rear guard. The group leaves the room, goes down the stairs, and eases into the yard, one by one. A crowd of people are warming themselves in the sun. Each man arrives casually at the Gypsies' barracks, and they climb the stairs. Lots of Poles and Russians are already going up or coming down, and some cast surprised glances at the *F* tags of the French, as if to ask, "What are the *Franzous* doing here?" But since it's none of their business, they move on.

The men arrive in front of the Gypsies' room to regroup. If only it's the right door! Gerard grabs the handle and violently pushes it inward. Then the impossible happens—the monkey wrench in the works. A Gypsy is behind the door, ready to go outside. In a split second, he confronts the intruders, then rushes forward and dives down the stairs. It's useless running after him, so the French team goes in, holding their clubs ready. Shit, there's hardly anyone about, just three greenish-looking Gypsies. They don't make a move but only stare fixedly at the attackers. The instruments are where they should be, on the right and within arm's reach. The three men quickly grab a violin, a balalaika, and a bandoneon. The three raiders get out, moving fast, and Gerard slams the door shut. It has all only lasted five seconds, but already, the Gypsies are bawling out the windows. For God's sake, thinks Gerard, let's get out of here and fast!

In the courtyard, the Gypsies who had been soaking up the sun now line up, each with a knife in his hand. The opponents the French had expected to take from behind are now facing them, and the elaborate strategy of the chief of the operation is now worthless. If the French don't hit them together in force, the anticipated military lark will turn into a bloodbath. In a glance, though, Gerard notes that the French-men are scattered, fighting with the Gypsies. He runs toward them, club held high, only to find two Gypsies armed with long blades in front of him. He reckons he's done for, but they make the mistake of attacking him one at a time. Thanks to the club, his reach is greater. The first plunges a knife toward him, but Gerard manages to strike him a terrible blow, and the Gypsy crashes down. The second, sur-prised, pauses for a second. It's a second too long, and the club strikes another devastating blow. Gerard can no longer see anything, but he can hear the clamor all around him; it's a stampede. So, with his club raised, he rushes toward his barracks, goes around the corner, climbs the stairs at full speed, and gets into the room.

One of his teammates has managed to bring the violin. Eyes popping out of his head, he stammers out nervously, "Hey, Gerard, you man-aged to get through, too?"

Gerard looks at the violinist "chief of staff" whose plan set off the operation. His eyes still hold the gleam of kill or be killed.

A little embarrassed, the artist lifts up the violin without trying to meet Gerard's angry stare.

"Hey, guys," he offers, "it's not my fault. The attack was well planned, but you weren't quick enough. But at last, now we can play our music."

★　　　★　　　★

Hugues succeeded in getting a blanket. In Bergen-Belsen, a blanket is a rare commodity. You have to look out for it nonstop if you don't want it to be stolen. He has teamed up with his partner, Robert, and, during the night, they huddle against each other, being careful to tuck the blanket tightly around their bodies. The nights are still very cold, and they need warmth.

Hugues has decided to go and scout for supplies. This means casu-ally looking around here and there for any useful remnant—a piece of string, a corpse with any useful clothing, perhaps even some leaves to chew. He must survive.

He has seen so many friends who, under the pretext of taking care of themselves, stay in bed all day long and finally die without being aware of it because they no longer possess the will to continue their bitter ex-istence. But Hugues wants to fight on, fight to the very end. However, in this respect, he worries about Robert, who doesn't move and sleeps all day. Hugues is no longer deceived. Maybe it will be tonight, maybe tomorrow, but he knows Robert won't live much beyond the next forty-eight hours. Robert has endured all that is humanly possible. The tunnel selections, the bitter cold, the cutting winds, the rains, torturous hunger and misery, plus the horrors of the evacuation have stripped him of all his remaining desire to survive. Robert is going to die on the sidelines. He simply cannot take any more.

"Look, Robert, I'm going to take a look around and see if I can find something for us two. So don't move, and look after the blanket. You mustn't let it be stolen."

"Okay, Hugues, you can count on me. I prefer to stay. I feel fine here. It's so good to stretch out for hours with nothing to do. Here, it's the good life."

"Poor soul," thinks Hugues, "you already look like one of the guys about to die, and we both know it. Your eyelids are almost closed, and you no longer shit. But be careful with that blanket." Hugues gets up and goes off on the prowl; there's always something to pick up along the way. He thinks about Robert again. It's been some months since they first teamed up, but now Robert is going to drift away. Their friendship will be over, but since no one is going to get out alive, does it really matter? "If my parents could see me," Hugues thinks, "they wouldn't even recognize me. They'd go by without even a glance in my direction. So why worry about things? Let's just get back on the right track and see what happens."

On the first floor, there is a large room filled with people, some dying, others just sleeping. Slightly apart from the masses of sleeping and expiring bodies, Hugues spots a woolen jersey, alone and magnificent. With an air of casual innocence, he sits down about a yard away from the wondrous woolen garment. Everything is OK. No one pays him any attention or even asks him what he's doing here. He takes it easy, relaxes, and moves closer and closer to the marvelous object. He glances to the left and right, but everyone nearby is sleeping soundly. It's quiet and perfectly calm. Why wait? Hugues takes the jersey and eases quickly out of the room.

Once outside, he strips off his coat and slips into the magnificent woolen jersey. Horrors! Suddenly he feels a thousand teeth biting his flesh, sucking and drawing out bits of his life. He tears off the garment and turns it inside out. It isn't even worth examining the seams; there are lice by the thousands, maybe millions. The owner preferred dying from the cold rather than being eaten alive. Hugues throws the moving mess to the ground, where some other unsuspecting victim will doubtless find it in his turn.

He climbs back to the top floor to check on Robert. The blanket is gone. Robert is doubled up in his sleep, his legs spasming strangely. Hugues knows he must find another blanket. In this coldness, his own legs also hurt, and he lacks strength. But it's time for action, and he will know how to summon the force necessary to protect their lives.

Some smaller rooms on the first floor have been occupied by Poles, former Stubendienst. They're organized to survive forever, with loaves of bread, tobacco, blankets, and everything. Why not try a surprise attack?

He reaches the door. Its handle fascinates him for an instant. Then he leans on it, pushes inward, and finds himself inside the room. A group of big Polacks are sitting, talking among themselves. They have their soup bowls on the floor and are dipping their spoons languidly into the brew. At a glance, Hugues spots a folded blanket within his reach. He pounces on it, races to the door, closing it behind him, and bounds up the concrete stairway.

Back on the top floor, he drapes the blanket over Robert, slips under it, and says to his partner, "It's OK, buddy, I've found some heat for us tonight, but get it tucked under you firmly. I'm not making any more trips tonight."

Robert hasn't heard a word. He is sleeping. He is going to die, but it's the loveliest day in his life.

★   ★   ★

Today is Sunday, April 15th. Bergen-Belsen is on the square for roll call. Everyone is there, including the destitute, the lame, and even the dying men being supported by their armpits. They're well lined up in the five-man ranks they've learned so well, no matter how dilapidated their bodies have become.

The lower and middle nobility are also with us, Stubendienst, Schreiber, Kapos, and barracks chiefs. They're all present, as they have always been and as they will always be as long as there are concentration camps. In spite of a cold breeze, the weather is fine for a change, and the sun reheats bodies badly in need of warmth.

Yesterday, late in the afternoon, the distant hum of combat could be heard. It wasn't the apocalyptic din of a great battle but the dull firing of medium-weight artillery and the sound of heavy machine guns, probably 12.7mm. An Allied unit must be out there, but is it near or far away? From the sound, it can't be more than ten miles distant. What direction will they take, and will troops be following up? However, night fell and nothing happened.

As the prisoners awake this morning at about eight o'clock, fighting is already under way. Automatic weapons and artillery can be heard perfectly, along with the sound of light arms. There is steady firing of heavy machine guns, the barking of artillery, and the isolated shots of individual rifles. And over all the sounds, there is the incredible noise of metal, the grating of metals crushing against each other. Tanks. It can't be anything else; it must be their cannons that we hear. If we can hear them this clearly, they can't be more than three or four miles away!

It's nine o'clock, the sacred hour for roll call. The Kapos and barracks chiefs, clubs in hand, survey the alignment of the prisoners. A roll call must be perfect; if not, it must be restarted all over again. What's happening outside the camp? They aren't concerned. They're doing their job and will do the same until the end of time. Ah, here come the SS.

The SS arrive, looking as spotless as always, caps at the correct angle upon their Aryan foreheads, boots gleaming, and the creases in their trousers as straight as blades. Around the improvised camp, the Hungarian SS look on stupidly.

The noise of battle seems to have toned down, but the metallic grinding of the tanks becomes louder. They are quite close.

The SS Blockführer come to the rows of prisoners and begin counting. They are cold and distant, as usual. With their sticks, they touch every second shoulder, ten, twenty, thirty. At the end of the column, they add the number of the night's dead, all well lined up for the tally. *Stimmt!* Everything is OK, the numbers are correct. There is no hint of nervousness or madness in them. Their well-trained muscles and nerves remain supple and ready.

Suddenly, on the road alongside the barracks, metallic monsters advance, their cannons pointing toward the camp. The first one swings around to the right and crushes the gate.

Immediately afterward, a small car armed with a machine gun smashes over the mass of barbed-wire fencing and stops on the square. The machine gunner is in position, his finger on the trigger. He is wearing a flat helmet; he's English.

My God, it's the liberation! This is it! There's an instantaneous clamor, an enormous clamor like nothing ever heard in history, gushing from every prisoner's throat. We've been freed, we are free. We're alive! *Alive!*

The moment of suspense passes, there are cries, shouts, and whistles. The SS draw their guns and begin firing as they flee. The commandant is gone. The Kapos and barracks chiefs, the club-carriers, try to get to a barracks for safety. But now, the horde of Russians get into action. They want revenge for all they have had to bear and for the horrors Germany has made them suffer. Cries rise from the Russians, cries of hate and murder. The hour has come for vengeance without pity.

Caught up in the crowd, one armlet-wearer blows his whistle desperately, then stops and begins to scream for help. But he is alone. His screaming stops and turns to sobs. An angry crowd is on top of him in an instant. When they stand back, his shape is stretched out and broken, with an eye out of its socket and trembling limbs. The once murderous little Kapo is still breathing. A man comes up, carrying a heavy boulder, and crushes his head, but the Kapo still lives, although his eyes are a strange distance apart. His arms and legs give out sporadic jerks, and his spinal column must be in a thousand bits. So a Russian goes up to him, undoes his fly, and pisses on him.

A group of Kapos and barracks chiefs have managed to clear a passage as far as a barracks, where they shut themselves inside. Well, you bastards, you've condemned yourselves. You wanted to keep your armlets until the very end, you infamous shits. Now it's time to pay for your beatings and murders. A crowd follows them. The whole of Europe is together to track them down. Men who, the night before, couldn't have lifted a foot now climb the stairs at full speed. They open the door to a room and discover a Kapo, green with fear, flat against the wall. He still has his truncheon in his hands, but they reckon he isn't about to use it. His limbs are frozen. He begins to sob. The horde of the cursed, the horde of tramps and dying men closes in slowly and quietly. They can taste their triumph. They are all there, every nationality, every poor soul. They laugh and close in. The Kapo's strength gives out, and he falls to his knees, his club only a toy between soft fingers. The crowd throws itself upon him and breaks him into a thousand pieces.

The doors are opened, one after another, and each one reveals a choice piece of wild game. Even if these murderers had taken off their armbands, they'd still be wearing their hooded jackets, riding britches, and boots. You don't get rid of these things easily; they've kept you alive and made you survive for years. But you kept them to the end, there's the mistake. Now you're going to die, just like all those you've slaughtered and crushed to bits during the years while you were kings of the concentration camps. Now your victims are throwing themselves upon you. The world is so unjust.

Another door is opened, and it's an anguished figure that is presented to the avenging crowd. In a great swirl, the former human terror is transformed into mincemeat, dead, still, rotten. The victims' boots and clothes make the poor devils happy. They move on.

In a room on the second floor, a shape presses against the wall. It's a small, lean, ridiculous-looking man with a large black beret perched on his little head. He is pale now and seized by twitching. Arching backward in his boots, he seems to be trying to melt into the wall. His club hangs at the end of his arm. A voice cries, "It's Follette!"

Follette, the skinny tyrant, a bloody barracks chief. Almost no one in this group knows him, having had enough to do with their own Block-ältester without bothering about the neighbors. But whether they know Follette or not isn't important. The guy is there; he's doomed.

The pack advances, slowly, quietly, and just a few laughs are heard. Follette regains the use of his legs. In an instant, they'll crush him, and the blood will spurt out of his body. Step by step, he gets closer to the window, still holding onto his club. The prisoners aren't hurrying and slowly close in on him. Follette, with his haggard eyes fixed on the crowd, scrapes his feet along the floor. He's in front of the window, with the small of his back against the ledge. The men keep closing in, almost touching him. Then Follette cries aloud and falls back over the window ledge. Two seconds of dropping, and he crunches into the yard on his back. Immediately, a swarm of insects is all over his body, vultures feasting on dead meat that will soon be only a shapeless mass.

Here and there, some cries and ranting can still be heard. Men tracked down, their eyes wild, howling out their fears. They are all going to die, one after the other, alone now against the terrible revolt of their former victims.

In the courtyard, men are crying, crying with joy. It's finished, and they are free. Many among them will die tomorrow. They've arrived at the end of their lives and can no longer hold on—but they have known that fabulous instant of liberation. Some others, already Moslems, are indifferent. They've already drifted into unconsciousness, their brains no longer working. They simply walk about in the crowd with their scarecrow silhouettes. Their guts are rotten, and with unsure steps, they make for the latrines.

Men are moving in every direction. They want to find their friends again, hug them, and shout with joy. It's over. In the name of God, it's over! Everyone is speaking to everyone else, and the different communities fall into each other's arms; it's the Great Brotherhood of the Destitute.

There are no more Kapos, barracks chiefs, and the like and no SS hierarchy. Each prisoner has become David, who has defied and beaten the giant. They have won. Their hollow, infested chests straighten a bit, and laughter comes to their ravaged faces. Their eyes, in the depths of their dark sockets, are intensely brilliant.

We look from right to left, we walk freely from one group to another, we laugh aloud, and we run toward the English, wanting to hug them. They're beautiful, they're gods. Thanks, guys, thank you, you the gods whose formidable weapons have ended the greatest misery ever known to mankind.

The tanks are still stopped on the roadway, with their turrets fixed on the camp. A lot of jeeps have come in, and some infantrymen carrying their rifles make up a sort of sanitary ring around the crowd. They're horrified, almost afraid to believe their own eyes. Bodies are strewn all about on the ground, and they see dying men crawling on all fours as well as Moslems with their vacant, indifferent look. They can see the skeletal silhouettes and protruding skullbones, the huge wounds swelling men's necks, their ripped clothing, and the unbelievable filth of this place. They can smell the dirt, the shit, the rot, and the death that rise from the group and assault their throats and nostrils.

Like all fighting soldiers, our liberators have seen the ravages of war upon human flesh. They've seen bodies disemboweled and cut in two, jawbones shot off, and limbs blown into the air. They've seen a lot but never anything like this. The tank crews have opened their trapdoors and come out to look, but they can't believe it. Things like this are just impossible.

An English officer arrives in his jeep and jumps out. He is small, dark, and without a doubt, the officer in charge. He asks if there is anyone who speaks English. A Frenchman steps forward. They converse for a moment, and then the prisoner leads him off to a building. Followed by a few armed soldiers, the officer climbs the steps. The Frenchman opens the door, and the English are overwhelmed to see the horror within. The room is filled with bodies piled head to toe from the floor to the ceiling. One row is of dirty, naked feet, and the alternate is of heads, dead eyes wide open, and jaws agape. The English seem to have received an electric shock. For a moment, they seem frozen in place. Then they move quickly outside, feeling sick, ready to collapse.

Meanwhile, the sun, rising slowly in the sky, bathes the courtyard. It will be a fine day.

★   ★   ★

Elsewhere, the morning of April 5th finds Dora like a ship adrift. Two large transfers of prisoners have been carried out, leaving things structureless and without any real organization. It's anarchy. The kommandos have been dismantled and broken up. The camp has become a place of wandering souls. There is only one solid section that is still functioning, and that's the infirmary. The doctors and hospital staff offer the last comfort to those who will undoubtedly not live to see the liberation.

Those who escaped the earlier great evacuation are there, those who, by ruse or by chance, managed to wriggle through the net awaiting their moment of destiny. There is nothing left to do, and any rebellion would be in vain. May God's wishes be met. Life or death is played at the toss of a coin, without knowing the rules of the game. Chance is the deciding factor.

An order comes from the gate, and the remaining prisoners are assembled. It would only have taken three large shipments to empty Dora, that obscene mastodon. Now it's our turn. The self-saving acts and cunning have been to no avail; we have to go. There are still the tramps, the less than nothing, the scum. There are also the wearers of armbands and the officials, the best and worst, those who saved their skins by assassination, and those who used their little jobs to save those whom they could.

The column seems curiously small, and yet there are a lot of prisoners. In ranks of five, they cross the camp gate. Dora is dead.

The group passes the tunnel entrance, bears left, follows a roadway, and arrives at Niedersachswerfen Station. A train waits alongside the platform. There are no civilians, no passengers. Nothing has been organized for the local population, which is fleeing the bombing by way of roads and highways. This station is reserved for the prisoners.

The column is divided, and the men board the rail trucks. They crowd in but nevertheless have room to move. On the platform, there are only the SS, the Posten, and a few Kapos. The SS issue orders, there is a clicking of heels, and the armed guards climb aboard. With that, everything changes. They push back the prisoners with their rifle butts, then take up a good third of the available space. The men crush each other, step on the feet of some, and dig their elbows into the ribs of others. Unbelievable pains attack their bodies. They shout and swear at each other. The weak, the smallest try to stretch upward, their mouths gasping for air. With a rolling and creaking, the door is closed. It's almost black inside. Spirits run wild; it's an uproar.

"Ruhe!" Shut up! The guard strikes the nearest silhouettes, which move back. The weakest feel their ribs groan. My God, we're going to die before we even get started.

The guard becomes extremely uncomfortable because of the smells of sickness, dirt, and misery that rapidly fill the car. He opens the door slightly. He has been around prisoners for several months but never in such close proximity. These rags are really filthy. What good is it to cart them around? Why not get rid of them straightaway?

The hours pass while the train waits at the station, then, finally, it's on its way. Adieu, Dora.

★   ★   ★

On the second day, the last train from Dora stops in the countryside. The convoy chiefs get down to meet military men and railroad officials. Conference. The guards also get down and pass back information. The track has been bombed a little further on and no longer exists. However, another train has been brought up on a track on the far side of the hill next to us. Everyone outside!

The prisoners jump down, and the ravages of the first hours on board the train can already be seen. If most of them are still in one piece after all that has happened to them in recent months, the weak and lame have suffered. They are haggard and doubled up in pain. They don't speak and have no more physical reactions.

"Zu fünf!" Columns of five. Here we go again.

The Kapos and Lagerschutz have their clubs in hand; for them, it is always useful. The column is forming up too slowly, in their view, so the armband-wearers attack. With vicious blows, they knock out the weakest, those who are wandering about, and those who can no longer follow along. In a rain of merciless clubbing, they liquidate all who might slow the column's steady pace. No need being burdened with stragglers, there will be enough still left alive. They are cutting out the deadwood.

The roadway is narrow and steep. The guards, feeling insufficient in their numbers, have asked some German prisoners to volunteer to fill out their ranks, thus completing the cordon on both sides of the prisoners. Their heavy artillery is at the rear, the SS with their machine guns. Everything seems perfect, so forward march!

Marching in formation is such a conditioned reflex with the prisoners that they fall in step automatically. There are weaklings everywhere, but their mates pull and push, trying to get them back into line. Exhaustion saps the men quickly, but it isn't the weariness of a good walk in the forest amid healthy air and birds chirping. No, it's the deadly enervation that depletes your strength and makes you think, "Do what you want with me; I couldn't care less. I can't go on."

The column now resembles a stretched-out worm in which some sick cells are beginning to waver, float loose, and roam about. Some prisoners shamble off to the right or left in uncertain strides, disturbing the orderliness of the formation. They fall by the roadside, and a blow from a club or a bullet in the head sends them directly to paradise. Others slow down little by little, ending up at the rear of the line. There, the artillery is waiting for them.

The column moves on, and the birds have flown. The marching becomes mechanical. As our grandfathers told us, the best way to walk is to put one foot in front of the other and continue doing the same.

By following grandfather's advice, we manage to reach the top of the hill. Of course, you mustn't look behind. Back there are the guys who have tasted freedom, just a finger's touch—but only a touch, and it isn't enough. No, you have to look ahead, and what a marvel: There is a train bellowing out steam at the bottom of the hill. Wait for us, blessed train, we're coming.

Once on the station platform, ranks are formed, the men are counted and then ordered to climb aboard the wagons. The guards follow, accompanied by the armband-wearers. They take up most of the space and push the prisoners into the corners. The train gives out a big, happy whistle and is off.

★   ★   ★

On the third day, the train wanders about, dawdling, coming and going, climbing up and down in this Germany that has become a trap that is relentlessly closing shut. We must have gone through a large station during the night, but no one knows which. Anyhow, what's the difference? We're still piled on top of each other, with the SS and Kapos raining terror all around them.

Somewhere ahead, all hell breaks loose. It's a bombing raid in front of the convoy. The war is here, just a few yards away, and not too far above us, the liberating angels are chewing their gum as they press their release buttons and let the bombs fall.

The train stops, and the guards rush outside. The prisoners? They have to stay put. The SS string themselves out, pointing their weapons at the train.

The planes are gone; end of the alert. The train moves off again. It still whistles out in an F-sharp or B-flat, which suits such a highly civilized nation. The grouping of prisoners by nationalities or preference has long since disappeared, and we are all crowded together in a corner. There are the dead, burdens we all wanted to get rid of, and their oblique positions hinder any kind of an orderly piling-up.

The train stops in the middle of nowhere; there must be another problem. Yet we hear no explosions near or far, no indication of another bombing raid. Some SS and Kapos begin searching among their collection of human trash. What can they want now? They have some fixed idea in mind because they are ignoring everything that is not French. The French interest them; they have flair and perspicacity. They haven't lived in the camps for years and not known everyone. So they look the French in the eyes and ask, "Are you a French officer?" "Yes." "Then outside the train." "Are you, also, a French officer?" "Yes." "Then you, too, outside."

The Germans collect a good number of French officers and line them up a few yards away. The shooting begins; the weapons fire, and the young officers fall to the ground.

The train moves on again.

★   ★   ★

It takes its time. Is it still on the ground? We don't know. It rolls along, it flies, shunts here, goes forward, reverses, stops, moves on again. Why worry? A train is a train; that is its life. Of course, on this train, there are some strange bodies set on surviving. But these guys are mad. What's the good of trying to keep a body in working condition when it's down to nothing more than a few pounds of bones? Maybe it's no use, but we'll never let go. The days and nights roll by, and we crowd into a corner of the wagon, for the honors. The skin and bones living on here are of interest to no one. We don't care about that; we resist on principle.

What does eating mean? Nothing at all. We couldn't even swallow a radish. We don't even think about food. We're piled up in our little corner with dead bodies as a burden. Yet these bodies are our friends. You hear? Our friends.

We've ridden for endless days and nights on the cursed railroads of this fucking country. We no longer know where we are, but that doesn't matter. As long as we aren't knocked out of it by a German rifle butt or a truncheon full in the face, we'll be here, and we'll hold on. There will always be one of us left to tell you that we won't let go.

More days pass, and the train rolls on. In the beginning, there were landmarks, and we could calculate the hours of travel. We looked at the sky and to the morning sun or simply counted days and nights. But slowly, everything drifted into a dulling uniformity, and no calculations were of any use. What good would it do, after all? We're alive or dead; nothing else is important.

★   ★   ★

The train arrives at a familiar destination, no doubt of that. When you're a veteran prisoner, you can recognize places that are for you and the others. You avoid places not for you; you wouldn't be welcomed there. But this place looks just right for us. Barbed wire is rolled up around the insulators. It's exactly our style. What's the name of this camp? Ravensbrück? We're at the women's camp. What are we doing in such a place? Well, no matter, Ravensbrück or wherever they send us isn't so important. As soon as we've gotten down from the train, this place will be like all the rest.

In column, we arrive at the camp. It shows signs of being recently occupied, then quickly evacuated. The barracks are empty, but straw and trash scattered on the floor indicate a rapid exit. Is the fencing electrified? Nobody dares try, and what's the use, anyhow? Maybe we've missed the liberation, but at least we're on familiar ground. With the barbed wire and the thin straw mattresses, we're back home, without a doubt.

Have the women lived here? It can't be true. It's as miserable as the camps for the men. A sudden silence develops, and every prisoner whose wife has been arrested feels a lump in his throat. "It's impossible. Did my wife live here? Perhaps she was right where I'm standing. What has become of her? Has she, too, gone on a hideous journey? Or is she . . . dead?"

The barracks are empty, without beds or mattresses. The men are shut inside, almost as jammed together as on the train. Fights break out.

Barracks chiefs reappear, and the camp administration comes back into control. They will be there till the end. They write down each number; count, count again, and subtract. Anarchy, leveling out, and anonymity will disappear. In another few months, the "Women's City" will become a model men's camp. Already, some hierarchies have developed and acquired positions.

Now the prisoners follow a strange routine that they haven't known for months or years. They don't work anymore. *"Arbeit macht frei,"* says the sign above the entrance to Buchenwald. "Work makes you free." So, wake up, gentlemen of the SS, you're letting the camps drift into ruin. There are, of course, some work parties, but most of the prisoners remain unoccupied. It's unheard of, but at the same time, they can't stroll around in the camp; it's both tiring and dangerous. So while waiting to be organized for work details, there is always the roll call. Afterward, we return to sit down or stretch out somewhere.

The authorities have come across some Red Cross parcels in a store and make a grotesque ritual of indignantly handing them out. The rations are so minimal as to be more symbolic than anything else, but nonetheless, these foodstuffs meant for healthy people are like bombs in the dilapidated, shrunken stomachs and intestines of the prisoners. These highly concentrated nourishments annihilate the weakest men quickly. There are also some new products, such as Nescafé, that bring about nervous spasms in systems that have been poised on the brink of starvation for months and years. Some who have drunk it have developed a state of extremely high tension and can't sleep at all. Even small amounts of normal food are very dangerous to anyone who, for so long, has been under the tender, loving care of the SS.

And so the days drag by, empty and sad. Despite the roll calls and reestablishing of a sort of central listing, the authorities don't manage to reshape this moving but formless mass. We drag about and die very quickly. It's another Black Hole of Calcutta.

★   ★   ★

"Assembly!"

The prisoners get up with difficulty, stiff and aching. It's eight o'clock in the morning. Everyone outside! Some of the men complain and show their wounds to the barracks chief. Others, exhausted and ill, don't move. The chief begins growling and threatens them, and soon the prisoners end up on the roll call square.

It's unusual. Instead of being lined up by barracks, they're grouped together in lots of three hundred.

Pierre is worried. What does all this mean? There are a few French, Belgians, and Dutchmen around him, making a small island of Western Europeans in the middle of a wave of Slavic prisoners. In Dora, Pierre had a small job working close to the SS. Because he spoke perfect German, they had given him permission to let his hair grow. The lords didn't allow their immediate servants to look like the rest of the inhuman trash under their rule.

The groups of three hundred are hemmed in at once by the SS, Lagerschutz, and Kapos. They are all armed. The word flies to every ear; we're evacuating the camp.

That's what it is! Here we go, back on the roads again, looking for . . . what? Do the SS think they're going to find an ideal spot, sheltered from the hurricane that is sweeping across Germany?

"Above all," says Pierre, "let's stay close together. If we don't get separated, we'll try to hold on. Maybe we'll be able to do something."

The gate opens, and, one after another, the columns leave the camp. They move off into the countryside. Slowly, the columns separate, and the distance between them increases as they march. Already, they can see the rejects from earlier groups strewn along the roadside. The ill and the injured and the old men of forty have all finished their lives in the ditches. The prisoners march on. The Kapos and Lagerschutz, in close ranks, liven the group's fervor with vicious swings of their clubs. At the rear, as is the usual German custom, the stragglers are liquidated with either a single bullet or a burst of machine-gun fire to the head. They march on.

The column comes to a farm, as ordinary as any can be with its farmhouse, stable, and barn. Guards open the doors of the barn. It's roomy, with a hard earthen floor and an upper floor filled with hay.

"Forward!"

The troop enters the building, and the doors close behind them. It's dark, and the men collapse on the spot, completely exhausted and shattered. There aren't even any fights; they can't do a thing.

"Hey, guys, let's go up there in the haymow." Pierre and his group climb the ladder and bury themselves in the hay. They push as far into the straw as possible, well away from the entryway trapdoor. Here and there, there is a brief confusion of noises and exchanged words. A few others are also in the haymow, but the majority of the prisoners haven't had the strength to climb up and have fallen asleep on the ground. Outside, the SS and their armband-wearing assistants talk and laugh.

★   ★   ★

Morning comes. *"Aufstehen!"* Outside, quick. Get up!

The barn doors have just been opened, and the guards are crying out their orders. They seem nervous and quite distracted. Everyone outside quickly! We must get moving again!

The prisoners, still completely tired out, form into columns again. They are counted. Bastards! There are people missing. Some SS and Kapos rush up to the haymow and swear as they search. In their corner, Pierre and his group don't need any advice. Whatever happens, don't move! The search continues, and from time to time, there are howls of pain followed by the sound of running footsteps. The Germans find some hideaways. They mix up, searching in the hay and shouting. The westerners hold their breath.

The guards go back down again, prodding the unlucky ones ahead of them. There are still a few missing, but the SS are pressed for time. The Russians must be near, and they have to leave on the double. "Forward, march!" The column moves off and marches back onto the roadway.

Outside, it's almost daylight. You can't hear a sound anywhere; there doesn't seem to be a living soul for miles.

Pierre and the others emerge from the hay. They keep very quiet, feeling like the fox that has shaken off the pack but knows that he can be found again at any moment. All is still; no sign of Germans, Russians, or civilians. Nothing. And they are tired out.

"Above all, we mustn't stay here."

The small group quickly leaves the farm and moves off. The weather is fine but cold. Their stomachs are already crying out with hunger. They must eat; they must find some food, no matter what sort. They walk onward.

They find a dead horse lying alongside the road, a fine white mare. It's on its side, the stomach swollen and legs wide apart. A prisoner with a knife begins cutting large slices out of its rear. The meat is frozen. The men put some lumps inside their shirts, and they move forward again.

A little further in their journey, they enter an almost deserted village; the inhabitants have fled for their lives. The men go into a house standing away from the others. It's empty, having been hurriedly deserted, but there is enough left in the fireplace to rekindle a small cookfire. The men quickly cook the bits of horseflesh, then swallow and gulp them down like hyenas devouring a carcass.

"Let's not stay here; let's get moving."

The group soon realizes that they haven't been liberated at all. They aren't free; they're on the run, a completely different thing. The world about them is filled with deadly dangers. If a troop of armed SS or even ordinary soldiers notice them, they'll be shot down immediately. Even German civilians are dangerous; they can alert the authorities, if any are left, and that will be the end of this little stroll. The country must be in complete hysteria. That simple phrase, "The Russians are coming!" is enough to drive them to any extreme.

A troop appears in the distance, heading right for the escapees. Everyone hides. The troop approaches. They are armed and speaking in French. It's a detachment of LVF, all volunteers in the German army. They pass by without noticing anything.

The prisoners can't stay in striped uniforms. It's too dangerous; they must find civilian clothes at all costs.

The fugitives reach a deserted hamlet and begin looking into the houses. Before long, they are all dressed in workaday clothing, even shoes instead of prisoners' clogs.

Until now, they have been moving in an empty world, but all at once, they are in the middle of the war. They take a road and there find the collapse in all its full absurdity. The road is flooded with trolleys, cars, bicycles, and people on foot. There are children and old people, with suitcases, cartons, and boxes—Germans and foreign workers from all over Europe. They are speaking German, Slav, French, Hungarian, and Bulgarian. They are fleeing for dear life to save themselves. "The Russians are coming!" is the cry. The old people are exhausted, and the children cry, but these four words keep the huge crowd on the move. They must flee, must escape from what is going to happen. They would rather get killed on the road than have to face such an awful fate.

Pierre and his mates slip through the mass of fleeing people. Nobody worries about them or even notices them. Where are we all going? Nobody knows, but surely toward the west.

In the evening, they come upon a hamlet with farm buildings and barns. "Let's go into that barn."

They open the door to find the place filled with German civilians, piled together in family groups. Their eyes are filled with fear. The escapees go into a corner together, exhausted, ill, and starving. All the assorted bits of humanity gathered there begin to fall asleep.

During the night, a noise outside becomes louder and louder, like a fleet of rusty trolleys. It draws nearer and nearer, and now it is here. It's the sound of tanks.

The barn doors open suddenly, and some small silhouettes appear. It's the Russians. The little men move into the barn. They point their machine guns at the groups inside and with kicks, push back the suitcases and burst open the boxes. The children cry.

"Dawai Uhre, bystro!" (Get your watches, quickly!)

They want everybody's watches, these little men with machine guns. They move from group to group and family to family. *"Bystro! Bystro!"* The civilians give them their watches, and the little men laugh and grin. They smell of war and of sweat. Meanwhile, outside, searchlights are sweeping back and forth over the little hamlet.

★   ★   ★

Are the prisoners free? No, they are not. Pierre realizes it at once when he tries in a lingua franca-germano-russian to explain their case to the Russian units that have taken the village.

"Franzouski! Who cares? Belgians? Dutch? What's all that? We don't give a shit." These are assault troops who hardly even speak Russian but demons who are damned quick on the trigger. They have swiftly picked the refugees clean. They have come from the very depths of Asia, and now they are pushing across to the west. You don't have to tell them about citizens' or human rights or of those who have suffered a thousand deaths in the German concentration camps. *"Yob troiou matj!"* (I fuck your mother!) These are the hordes of Attila!

The detachment is equipped mainly with American material, from the lightest to the heaviest, except perhaps for the Kalashnikov machine guns and Nagant revolvers. But the weapons, no matter their origin, and the men who use them so readily create an indelible impression of strength.

Pierre and his buddies can't obtain anything for themselves. They're not considered as enemies, but neither are they regarded as friends. The Russians don't have time to study the problem, and moreover, they laugh at them. The westerners are tolerated.

The Russians have captured a unit of German infantry that had been wandering in the area. The Germans are sitting with their light arms, mostly Mauser rifles, with no ammunition. Their Schmeisser machine guns have swiftly disappeared, souvenirs of the war. Some Russians surround the pile of rifles. They take them, one by one, and, laughing, smash the butts at the small of the stock. The German prisoners in a group in front of them look on. Suddenly, several men go forward and, with signs, explain that they want to do the work. The Russians, still laughing, give their OK. So the Germans, with efforts like lumberjacks, take their own weapons and smash them.

The Russian shock troops have been replaced by others and continue their advance. Berlin is about fifty miles to the south, and that's where the last battle will be fought.

After much discussion and explaining, the prisoners have managed to obtain a certain freedom of movement. They decide to make a break, to try to escape to the west because with the Russians, they'll never be free. They discover their chance in the form of bicycles they have found hidden in a corner. While the Russians sleep, they slip away.

The countryside is flat and desolate. A world has vanished, and there are only a few wandering souls to be seen. They pedal onward. The miles roll by through an area free from fighting. Obviously, all the armies are driving toward Berlin. The rest is left to its own means. But they keep pedaling. Are they free? Are they still fleeing? They don't know. Are they friends? Or enemies? And whose friends? Whose enemies? In this insane world, it's impossible to tell. They have to get out of this mess, so they pedal on. They meet some American prisoners wandering the roads; they're making for the west as well. Everything has become irrational; they pedal onward. "In the name of God, Russians!"

There is a Russian guard post just in front of them. It's too late to avoid it. The group goes on as far as the post. The Russians are out in force and don't seem inclined to let the group pass.

"Papers!"

You can travel every country in the world, even without understanding any languages, but when you encounter a barrier of uniformed people who stop you and speak, you know they want to check your papers. But what papers for us? Nobody has any. But, yes, Pierre has something. From within his jacket, he produces a small, carefully folded sheet and presents it to the Russian duty officer. This small, typewritten sheet, with rubber stamps and German signatures, is the document authorizing that his hair is not to be cut short. The Russian carefully scans the paper, while the prisoners hold their breath.

"Karacho!"

With that, the Russian gives the signal for us to pass through. And there you are! If you have a good head of hair, you can travel the world. The little group moves forward again.

But where is the demarcation line? There must surely be one, agreed upon well in advance. Otherwise, the Allied armies advancing would risk firing on each other. The guys from Dora, however, would very much like to get through. But it would only take a nervous tank commander and the whole group could go up in a single smoking explosion. War is war, and such losses aren't even considered. Tough luck. Well, guys, we'll see, and they pedal on.

Ahead, the men see a medium-sized river. It's the Elbe. A strong Russian contingent is set up there, the men wearing boots and overalls secured with belts. They are quiet, but there are arms and equipment set up everywhere. It seems more like a frontier, a different world. My God, is this where we try to cross to the west?

Pierre and his buddies arrive in front of the control post, which is full of Russians. Two of the soldiers are dressed differently than the rest. Americans. Pierre approaches them.

"We are prisoners from Dora concentration camp. I'm with French, Belgians, and Dutchmen. We want to cross to the other side."

There are discussions among the military men. The Americans and the Russians decide that a Frenchman will go across to explain their situation to the Americans, and this is done. After what seems a very long time to the others, a motorboat makes out from the far side and draws up alongside the Russian detachment.

"Climb in, guys."

Everybody climbs aboard, and the boat moves outward from the riverbank. They are in the middle of the Elbe when the Russians start firing on them. They lie flat on the lower deck. Then the boat reaches the American bank, and they climb ashore quickly. They are free!

★   ★   ★

A column advances along a German road. It's a collection of prisoners from Dora and all the satellite camps. They have been traveling many days and nights. The train has taken them in all directions: forward, back, to the left and right. In the railcars, it's maddening. Men crush each other; they cry, they die. The days drag by one after another as their numbers dwindle. There are dead everywhere. My God, let's get out of this train, for pity's sake.

"Everyone outside!"

The train has stopped, and the doors open. The men get down onto the platform, at least those who are still alive. They look like zombies.

"Rows of five!"

The prisoners line up and are counted. There are still a few more than a thousand alive. They leave the station immediately and are quickly marched into the countryside. They must march on, it doesn't matter. Anything is better than that train of death.

The troop makes its way along the road. The miles mount up. Where are we going? What's going to happen to us? If the SS keep dragging us all over the place, perhaps they don't have an intention—or the orders—to kill us; otherwise, it would have been done before now. Perhaps there's a slight chance of our getting through. So, if everything isn't lost, we must go on, go on walking, and hold on. For every hour and even for every minute that goes by, the Allies get closer.

Now the column arrives in a town named Gardelegen. It follows a street leading to some large buildings that look like barracks. Everyone goes in. Are they going to keep us here till the end? It's quite reassuring to be in a town since we don't think they would liquidate us within the sight and knowledge of the whole civilian population.

The prisoners rest. These are tough people. For days now, they have gone through all the trials, hunger, thirst, misery, and executions the SS can devise. They want to hold on until the end.

★   ★   ★

"Assembly!"

It's not possible. Are we leaving again? Ah, yes, we must go. The SS and the Kapos shout the orders and strike out with their clubs, and the men re-form into columns. They leave Gardelegen.

The troop arrives in front of a barn. The SS open the door, and the thousand men go inside. Straw is scattered all about everywhere. The door closes behind them, but, for Christ's sake, what a smell of gasoline! No need to paint a picture; the prisoners understand everything. The Germans have set up a giant grill. It's the end.

The SS half-open the door and throw some burning torches inside. The fire spreads rapidly. Screams burst out in every language; the fire must be put out! So the SS open the door again, just enough to throw some incendiary grenades inside. The prisoners rush onto the flames to put them out, and the SS fire into them. Now there is a considerable pile of bodies in front of the door. More prisoners go forward to put out the fire, and they are killed in turn. Still more men rush forward, but with the same result. The German machine guns and rifles spray death into these demons who are trying to survive.

But the fight is uneven. The fire has spread, and the prisoners can no longer contain it. The flames turn men into torches, piles of charcoal. There is nothing left but the agony of being grilled. They will say prayers before the end but fight until then. All through the last horrible night, these Untermenschen, these lesser humans fight the fire or rush toward the SS, who kill them. They'll never let go; not for the convenience of the SS or Hitler's murderous hatreds or the greater glory of the German Reich!

By the following morning, the barn has been completely burned to the ground. The SS and Kapos start to get the bodies out and bury the evidence of their murderous success. But now time is running out. The Allies are coming, so the killers abandon their task and disappear.

In the barn, only the powdery remains of men eaten by the flames can be seen. Everyone is dead. All of them? No. There are eight men left from Dora, eight demons who never gave up and managed to stay alive. One after the other, they emerge from beneath the killing place. They have lived to tell the tale.

★   ★   ★

And there we are; everything is finished. The strange voyage is over. The Planet Dora has exploded, scattering its flames, smoke, and gases all over Europe. Debris—both living and dead—has followed incredible trajectories and fabulous parabolas to land in the north, south, east, and west. The residues from the explosion have defied all laws of ballistics by falling in incoherent places impossible to predict or calculate. But they have just as equally defied another law—the law of human ability to survive, the law of limits not to be broken. These limits have been pulverized by some. How many were they? And when were they liberated, these champions among all who resisted? It's impossible to say or even to calculate their numbers.

One day in April 1945, Dora opened its gates and threw thousands of men, in little groups, men who had already passed the barriers of human survivability into freedom at last. They wandered on roads and railroads, mixed with prisoners from other camps, escaped, or joined the dead in the bone house or at the bottom of a ditch. So many millions had been murdered—clubbed, tortured, gassed, hung, burned alive with flamethrowers, or gunned down in the corner of some forgotten wood. But the day of liberation had arrived.

The Allied forces regrouped them and, in time, sent them back to their own countries, some after a few days and others after months of recovery and treatment. Many lived only a few hours after the liberators arrived. Others died in hospitals or on arriving at home. But before all this, the crematorium furnace daily swallowed up increasing numbers of prisoners and reduced them to windborne smoke and ashes.

But these men at Dora, Ellrich, and Harzungen, in the small kommandos or during the evacuation, had held on. Even dead, burned, or thrown upon a pile of human trash, they were the victors. They had shown and proved with their martyred bodies that human beings must never give in, never surrender, never submit to tyranny. They had proved it hour after hour through agonized weeks, months, and centuries.

Many years have passed since Dora ended. You would think that its story was over and done with. It isn't. At the end of the war, the great powers shared the engineers, the creators, and the fathers of the V-1s and V-2s.

Far from punishing them, they supplied them with laboratories, study offices, and factories. They were also showered with praise and with money, honors, and glory. Nothing was too good for them, and some were shown off as good examples to schoolchildren.

These men took up their work, which the misfortunes of war had forced them to abandon. And they have succeeded beyond all expectations.

Today, throughout the world, there are silos in place and ready to launch. And in these silos, there are rockets, the direct descendants of the V-2s of Dora. The fruits of modern science and technology, these fantastic machines can, within a few minutes, destroy all that exists on the surface of the Planet Earth.

Dora will live on—as long as there are men, as long as the Earth exists.

GLOSSARY

Arbeitseinsatz—manpower allocation office
Arbeitsstatistik—manpower records office
Barakenbau-Kommando—barracks construction teams
Barakenbau-Tischlerei—barracks construction carpentry shop
Blockältester—barracks chief
Blockführer—SS man in charge of barracks
Effektenkammer—clothing store for prisoners
Gummis—electric cables covered with rubber and used for beatings
Häftling—prisoner
Kapo—team leader, a prisoner
Kommando—work team
Konzentrationslager—concentration camp
Lagerältester—camp chief, a prisoner
Lagerdolmetscher—chief interpreter, a prisoner
Lagerführer—SS officer, subordinate to the camp commandant, responsible for
    the prisoners
Lagerkommando—camp maintenance team
Lagerschutz—camp police
Meister—German civilian foreman
Moslems—camp term for men at the lowest level of decay, unresponsive, and
    near death
Mützen—prisoner caps
Politische Abteilung—political section, camp security
Posten—SS guards
Rapportführer—SS officer in charge of the link between inmate responsibili-
    ties and the SS camp administration
Schreiber—secretary, bookkeeper
Schreibstube—secretarial office
Stalag—POW camp
Stubendienst—male orderly, a prisoner
Stücke—pieces, an SS term of contempt for prisoners
Tischlerei—carpentry shop
Todträger—prisoners who handle the dead
Untermenschen—subhumans, in the Nazi worldview
Vorarbeiter—foreman, a prisoner
Waschraum—washroom
Zawatsky Company—Mittelwerk GmbH, the German company in charge of
    rocket production

ABOUT THE BOOK, THE AUTHOR, AND THE EDITOR

An extraordinary memoir by a survivor of the Nazi camps, Yves Béon, *Planet Dora* is a recollection of life and death in a concentration camp like no other. Dora was a cavernous underground factory cut out of solid rock, where life was like a nightmarish scene from Dante: thousands of prisoners beaten, starved, killed, and living underground for weeks at a time. The purpose of all this brutality was to build the world's first operational rockets: the V-1 and V-2 missiles, Hitler's vengeance weapons.

Some of Germany's most brilliant scientists were involved with production at Dora, including Wernher von Braun, who after the war went on to become the father of the American space program. It was his Saturn V rocket, designed with the help of his wartime comrades, that put the first man on the moon, while the Saturn V project was headed by the man who had been the director of slave labor in Dora. In fact, some of the very rockets built in Dora were packed up after the war and shipped to New Mexico to serve as the seeds of the U.S. space program. In a very real sense, the greatest technological achievement of the twentieth century had its origins in the enslavement and murder of thousands of innocent people, the down payment of a Faustian bargain that still tarnishes our reach for the stars.

Planet Dora was originally published in France; this American edition is prefaced by a historical introduction by Michael Neufeld, author of *The Rocket and the Reich*, the definitive work on the German rockets. Once you read *Planet Dora*, horrifying in its implications, you will never watch the launching of the space shuttle the same way again.

Active in the French Resistance from age fifteen until he was captured by the Germans, **Yves Béon** is a survivor of the Buchenwald, Dora, and Bergen-Belsen concentration camps. **Michael J. Neufeld** is a curator at the Smithsonian's National Air and Space Museum and the author of *The Rocket and the Reich*.